PHIL *'The Power'* **TAYLOR**
Staying Power

PHIL
'The Power'
TAYLOR

Staying Power

A Year In My Life

With Mike Walters

HODDER &
STOUGHTON

First published in Great Britain in 2014 by Hodder & Stoughton
An Hachette UK company

1

A CIP catalogue record for this title is available from the British Library

ISBN 978 1 444 79728 2
Trade Paperback ISBN 978 1 473 60851 1
Ebook ISBN 978 1 444 79729 9

Typeset in Plantin by Palimpsest Book Production Ltd, Falkirk, Stirlingshire

Printed and bound by Clays Ltd, St Ives plc

Hodder & Stoughton policy is to use papers that are natural, renewable and recyclable products and made from wood grown in sustainable forests. The logging and manufacturing processes are expected to conform to the environmental regulations of the country of origin.

Hodder & Stoughton Ltd
338 Euston Road
London NW1 3BH

www.hodder.co.uk

For Mum – always there.

CONTENTS

Acknowledgements

IT was a nice surprise when I was asked to do this book, and even more gratifying that so many people swung behind me to help pull it all together. I must start by thanking Roddy Bloomfield, the eminent scholar and consultant at publishers Hodder & Stoughton, who was the driving force behind it, and editorial assistant Fiona Rose for keeping us up to speed; my manager Barry Hearn, Professional Darts Corporation chief executive Matt Porter and PDC media manager Dave Allen for their flawless efficiency; my daughter, Lisa, for running my diary and making sure I am in the right places at the right times and on the right days; my other children Chris, Kelly and Natalie, for keeping me honest; photographer Lawrence Lustig, for his exhaustive picture research; and my enthusiastic 'ghost' and collaborator, Mike Walters, for bringing a year in my life and an assortment of my career highlights to print.

I remain forever grateful for the love and support of my mum, and the enduring work ethic I inherited from my late father, whose memory I shall always respect. And in testing times, you find out who your real friends are. I am lucky to count Bob Glenn, Garry Plummer, Scott McArthur,

Shaun Rutter, Pete Williams and Eric Bristow, to name but a few, among my pals.

We are not here for a long time; we're here for a good time!

Photographic Acknowledgements

Photographs reproduced with kind permission from Lawrence Lustig, ITV and Fremantle Media.

FOREWORD

GOOD grief, was it almost twenty-five years ago that I won my first World Championship? Back in 1990, Margaret Thatcher was still Prime Minister, Sir Alex Ferguson had not yet won his first trophy as Manchester United manager and A.P. McCoy was still to ride his first winner. I was a father of three – soon to be father of four – and now I have four grandchildren, greying hair and my eyesight's a bit wonky. Where did that quarter of a century go?

I had described my occupation as 'unemployed engineer' on the entry form for the Lakeside World Championship. I was a rank 125–1 outsider, and found myself facing Eric Bristow, my mentor, in the final. I beat him 6–1. Eric may not have been the force he was in the mid-1980s, when he became the original superstar of darts, but I was very ambitious and wanted it badly. When you have been collecting £74 a week in a ceramics factory you don't hang about if someone is dangling a cheque for £24,000 in front of you.

When I look back on the trophies, the titles and the pay cheques since 1990, I can only reflect how fortunate I have been. From living in a council house where we all had to sleep on the ground floor because the stairs were condemned, and wake-up calls from my mother – cold buckets of water were a sure-fire way to get me out of bed first thing in the morning – my life has changed beyond recognition. Darts, too, has changed from a seasonal side-show to big business. When I won my first tournament in 1988, the coveted Burslem Open title, it was a game played in smoky halls; now, when we walk on stage, we feel like rock stars. And the sport once lampooned as a drinking competition, where competitors threw darts to pass the time in between sinking pints or shots, is now based on a more clean-cut image. Players drink nothing stronger than water on stage, and we are subject to the same anti-doping rules as Olympic sprinters.

In the last twenty-five years we've had Lady Thatcher, John Major, Tony Blair, Gordon Brown and David Cameron running the country. Some of them have done it better than others. Liverpool, Arsenal, Leeds, Manchester United, Blackburn, Chelsea and Manchester City have all been champions, A.P. McCoy has become the first jockey to ride 4,000 winners . . . and I've been on an incredible journey. This book is not so much a diary or a yearbook as a snapshot of the life of a darts player who has been lucky enough to win sixteen world titles – and who would dearly love to win one more.

I've had my ups and downs – on top of the world one minute, in the dark depths of despair the next – and there are so many people to thank that I am scared to compile a list in case I omit any deserving names. But as you join me on the road for a twelve-month period from July 2013, my greatest debt as a darts player is to you, the public. You buy the tickets and help to sell out every venue. You drive TV ratings through the roof by following major tournaments in such great numbers on the box. You sing our names, you share our joys and disappointments, you make us laugh with your fancy-dress outfits.

But above all, you make a 54-year-old grandfather grateful to be competing in world-class fields at an age where most sportsmen would be content to watch from a safe distance. You even voted for me in such numbers that I was runner-up in the BBC Sports Personality of the Year in 2010, behind the great A.P. McCoy himself. When I retired, briefly, from darts in 2004, it was public support that made me change my mind just eleven days later. It was the public who besieged my shopping trolley in the supermarket aisles, begging me to reconsider. It was strangers from the great British public who came to my front door in the Potteries with flowers and oatcakes, pleading with me to stay in the sport.

You have made the last twenty-five years worth every second of the ride. I have come a long way from growing up in a terraced house in Tunstall where there was no electricity or running water, and we had to wash in the yard. There may come a time, before I check out for the last time on the oche, when I will need batteries to keep me going. But nothing has sustained me like public support, for which I will always be truly thankful.

Phil Taylor,
Stoke-on-Trent

1

CHEAT

July 2013

At first, I couldn't make out what they were saying. It was just your usual, thirsty darts crowd having a good time, except that a handful of punters were determined to get themselves noticed. When I tried to shut it out as background noise, it sounded like 'cheap' or 'chief', but then the penny dropped. In Blackpool's Winter Gardens – one of my favourite venues, which has brought me more success than any other stage – these voluble critics were calling me a cheat.

There may have been more than one pocket of customers trying to put me off as I released each dart, but I didn't need to look for them. You could hear the venom behind every burst of 'Cheat, Cheat, Cheat.' Each one was like a dagger in my back. It was nothing to do with my quarter-final match against Justin Pipe at the World Matchplay, a tournament I had won thirteen times before. They were on my case about a controversial leg at an event in Gibraltar the previous month. It had been dredged up by someone with a grudge and fed to the *Sun*, who had run a sizeable story – not in the Sports section at the back of the paper, but on their news pages – insinuating that I had pocketed the winner's £20,000 prize money unfairly.

Let me tell you how it feels to be labelled a cheat. It is probably the nastiest, most damaging charge you can level at any sportsman. It didn't do much for Ben Johnson's career after his Olympic gold medal in 1988 was found to have been fuelled by diesel when he was only allowed to put unleaded petrol in the tank. When someone calls you a cheat, they are basically saying that your whole career is based on a lie. That you are a fraud. That you are stealing a living. It's not very nice.

Initially, I tried to blank it out. I was playing well enough, I had got Pipe where I wanted him, and there was no need to let these people's harsh criticism get to me. But, once you are aware of it, sadly it's not easy to pretend you can't hear fifteen or twenty grown men calling you a cheat, and I'm afraid I let it get to me. After sharing the first ten legs, I eventually managed to find another gear and won the match 16–10. But inside I was feeling ripped apart by those hurtful allegations about my sense of sportsmanship and fair play. It spoilt my week in Blackpool, even though I went on to beat Adrian Lewis 18–13 in a high-quality final with an average of 111.23. Ultimately, it was like cracking open a bottle of champagne to celebrate and finding the

Bollinger was corked. It was a bitter-sweet experience and I am in no hurry to ever go through it again.

Blackpool will always have a special place in my heart. I could happily live there all year round if it was easier to get home from tournaments further south. My waxwork stands in Madame Tussauds on the seafront there beside Hollywood celebrities, pop stars and heads of state. I still find that incredible whenever I go past it on the Golden Mile. Little old me, a former ceramics factory worker from the Potteries, mingling with all those famous people's replica statues. Each year at the World Matchplay I have slipped into a routine that makes me feel settled and able to produce my best form at the Winter Gardens. Instead of a hotel – and every place is always banged out during peak holiday season – for the past few years I have stayed at my own place, a private lodge at Ribby Hall on the Fylde coast near Lytham St Annes. A bit of self-catering now and again never hurt anybody, and I always feel relaxed up there.

But this time, it was different. I was more afraid to show my face in public. I didn't venture out for walks as much as I used to, even though it was glorious weather. I was worried people would be pointing at me, talking behind my back. I wouldn't say I became a hermit, or a recluse, but suddenly I was more aware of furtive glances, pointed fingers and secretive whispers – even though they were probably nothing to do with me, my conscience was clear and, in my own mind, I had nothing to be paranoid about.

The source of all the nastiness was my second-round tie against Dean Winstanley at the Gibraltar Darts Trophy a month earlier. On the ever-expanding Professional Darts Corporation (PDC) roster, the tournament was being held for the first time at the Victoria Stadium complex on the famous Rock peninsula. Being a keen missionary for the sport, I was happy to spread the gospel to a new outpost for darts, especially to a British colony, and I travelled in good heart after winning the UK Open title a couple of weeks earlier. The £100,000 prize fund, stumped up by the local government, was attractive too. For three days' work, £20,000 to the winner seemed like a good deal.

Although it was later covered by Sky Sports in a highlights programme, who screen the vast majority of televised PDC dates in the calendar, crucially the Gibraltar tournament was not shown live, although it was streamed online. This meant that the lighting in the venue was not as bright, and the lux not as powerful, as in other major title events. Normally, when you are on stage at a televised tournament, the lighting is so fierce it can melt an ice cream in thirty seconds, but this was not so intense. I must have been relaxed enough with the temperature in the first round, because I beat Gino Vos 6–2 with a 115 average. Happy enough with that.

In the next round, I was up against Winstanley, a Lakeside World Championship finalist in 2011 and a Grand Slam semi-finalist in his first year on the PDC circuit. On his day, he can beat anybody, so I wasn't going to take him lightly, and in the event I didn't play very well. Leading 2–1, I needed 68 to check out and put a break of serve between us. Single 20, single 16, double 16 would do nicely – except that my first dart slipped down the leg side, so to speak, into the single five bed. Bugger. No matter – treble 13 would retrieve the damage, and my second dart was bang on the money, leaving double 12 (around 10 o'clock on the dial) to seal the deal.

When the dart left my hand, it felt good enough and I thought it had located the target area under the top wire – and so did Russ Bray, widely considered to be the best referee in darts. Russ, whose distinctive, rasping voice makes him instantly recognisable by ear, if not by sight, called game shot, and as I sauntered up to the board to collect my arrows, I was probably thinking ahead to the next leg. You never dwell on your last shot in darts, it's always best to focus on the next one. I simply didn't notice that the double 12 had nestled against the wrong side of the wire, to the north, because Russ had called it, and as far as I was aware, that was that. With the benefit of replays, zoom lenses and hindsight, of course, the proof of the pudding is that my dart missed its target. That's the top and bottom of it. But for all the conspiracy theories that surfaced later, the truth is there was nothing more to it than human error.

What I will say is that there were shadows across the board, if not across the arena as a whole. Tournament director Tommy Cox had a lot of complaints from players about the standard of lighting that week. Look at the footage on YouTube, or elsewhere on the internet, and you'll see exactly what I mean. When I toed the oche, half of my face was illuminated, the other half was in shadow. That's no exaggeration, it's quite pronounced. And Russ, like me, was also fooled by the angle when my dart landed. I'm not a player who rams every shot into the board like a spear at Rorke's Drift – the trajectory of my throw sometimes leaves the flight sitting lower than the barrel, which can obscure a player or referee's view. In the commentary box, they were unsure. Rod Harrington, who happened to be on air at the time, said, 'It didn't look in at first, did it?' But when Russ, who was the official on stage when I hit my first televised nine-darter at the World Matchplay in 2002, called game shot, I never gave it a moment's thought that he could be mistaken – or that there might be any repercussions for me further down the line.

Winstanley, a down-to-earth Yorkshireman and a really nice lad, never said a word to me on stage at the time. On the video footage, as I prepare to throw first in the fifth leg, he looks over his shoulder towards a PDC official statistician sitting just below the stage, presumably to ask if that last dart was good. But we were backstage, after I had gone on to win the match 6–1, before I knew there was anything amiss. Dean was upset because he had missed out on qualifying for the World Matchplay at the Winter Gardens. When he said, 'That double has cost me', at first I thought he was talking about the winning double, the last dart of the match. I just told him he was a good enough player to make the cut at other televised tournaments, but he was still agitated because I clearly hadn't addressed his concern.

Let me make it clear, from the outset, that Dean handled the whole thing very professionally. He had every right to be upset, but he didn't rant and rave or make a great scene. If my shot at double 12 had not counted, he would have had a chance of levelling the match at 2–2, and who knows what might have happened after that? Let me also make it very clear that I don't like winning games under false pretences. I've been lucky enough to win eighty-odd televised tournaments in the last twenty-five years, and I've always taken pride in knowing that every penny of prize money, every penny of sponsorship, every penny from private appearances has been earned fair and square. An honest day's work for an honest day's pay – because I remember what it was like to grow up in a household where there was very little money.

So when Dean flagged up the problem with that double 12, I was troubled. I didn't want his career to suffer because of an honest mistake, so I offered to replay the game, or forfeit the game and forfeit the prize money. The PDC would not let me do that because replaying matches was inadmissible under the rules. Tommy Cox assured me I had nothing to worry about because Dean had not raised any concerns at the time and Russ had called game shot in good faith. I went on to win the tournament, beating Jamie Lewis 6–1 in the final, and I was happy enough with that. But on social networks the poison had already started to circulate.

I joined the Twitter revolution relatively late in the day, and don't spend hours logged on to find out who's been saying what about me. I don't consider myself famous, so I don't lie awake at night worrying what the huddled masses and keyboard warriors might be spreading on the World Wide Web. I wasn't really aware of any major revolt in the shires until we got to Blackpool, where the flames of controversy were expertly fanned by the press.

At this point, it's worth reminding ourselves that cheating in darts – at least by falsifying the score – is virtually impossible. Unlike boxing, ice skating, synchronised swimming, diving, gymnastics and equestrian dressage, which are all Olympic sports, games of darts do not rely on judges marking what they see. Counting down from 501 is a quantifiable process. Basically, you can't knowingly cheat simply because you won't get away with it. And if the referee makes a mistake, the TV cameras will soon catch you out.

I am well aware of my responsibility to the wider image of darts, and the importance of policing the sport starts with the players themselves. Other sports set a prohibitive tariff on cheating as a deterrent, and darts should be no different. In golf you are quickly ostracised by fellow professionals if you ground your club in a bunker without declaring it, or inadvertently move the ball a single millimetre when lining up a putt. In snooker, it's a complete no-no to move a ball as you reach across the table without calling a penalty against yourself. Cricket has clamped down hard on ball-tampering and spot-fixing. We've had doping, fake blood injuries with tomato ketchup, diving footballers and I even read once about an Olympic fencer who rigged his electric épée to record blows where none was landed. Cheating is not attractive, whatever the sport, so I said it at the time and I'll say it again now: I would never in a million years want to win at darts by cheating, and I felt stabbed in the back when the business in Gibraltar reared its ugly head again at the World Matchplay.

I was incensed when I picked up a paper on 24 July and saw headlines in which, at face value, my old mentor Eric Bristow was slagging me off for being a cheat. And although the PDC had put out a statement exonerating me, it did little to lift my mood. Their statement read:

> Following speculation and discussion on various online and social media forums, the PDC can confirm it has reviewed footage of the conclusion of the fourth leg of the Gibraltar Darts Trophy second round match between Phil Taylor and Dean Winstanley, where Taylor was awarded game shot on a finish of double 12. The footage shows the dart landed outside the double 12 segment. However, Taylor and referee Russ Bray have confirmed they were unaware of this, while Winstanley did not raise his concerns at the time.
>
> PDC tournament director Tommy Cox said: 'I spoke

> with both players and the referee, and Phil offered to replay the match, which is not an option under the rules, and Dean confirmed he wants to put the incident behind him and concentrate on his next event. I would like to reassure the public that fairness, transparency and integrity are top priorities of the PDC, and this unusual episode is purely attributable to a rare instance of human error from the referee.' The PDC now regards the matter as closed.

Closed? For me, the nightmare had barely started. Bristow's comment in the *Sun* gave the conspiracy theories an air of legitimacy, and appeared to be a direct criticism of me. 'The player knows if it's not in and he has to declare it. You don't want cheats.'

I couldn't believe my eyes. It appeared that here was the man who had taken me under his wing as an apprentice, and financed the early stages of my darts career – a man I held in the esteem of a brother – calling my honesty and fair play into question. It felt like the end of the world. Later, on reflection, I came to realise that the whole episode was a sign of the times. Footballers get sworn at, and called every name under the sun, every week. They are accused of cheating by diving to win a penalty, even if the tackles nearly break their legs. Their private lives are scrutinised. And they end up in the newspapers and on internet forums based on what they achieve as sportsmen, what they eat for dinner or who they are seen with on a night out. They have become public property, and, whether they like it or not, are regarded as role models. As a darts player, I never thought the same thing could happen to me, but when you are playing on a circuit where the prize money is now above £6 million every year, and rising fast, I guess 'fame' and all its trappings are part of the ticket.

Make no bones about it, I was furious when I read that quote from Eric. I hated the very thought that he might think I was a cheat, absolutely hated it. After beating Lewis in the World Matchplay final, I made some comments to my local paper, the *Sentinel*, which I would later regret. 'The World Matchplay was probably the hardest tournament I've ever won, and Eric saying I'm a cheat made it all the harder,' I said. 'I will never talk to Eric again as long as I live. I have never cheated in my life, and when someone goes out and says you're a cheat, it breaks your heart, but I'm over it now. Eric's still laughing and joking with everyone because he thinks he's done nowt wrong – but in my eyes he has.'

With hindsight, it would have been better to clear the air with Eric there and then – a night out in Blackpool, a frank exchange of views, lance the boil and get it out of my system. But that August marked a break in the PDC schedule, and the next stop was on the other side of the world for the inaugural Sydney Masters in Australia so, for one reason or another, our paths didn't cross for a while. By the time the Grand Slam of Darts in Wolverhampton came round in mid-November 2013, the 'cheat' business was still a running sore with me. I didn't want to sit down to dinner with him. As far as I was concerned, the whole thing was a load of rubbish.

Ours is a sport where you can't set out to cheat because there are three officials – one referee and two markers – either side of the board. If they don't spot a dart landing the wrong side of the wire, does that make them cheats? Of course not. All along, I had maintained that the lighting in Gibraltar wasn't great, that there were shadows on the board – and other players had agreed with me. But as a sixteen-times world champion, I was considered fair game for controversy. And at the back end of the World Matchplay, it was suddenly open season.

Some of the garbage doing the rounds was so outrageous I would have laughed out loud if the allegations had not been levelled at me. Not that I practise them personally, but there are dark arts in darts – ways and means of distracting your opponent when he is on the oche – and you get to hear most of them from talking to players backstage or on the practice boards. Tapping your feet, clearing your throat, humming, sniffing, snorting, sneezing, swearing under your breath so nobody can lip-read . . . I thought I'd heard them all. And one or two critics even recycled an old falsehood that had lingered like a bad smell a few years earlier.

Back in 2005, I was accused of breaking wind as my opponent lined up his third dart so he would be put off by the evil bodily fragrance drifting across the stage. A chap named Alex Roy, who had lost 4–0 against me in the third round of the World Championship at the Circus Tavern, allegedly claimed I had gained an unfair advantage by causing a stink. 'Phil is a great player, but the fact is he is very flatulent,' said Roy. I was so flattered, I had to look up the word to see what it meant. 'It's hard enough trying to concentrate, but when there is a horrific stench filling your nostrils, it's even worse. I don't know what his pre-match meal is, but maybe he should consider changing it. Phil says he was busy practising over Christmas, but if you ask me he ate too many Brussels sprouts with his Christmas dinner. Everyone "trumps", but there is a time and a place for it, and he shouldn't do it on stage. It's very unprofessional.'

You couldn't make it up. Breaking wind on stage to order? I've never heard such tommyrot. I'm sure there's a joke out there about an ill wind that blows in such wild accusations, but it's no laughing matter when it's your own integrity on the line. And slurs about being a cheat can destroy careers unless you're careful. As it happens, somebody may have been making it up. Alex subsequently complained one or two press guys had egged him on about the farting story, and had put words in his mouth, so to speak.

Fortunately, a phone call from Keith Deller not only lifted my mood but put Eric's damaging comments in the paper into a more enlightened context. Seven years before I won my first title, Keith had become the first qualifier to be crowned world champion when he beat Eric in the final with a 138 checkout. Treble 20, treble 18, double 12 – there it is again, double 12 – is still called a 'Deller' by commentators. Like Eric, he does a lot of work for Sky Sports as a 'spotter' in the production trucks behind the scenes: spotters are the expert former professionals whose knowledge of players' preferred scoring shots and the combinations available help the director and cameramen to predict where the next dart will land – they are an essential part of any live TV production.

Keith and Eric still appear at exhibition nights all over the country, often travelling to venues in the same car, and in conversation Keith asked how I was getting on with my old mentor in the light of the Gibraltar affair. I think I muttered something about life being too short to hold grudges or fall out with people when he told me, 'He never used your name, you know.' Sorry, what was that again? Keith told me he had been sitting next to Eric in the car when he took that call from the *Sun* reporter. Yes, he had said we don't want cheats in darts. And, yes, he had said a player should declare it to the referee if he is credited with the wrong score. But did Eric use the name Phil Taylor? Not according to the bloke sitting next to him and ear-wigging the conversation. Not according to the man himself. That does not prove the question was directly about the incident involving me in Gibraltar, but as far as I'm concerned it means Eric did not slag me off. There is a big difference between making a point of principle and a personal attack on a friend. The next time I saw

Eric I told him, 'Look, bud, I know what you said – I may have got the wrong end of the stick.' We are fine now.

But it doesn't change the disquiet I felt about people in the crowd at the Winter Gardens calling me a cheat. It spoilt my week. Mud sticks, and I'm grateful that the vast majority of people who come to watch darts have accepted an honest mistake for what it was. I had offered to forfeit the game against Dean, and to hand back my prize money. I'm not sure what else I could have done in retrospect. I certainly would not want any of my fellow players' integrity to be questioned when they go on stage because it hurts. We all enjoy the rock 'n' roll crowds having a good time, but there is a football element to some of the chanting and 'banter' that we could do without.

The PDC ban football shirts and colours from tournament venues to make sure there is no tribal rivalry between factions of rival clubs in the audience, but the punters will always have their favourites, or want one player to win more than another. That's human nature, and nobody can grumble about that. But I have seen players come back into the practice room in tears after they have been ripped to pieces by the crowd – from shouting out as they release the dart, usually on a checkout, to the kind of personal abuse you would not tolerate in the pub. As we attract bigger audiences, we have to accept that among 10,000 paying customers there may be a handful of wrong 'uns. You get them at football, you get them on big nights of boxing, but it's not easy to land a dart on target, with only millimetres of margin for error, when these people are giving you an earful.

For months afterwards, I could not understand why people wanted to nail me to the cross. I'm just a plump darts player from Stoke who has won a few matches down the years. I'm just a working man who has earned a decent living. I don't feel famous. I live a dull life. I don't fall out of nightclubs at 4 a.m. three sheets to the wind. If I'm not playing darts, I'm usually tucked up in bed before the 'bongs' on *News At Ten*. I don't know why they picked on me over the Gibraltar Trophy. My manager Barry Hearn says I should take it as a compliment – although people hissing 'Cheat, Cheat' below the stage didn't feel like much of a compliment at the time. I don't know if the story helped to sell any extra newspapers, but I guess the fish and chips enjoyed it.

Let me just say I did not receive one piece of abusive correspondence about it through the post (for those of you who remember the time when we used to write letters) and I received nothing on Twitter that I felt my family should have been shielded from. But it's amazing how darts has become public property all of a sudden.

Once more, for the record: I am not a cheat. I'd rather stick pins in my eyes than win a tournament unfairly.

2

ERIC

FORTUNATELY, my relationship with Eric Bristow was not damaged in the long term by the 'cheat' nonsense in Gibraltar. It would take an earthquake to undermine such a long-standing friendship beyond repair. The only way it has changed over the last twenty-five years is that we don't see as much of each other as we once did because we are both so busy.

My defining memory of Eric will always be sitting up in bed, in our twin room at the Lakeside Country Club, eating fish and chips on New Year's Eve before the 1990 World Championship, listening to everyone downstairs having a ball. We must have looked like Morecambe and Wise in that sketch where a police car goes hurtling past, siren blaring, and Eric says, 'He'll never sell any ice cream going that fast.' It was our custom to set aside one night of the year, usually in the build-up to Christmas, to go out and enjoy ourselves, have the odd shandy and a game of cards, let down our guard and forget about darts. But at Christmas, we always fitted the turkey around practice on the board – not the other way round – and when it came to New Year, with the World Championship upon us, there were no party hats, no streamers and no waking up with a sore head on 1 January. When it came to business, Eric always knew when it was time to be deadly serious.

I'm always a bit baffled when I meet strangers and they flatter me with praise about being the greatest player who ever hit a bullseye because, for me, Eric Bristow was the original superstar of darts – and he always will be the king. To be honest, when I first watched him on TV in the early 1980s, I didn't particularly like the bloke. He was brash, arrogant and came across as a bit too cocky for my liking. It is well-documented that Eric became my mentor and coach after we played county matches together for Staffordshire. He was a hard taskmaster at times, and we fell out more than once, but it was he, more than anyone, who was responsible for drumming it into me that winning is the greatest medicine known to mankind.

We couldn't believe our luck in the Potteries when the Crafty Cockney himself upped sticks from his manor in Stoke Newington and relocated to Stoke-on-Trent. As the great Sid Waddell once observed, it was like Jesus Christ forsaking the Holy Land and settling in Milton Keynes. And I couldn't believe my luck when Eric adopted me as his protégé. Throughout countless hours, which must have run into thousands, on the practice board, we always got on like a house on fire, playing hard before shaking hands and doing it all over again the next day. He was like a lion teaching its cub to hunt until the cub was ready to go out and fend for itself in the wild.

I don't think Eric expected me to turn out as successful as I became, but he always wanted me to win. I guess his reputation was on the line as much as mine, and it reflected well on him as a mentor when I lived up to his bravado. When his career as a world-beater was curtailed by 'dartitis' – the equivalent of golf's 'yips' – I sometimes wondered if I was living the legend he had left behind. But I will always remember the day in 1988 when he offered to sponsor me as a professional so I could play in tournaments all over the world. It was a big step, which involved me taking voluntary redundancy from my job at a ceramics factory making beer pump handles. There was no contract as such, no legal formalities. He just said, 'Pay me back if you win anything.'

Until my first world title in 1990, when I beat Eric in the final at Lakeside, just about every penny I earned in prize money on the darts circuit went towards paying Eric back. If I rang him from a tournament and told him I had reached the semi-finals, he would just snap, 'Ring me back when you've won a final' and slam the phone down. It was his way of keeping me hungry. We hardly spoke for six months after the 125–1 rank outsider had beaten him 6–1 in that Lakeside final and I had played him exactly the same way he had taught me to compete – like a bully, keeping the pressure on at every opportunity, never giving him the chance to bite back like a rattlesnake.

We didn't socialise much or meet up for a coffee to pass the time of day like bored housewives. We were friends because of one common denominator – darts – and most of our disagreements have been about darts. If he lost against a player he felt he should have been beating with his eyes closed, he would often take out his frustration on me. Then there would be a protracted silence between us, running into weeks, until I lost a match he felt I should have won and he would appear over my shoulder and snarl, 'Get back on the practice board, you idle git.' I never resented him for it, and I've always thought we got on more like brothers than best mates. As an only son, I look up to Eric as the older brother I never had.

Although he comes across as straight-talking and abrupt, if not actually blunt, Eric is as bright as a button. Anything to do with numbers, he's the sharpest tool in the box. Ask him the route to any checkout and he'll come up with the combination in a flash – 'A 149 finish? That'll be treble 20, treble 19, double 16' – before most of us have even worked out that 149 comes after 148. That's why Sky Sports value him so much as a 'spotter' in the production truck backstage. And don't underestimate his brain power where sport is concerned. He knows his football – I've no idea how a bloke born in the East End comes to support Chelsea, although he stayed loyal to his roots with that 'Crafty Cockney' nickname. (He borrowed it from the name of a bar from somewhere in California. Santa Monica, I think.)

Our sport has changed a lot since he was cock of the

walk and I was making toilet flush handles and beer pump handles in a factory. When you watch footage of big tournaments now, the venues are often immersed in a fog of smoke. I've never been especially militant about passive smoking, but recent medical check-ups have revealed damage to my vocal cords. Doctors are pretty certain that's the legacy of playing in pubs, clubs and big venues full of tobacco smoke before the government introduced smoking bans in public places in 2007. I don't know if it will have consequences for me further down the line, but if anyone doesn't believe in the potential of passive smoking to seriously damage your health, I would invite them to wake up and look at the evidence.

As I've previously intimated, the public perception of darts players has also changed a lot since Eric's rivalry with Jocky Wilson and John Lowe set new standards for the game. It was a fantastic compliment for the sport when Eric was signed up to appear in ITV's annual caper round a camp fire in the Australian bush, *I'm A Celebrity, Get Me Out Of Here!* Of course, I was looking forward to seeing how he would get on if he was selected to perform one of the dreaded bush tucker trials – those exercises in public cruelty where contestants are expected to eat raw kangaroo testicles, witchetty grubs, crocodile nostrils and ostrich prostate glands while having buckets of cockroaches tipped down their boxer shorts. All with your genial hosts, Ant and Dec, standing over them like a pair of giggling schoolboys. To be fair, it's great television, isn't it?

In truth, I felt sorry for the bush tucker. If you put innocent bugs, insects and rodents in a sealed chamber with Bristow, there's only going to be one winner. I thought Eric handled it all brilliantly. When you put a dozen celebrities – some of them more famous than others – in the jungle, you soon unmask those who are playing to win and those who are true to themselves. I did wonder if the heat, boredom and basic diet would get to Eric and a dark side of his personality might come to the fore, but he came across exactly as the person I had known most of my adult life: straight-talking, honest and a man who doesn't suffer fools gladly. On too many reality TV shows, you get devious, manipulative people who play one character off against another. But Eric played it straight down the line. What you saw is what he is really like.

When he told that girl from *Coronation Street*, Helen Flanagan, that her skin was pimpled without make-up because there was too much chocolate in her diet, he didn't intend to cause offence – that's his natural charm! And when he told TV chef Rosemary Shrager to get back to the kitchen, I don't think he was being gratuitously sexist. He just has a gift for it. That's the congenital bluntness I know so well from our time as master and apprentice. The only time I've seen Eric's character change is when he's had a few pints, but he's not a violent drunk. Let's just say the nectar makes him even more belligerent than normal.

Towards the end of 2013, Eric was featured on prime-time television again, in an award-winning documentary series on ITV about sporting icons. They got him absolutely spot-on. (Even now, thirty years on from his career being at its peak, a bar or members' club comes alive when he walks into the room.) But more than anything, the programme was a reminder of Bristow as a world-class wind-up merchant. If he was on stage against someone who was playing better than him at the time, he would get under their skin and beat them. He had the nerve to plant a kiss on Bobby George's cheek and he had the nerve to beat Jocky Wilson in front of a baying Scottish crowd when a full can of beer, intended for Eric, hit the backboard.

It's a shame to admit it, but you couldn't get away with winding up your opponents so blatantly now. The younger players simply wouldn't put up with it – they would just laugh in your face on stage and tell your fortune to your face back in the practice room afterwards. Eric's main rivals, at the height of his success, were people like John Lowe, Jocky and Bobby – that generation was full of respect. Don't get me wrong, they were great characters, but the new posse of talent on the PDC circuit simply won't put up with any showman's bluster these days. They just want to beat you, have the shirt off your back and the tattoos off your arm if they can.

In years to come, I believe Eric Bristow will still be regarded as the icon of darts, much as Muhammad Ali has remained the untouchable face of boxing for half a century, or Jonny Wilkinson will always be the man with the golden boot who won the rugby World Cup for England. I may not always show it, but I will always be grateful that he took me under his wing and gave me the support to help me become a success in my own right. He taught me how to prepare for tournaments, how to unnerve opponents just like *he* did, how to become a champion, how to feel that winner's cheque in your hands. As I watched that documentary about Bristow, I felt a few pangs of nostalgia because I suddenly realised it was twenty-five years since he had coaxed me to my first sizeable payday, at the Canadian Open in 1988.

I can still remember the excitement, my hands almost quivering, as I took delivery of that cheque for $5,000 after beating Bob Anderson in the final – although the euphoria lasted all of two minutes. Before the sense of triumph had even sunk in, as I walked off the stage, still waving to the crowd, Eric was waiting for me. We shook hands . . . and then he took the cheque off me. 'Payback, old son – your first instalment,' he grinned. He said it was my coming of age as a professional, and that was the first time I had really felt like the full ticket: air travel, accommodation, entry fees, practising hard and then relaxing by going to watch *Rambo* at the cinema – it had all unfurled exactly as I would have wanted. That was not the biggest win of my career, either in terms of money or prestige, but it set a template. And Eric was the master who set it all up.

As I consolidated my place in the rankings, he would

sometimes bawl me out across a practice room when I was having a pint with some of the lads on the circuit, telling me to get off my fat arse and get back to the board because I still owed him thousands. It made me feel about two feet tall, but it was Eric's way of keeping me on my toes – and in a sense, nothing has changed. I know, for a fact, that he has forgiven me for beating him in that 1990 World Championship final, for knocking him out in the semi-finals seven years later and for going past his record of five world titles. He has never told me so to my face, but people tell me he never stops talking about me when I'm not in the room.

If there's one person who hates me losing more than myself, it's Eric. Although I'm a grandfather and I'm old enough to take disappointments on the chin, I know he doesn't like it when I get beaten. He still takes it personally, like a football manager taking responsibility when his team is turned over. When I won my sixth world title in 1998, there had been a lot of uninformed speculation that Eric would be cheesed off if I broke his record, but nothing could have been further from the truth. When he was asked if he now regretted investing his own money in me as a scholarship, he replied, 'Everybody deserves a break in life – and I gave him his.'

Every now and then, I like to think I've paid him back – at the bookies. More often than not, when he's backed me to do well at a tournament, I've not just given him a run for his money, or refunded his stake, but left him quids in. When I won my sixteenth world title against Michael van Gerwen in January 2013, I came back from 4–2 down to win 7–4. When I bumped into Eric behind the stage at Alexandra Palace, he planted a big kiss on my cheek and hollered, 'Taylor, you beauty! I had a few bob on you to win 7–4. Knew you wouldn't let me down, my son.'

I'll settle for that. As I remarked earlier, Eric Bristow is the brother I never had. Sometimes we fall out, but I've never lost sight of his part in my success. I couldn't have done it without him. Eric will always be the superstar of darts.

3

G'DAY

August 2013

THE first time I ever set foot on Australian soil, in August 2012, I had not long landed when I got a phone call to say my great pal, if not my shadow, Sid Waddell, had passed away. Sid had been diagnosed, eleven months earlier, with cancer of the bowel, and deep down I knew he was fighting for his life. But as the voice of darts, the man who brought our sport to life on television, it just didn't seem possible that he was gone. I don't mind admitting I shed a few tears because we were so close. It put a real downer on my first trip to the land of the great outdoors, which didn't quite live up to its billing because it turns out they play darts indoors over there like everyone else. I was devastated that I could not go to the Geordie bard's funeral because I was 10,000 miles away, but my absence did not diminish the respect I had for him. He was probably the most intelligent man

I ever met, and I will always regret that I never had the chance to say goodbye.

I had flown to Australia for an exhibition tour, taking in the Gold Coast, Melbourne and Adelaide, where the temperature grew progressively colder in the southern hemisphere the further south I ventured. It was hot enough for 'budgie smugglers', as they call them, in Queensland, and brass monkeys in the two state capitals, but I absolutely loved the country and its people – so I was chuffed to bits, as you can imagine, when Barry Hearn announced that Australia would join the PDC roster in 2013 with the inaugural Sydney Masters.

Barry had spoken, in the media, a couple of years earlier about generating an 'Ashes' culture in darts, and finding a vehicle to forge a bit of Anglo-Australian rivalry. And when Barry spots a gap in the market, there is nobody more likely to exploit it. Staged in the Big Top at Luna Park, a funfair built on the site of old railway sidings used during the construction of the iconic Harbour Bridge, the Sydney Masters was well worth the effort financially: on a par with the Gibraltar Trophy, there was £20,000 for the winner of a three-day tournament. Give or take Dame Edna Everage in the first round, and Kylie Minogue in the crowd, what more could you ask?

For the first time that I can recall in my career, the majority of the sixteen-man field was Australian – the top eight in the PDC Order of Merit, which included Australian internationals Simon Whitlock and Paul Nicholson (a late replacement for James Wade, who was unavailable because of a disciplinary matter), plus eight qualifiers, who were all Aussies and New Zealanders. If Barry had reckoned on big, partisan crowds giving the event instant popular appeal, he was not disappointed. The Aussies were some of the noisiest, and most hostile, supporters I've ever come across. There's nothing like a bit of edge to make the sap rise in an old scrapper from the Potteries. I loved it. In each of my three games en route to the final, I was the bad guy with a target on my back and a bounty on my head. Against Kyle Anderson in the first round, Nicholson in the last eight and Whitlock in the semi-finals, the atmosphere was febrile and the beans were jumping. Happy days.

There may have been a few remnants of jetlag when I beat Anderson 6–1. The winning margin was comfortable enough, but my 98.19 average was nothing special, and it was perhaps significant that my level of performance cranked up with each game as the competition unfolded. Nicholson – a Geordie by birth and accent, but an Aussie through marriage and passport – had knocked me out of the UK Open in 2011, so I was never going to take him lightly. I blew him away 8–2 with a three-dart average of 108.31. That was more like it. Next up was Whitlock, who has been established in the PDC top ten pretty much since the day he joined us from the British Darts Organisation (BDO) circuit. The 'Wizard of Oz', with his distinctive ponytail and long goatee beard, is very much the standard-bearer for Aussies on the oche, and this was the most feverish atmosphere of the lot.

I've been spat at, had coins thrown at me (not as charitable donations) and been showered with lager in Scotland before, but going on stage to face Whitlock in front of his home crowd must be like an England batsman walking out to bat in an Ashes Test at the Sydney Cricket Ground. Although you could barely hear yourself think, I was left in little doubt that the majority wanted me to fail, despite a sizeable ex-pat contingent among the audience. As it turned out, the pressure got to Simon more than it affected me. I soon opened up a 4–1 lead and never looked like relinquishing my advantage, running out a comfortable 10–6 winner. 'Phil got ahead of me early on, and I left myself with too much to do,' said Whitlock afterwards. 'But it's been an amazing week for me and for darts in Australia. It's great for us to have such a big event here in Sydney, and hopefully it's just the start of massive things for the sport in Australia.'

For me, however, the best part of the tournament was still to come. In the final, against Michael van Gerwen, I took the first four legs and never really gave him a chink of light at the end of the tunnel, checking out with 134 to seal a 10–3 triumph with a 109.42 average. Even against players of Michael's heavy scoring power, you are going to win 99 per cent of finals when you are nudging the 110 mark. I was pretty happy with my week in Oz – and none too miffed with the £20,000 prize money. Sure, the crowds were noisy, but sometimes I thrive on the animosity. There's nothing wrong with a partisan atmosphere as long as you don't have people hurling personal abuse, trying to put you off as you throw, or, worse still, calling you a cheat.

It tells you everything about the success of the Sydney Masters that a second event in Australia was added to the 2014 World Series of Darts calendar, in Perth. Coast to coast – and it takes four hours to fly from one side of the Australian mainland to the other – they have caught the darts bug. On Premier League nights in Britain, when we are performing in front of 10,000-strong crowds, it's breakfast time on Friday morning Down Under . . . and the Aussies tune in to watch us in droves. They are used to watching live broadcasts of English football at strange times of the day and night, and now they are adjusting their sleep patterns to follow the 'arrows' as well.

Who knows where it will lead? Before I throw my last dart in competition, I would love to play in an international with the Ashes at stake on the oche. Sydney Opera House would be a nice place to stage it – the punters would be disappointed if they heard me sing, but I would give them the full kit and caboodle on that stage. The Aussies packed out the Big Top, they see all the major PDC events live on the Fox Sports channel now, and it is only a matter of time before they produce a darts World Champion. Whitlock came close in 2010, but I beat him 7–3 in the final at Alexandra Palace, and Nicholson has the stage presence, the charisma and the talent – if he puts them all together and adds a bit more consistency, he has the game to give Waltzing Matilda a spring in her step.

Nicholson is a canny lad, as they say in his Geordie heartland. He cultivated an image as the 'bad boy of darts', wearing dark glasses and a certain look that was guaranteed to exercise the crowd, one way or another. When crowds in Britain took to him, he relished it; but when they decided he was the pantomime villain, I felt the criticism got under his skin and it didn't always help him. As far as I can recall, I've only fallen out with him once – when he beat me at the UK Open in Bolton. No complaints about the result, he beat me good and proper, but I pulled him up later because TV cameras appeared to capture him waving me a sarcastic 'cheerio' as I made my way off the stage. He explained that he was only waving goodbye to the demons that had prevented him from producing his best form on the big occasion, and we left it at that. There was another episode, at the 2011 World Matchplay, where he said he would 'put me to bed' if I wasn't at my best. But I am old enough to understand that Sky are happy to hype up any rivalry between us, but it's nothing more than words intended to build up big games. If the Aussies can bring through another couple of world-class performers like Whitlock and Nicholson – I'm talking about players who regularly make the last sixteen, or the last eight, of tournaments on the box – they will be a real force as a darting nation.

But you can take it as read that I loved going to Oz, in the week after England's cricketers had won the Ashes 3–0 in August 2013, and flying the Cross of St George above the Big Top at Luna Park. Take that, cobbers.

4

DAD

MOST of us are lucky enough to grow up regarding our father as a role model and a best mate. Some of us are luckier still – we get a second 'dad' whose son is a worldwide pop star, but who still finds the time to be the perfect sounding board when you need a cup of tea and a chat. Losing my dad to cancer in October 1997 left a huge void in my life. Although I was a multiple world champion, a father of four and I was doing well financially, it was a major setback. It happens to us all, but the trouble with dads is that you always think they are indestructible; it would be much nearer the truth to say they are irreplaceable.

My father, Douglas – my middle name is an indelible tribute to his memory – was a decent, hard-working, honest man. He was as thin as a rake – mainly because of the unglamorous manual jobs he did, from apprentice builder to making quarry and floor tiles, shifting tons of clay in and out of the kilns by hand. Although I grew up in a household where we lived hand-to-mouth out of necessity rather than by choice, Dad gave us the odd treat when there was any slack in the purse-strings. Once he won £41 on the pools, for twenty-three points on his coupon, and spent it on a week-long family holiday at Butlins.

As well as acquiring his work ethic, I hope his honesty will be passed down through generations of the Taylor clan. If anyone gave him too much change at the checkout, he would refund the overpayment. And, unlike Premier League footballers who park in bays for disabled drivers, he wouldn't even wait for ten seconds on a double yellow line. Traffic wardens would be an extinct breed if motorists were all as straight as my old man. Despite being a prodigious smoker who went through up to thirty fags a day, he was as fit as a butcher's dog and never had a day off work in thirty years. It was a terrible shock when he began passing blood and was diagnosed with cancer of the bowel. Shortly before he passed away, I took him and Mum to Lourdes. Yes, I was hoping for a miracle, but towards the end I like to think it was also a source of spiritual comfort for both my parents.

I knew that Lourdes was in the south of France, so I booked us on a flight to Nice. Nobody told me the south of France was that big, or that Lourdes was a seven-hour drive across virtually the whole radius of the country from Nice. Maybe I should have paid more attention at the back of the class during Geography at school. When we finally made it to our destination, having flown to the wrong part of France, there was a pilgrimage on and every hotel room for miles around was booked up. It took us several more hours before we managed to find somewhere to stay for the night, out in the back of beyond. In Lourdes, people were being pushed around the streets in wheelchairs and, in some cases, their beds. The queues for treatment with spring water from the grotto, which is supposed to have healing properties, were massive. Around 200 million people are said to have visited the holy shrine in the last 150 years. Most of them seemed to be there when Taylor Tours arrived on the spur of the moment.

Judging by some of the noises coming from behind the screens, the treatment either killed you or cured you. (Mum thought she was going to watch a film, and that the squeals and shrieks were all part of the screenplay.) Although the trip was more demanding than I had intended, in terms of travel arrangements, I hope it conveyed to Dad how much I was grateful for everything he had done for me. He was probably the last of his generation, a good-hearted man who was never inclined to poke his nose into someone else's affairs, let alone revel in someone else's misfortune. If you told him the latest gossip about the neighbours, or people from across town he once knew, his stock answer was always the same: 'Nothing to do with me, it's none of my business.' I wish there were a few more like him now.

Although there were not as many TV channels forty years ago, he never used to watch much TV – apart from sport and the odd comedy. He would always rather go out and have a couple of pints. But you don't realise how much fathers do for you until they are gone: all the running around, all the chores, all the sacrifices. When I was still a toddler and we didn't have two brass farthings to rub together, Dad used to drop me off at 6.30 a.m. every morning with a lady who was effectively my child-minder, perching me on the crossbar of an old police bike with only one pedal.

In adolescence, I used to lift weights and work out like a boxer. I wasn't too bothered about being punched in the face or hit below the belt, but I used to watch big fights on TV with my dad and, it's fair to say, I was lighter on my feet than I am as a grandfather these days. If Dad came in after a hard day at work and found me slumped in front of the box, he used to chide: 'Have you done your weights yet? I bet John Conteh isn't sat around watching *Coronation Street.*' It was good preparation for my future teacher–pupil relationship with Eric Bristow, and all the times he told me to get off my fat arse and get back to the practice board. Just as Eric could be tough, if only to drive my standards as high as possible, my dad was not a nag just for the sake of it either. He didn't want me to grow up as a couch potato. I hope he was proud of the way I turned out.

When I won my sixth world title at the 1998 PDC World Championships, breaking Eric's record of five, how I wished my dad could have been there to see it. At the presentation ceremony, I just about managed to hold myself together, but the minute I walked off stage, I couldn't keep the waterworks at bay any longer. My mum is an incredible lady, and I owe her more than any figure on a winner's cheque at a darts tournament, but I've always been grateful that I inherited my dad's genes for accuracy with a projectile. In his playing days, he was a decent club cricketer, a formidable fast bowler with a reputation for a nagging line and length. Now I am affluent enough to own two holiday homes, I wish he was still around so he could live the life of Riley in one of them. I really wish that after a lifetime of working hard, paying his taxes and bringing up his family as best as he could, my dad could have retired to a life in the sun.

Even when he was made redundant from his job, he picked up the gauntlet when I took over the Cricketers Arms, a run-down, boarded-up pub in the May Bank district of Newcastle-under-Lyme, as a business investment in 1993. Dad ran the place for me, even though he would have preferred to spend his time on the other side of the bar instead of pulling pints for the punters, stock-taking and playing mine host, even though he wasn't especially talkative by nature. We had a terrific crowd of regulars who loved a chat, but my dad was never a fan of small-talk. He was happy just to keep the cellar in order, make sure there was ale in the barrels and then go home to Mum for his tea. But he ran the Cricketers Arms like a bank manager in charge of a hole in the wall – every penny had to be accounted for. He was so honest, so diligent, that if I took £1 out of the till to buy the kids a bar of chocolate, he was on my case if it hadn't been replaced within a couple of hours. Every time he wanted to balance the books, he would send one of the kids upstairs to the living quarters with the message, 'Grandad says you have to put a pound back in the till.'

Of course, you can only admire his determination to run the business along such ramrod straight lines, but he would drive me crackers. I would protest, 'It's my pub, my till, my money – surely I can do what I please as long as the bills are paid on time?' Bless him, Dad would not have any of it. But I wish to God he was still with us, soaking up the sunshine somewhere nice like Tenerife.

As it happens, I have 'adopted' a second father with many of my old man's traits: Peter Williams. I grew up in the backstreets of Burslem, just down the road from him and his son – a kid who would become a true superstar. Robbie Williams is thirteen years younger than me, and our paths never crossed socially when we were growing up in the Potteries. He wasn't involved in the raiding parties that would do a bunk over the fence at the sweet factory near his house and nick jars of the rejects, although there didn't seem to be a lot wrong with the fruit drops and toffees we pilfered – they could still rot your teeth in five minutes. Robbie says he remembers me knocking around in the neighbourhood when I was cock of the walk in my late teens, but I can't honestly say that I have any recollection of him from those days.

Apart from attending Mill Hill infants school, like Robbie, and lobbing some of my first darts in the games room at Ryan Hall Catholic Club – where he performed some of his earliest gigs – my first connection with his family was over the bar. Whether it was through playing darts or as a one-time publican myself, I knew a lot of the pubs around Stoke, and as an act of solidarity with the licensed victuallers who ran them, I knew quite a few of the landlords too. Peter and Jan Williams ran the Red Lion in Burslem when I was a young hustler, and around the time I won my first world title, their son Robbie joined a boy band called Take That as their youngest member. He has also done all right for himself as a solo artist, and as I write he has just played a sell-out gig in the Czech Republic capital, Prague. I know Pete has joined him on tour because he's just texted me to say what a great place it is.

Pete Conway, to use his stage name, is a retired comedian and club singer – and, like many stage performers, he is at his most entertaining, and most informative, in conversation. Although we knew each other before Robbie was famous, he has become my guru since my father died. Whenever I've got a problem, or if something's on my mind, he's the one who lends an ear and a kind word. That's why I have come to regard him as my second dad. When we get together, normally it just starts with one of us ringing the other and asking, 'Fancy a cup of tea?' And normally, it will turn into an all-night brew-up, if you get my drift. Often I'll turn up on Peter's doorstep just in time to catch the first race of the afternoon on TV. We'll sift through the cards, study the form – my knowledge of horse-racing is so limited that I might as well be studying a Chinese telephone directory – and put a fiver on each race. Nothing daft, no staking your mortgage on a dead cert only to find you've backed a three-legged donkey, just a bit of fun. We'll put the kettle on, channel-hop between one race meeting and another, and put the world to rights. When the last nag has trailed home, and the bookies have had the shirt off my back, £5 at a time, we might have a glass of wine – and if neither of us has to be up early the following day, we might even drain a bottle. Before you can say Red Rum, it's 4 a.m. and we haven't just put the world to rights: we've cured it of most known diseases.

Having a son who is so famous, Peter is the perfect source of advice I turn to if I've been upset by something in the papers or a bit of nonsense on the internet. Down the years, Robbie has had to put up with all sorts of headlines – some of them true, some of them rubbish, some of them scandalous, some of them heart-warming – and Peter has seen him come through them all. We also share a love of our local football club, Port Vale. There have been times when some fans wish Robbie would just buy the place lock, stock and barrel, and take them on a magic carpet ride like Elton John did at Watford when I was a youngster. But I know he bought a fistful of shares in the club back in 2006, and Peter used to run the social club at Vale Park. I think he's got a lifetime membership at Port Vale now, and the club look after him when he goes to home games.

I was absolutely thrilled for Peter when he got married again in May 2013, to a lovely girl called Melanie who he met through the Donna Louise Trust, a local charity based in Trentham Lakes, where she is director of fundraising. The Donna Louise Children's Hospice provides specialist care for children with reduced life expectancy and respite care for their families – it's a charity that does wonderful work, although it's heartbreaking when you walk in there and see the angelic little faces of kids who might not be there the next time you pay a visit. I believe Pete, who split up with his first wife when Robbie was still a toddler, serenaded his new bride at the reception that night on the karaoke – and then Robbie serenaded the happy couple.

Whether it was my dad ticking me off for sprawling on the couch when I should have been lifting weights, or Pete dispensing paternal advice as we pore over the runners and riders in the 2.30 at Haydock Park, I have been blessed with two fathers. But I know both of them stand by one golden rule in life: Everything you achieve, you have to earn.

5

BLARNEY

October 2013

RUNNING the gauntlet of partisan Aussie fans barracking for Simon Whitlock at the Sydney Masters is a piece of cake if you've ever been drawn to face Brendan Dolan at the World Grand Prix in Dublin and you're an Englishman with fifteen world titles to your name.

In 2011, it was my privilege to beat Brendan 6–3 in the final at the Citywest Conference and Events Centre, and in the previous year I had whitewashed him in the first round without even allowing him a single dart at a double. I would have been more popular if I had been the child-catcher from *Chitty Chitty Bang Bang* at a kids' Christmas party. For a raucous crowd, almost unanimous in its support of my opponent, I think only my World Championship semi-final against Eric Bristow at the Circus Tavern in 1997, when my old mentor had rolled back the years, tops that for an audience utterly one-sided in their loyalties.

The night before our final, Brendan had hit a perfect nine-dart finish in the semis against James Wade, and the place was absolutely jumping. So it was with a little trepidation, but a lot of excitement, that I headed to the Emerald Isle in search of my fourth major title of 2013.

The Grand Prix is unique among the big tournaments because it's double start and double finish to each leg. In my book that makes it the hardest trophy of all to win, especially if you have to play Dolan and his cheerleaders. Nothing personal against Dolan – he is one of the most easy-going, affable characters on the circuit – but it was almost a relief to avoid him when I was paired with fellow Englishman Jamie Caven in the first round. No problems there, nor against Paul Nicholson, Gary Anderson and James Wade on my way to the final. With the exception of the second round against Nicholson, when I was nowhere near my best, I was happy enough to nudge a 100 average every time, which is decent scoring in the double-start format, and I was particularly pleased to put Wade away 5–1 in the semi-finals because he had won the tournament twice before, even if James fell way below his usual standards and appeared to lose heart before the end.

Following that game, however, I was less amused by my post-match TV interview with Sky Sports' Rod Studd. My opponent in the final was to be Dave Chisnall, a player I had beaten many times before – but Rod decided to stir the pot by reminding me that Chizzy had knocked me out of the World Championship almost two years earlier, and asked whether that would be playing on my mind. I know TV interviews are all part of the game, and you don't want to fill airtime with meaningless, bland platitudes, but I didn't appreciate Rod's question. It's like asking a motorist who has driven half a million miles if he's haunted by the one time he's picked up a parking ticket. I told Rod he was out of order and cut short the interview, like a politician abruptly walking out on Jeremy Paxman after a hostile line of questioning on *Newsnight*.

In the feedback, some viewers thought I was being a bit precious, while others said the world No.1 should set a better example. They may be right. Look, I'm only human. But if that had been Adrian Lewis, Raymond van Barneveld or Michael van Gerwen going through to the final, do you think Sky would have jogged their memory by reminding them of a previous occasion when Chisnall had beaten them? Not on your nelly. Not on your telly. I don't expect broadcasters to fawn over me or to be painfully sycophantic – but there are times when I feel judged by a different set of rules than everyone else.

To be fair, in any major tournament the semi-final stage is where you make your biggest 'push' – or where you reach the greatest intensity. Reach the final, and you are on to a good payday, win or lose; miss out on the final and you feel as if all the practice, all your hard work over the week, has just come up short. It's a bit like being on the TV quiz show *Who Wants To Be A Millionaire?* The further you go in the competition, the bigger the drop in prize money if you get knocked out. But sometimes that extra intensity comes with an extra pressure. You're like a kettle reaching boiling point, ready to whistle and for the lid to blow off. Is it any coincidence that some of the biggest controversies you see in darts these days seem to occur in big semi-finals? That's not for me to judge, but I've been involved in one or two episodes I regret, and, like my little fall-out with Rod Studd – which was patched up and, hopefully, forgotten overnight – they have seemed to happen after games in the last four, when you come off stage and your mind is still racing.

Whenever I reach a final, I tend to be more relaxed where a lot of players, especially the ones looking for a breakthrough win to announce themselves on the PDC circuit, often clam up. The 2013 World Grand Prix final against Chizzy was a case in point. The poor lad was a rabbit caught in the headlights. He just froze – which is no mean achievement when you are being roasted at gas mark seven under those TV lights. I whitewashed him 6–0, and although you do feel pangs of remorse afterwards, on stage you can't give opponents even a moment's respite. In all those lessons and hours of tutelage from Eric Bristow, he drummed it into me: Put the other bloke under pressure from the first dart, jump on them straight away. I've won a few tournaments, and lost a couple of finals, where the decisive factor was a killer instinct that went missing at critical moments.

Time and again, Eric would tell me to keep pressurising my opponent. Make him sweat, make him pay. No mercy, no let-up, no exceptions. Chisnall was game, and he kept going, but he had been unhappy on the practice board backstage and I remember thinking, 'Crikey, if he's getting a bit down on himself when there's nobody watching, how's he going to cope in front of a live audience and the glare of TV cameras?' The answer was emphatic – I beat him 6–0, winning eighteen legs to Chizzy's two. And the two legs he did win both came in the final set. Eric would have been proud of my ruthlessness, and I make no excuses for it. As a spectacle, I'm sure it was more one-sided than Sky Sports would have liked, but I'm not here to fill their airtime by fleshing out contests into sudden-death thrillers just to give the other fella a chance. When you're fifty-three years old, and playing someone twenty years younger, trust me, you don't hang around on that stage a second longer than necessary. Given the chance, I know for a fact that there are plenty of young guns who would happily do exactly the same thing to an old grandad.

Chisnall didn't feel sorry for me when he knocked me out of the World Championship – the result Rod Studd was so keen to remind me about – and I would not expect his tea and sympathy. What goes around comes around, and although I didn't consider that whitewash as payback for what Chizzy did to me at Ally Pally twenty-two months earlier, it's all part and parcel of our job. Don't forget, after twenty-five years at this level, my head-to-head record against nearly everyone is better than theirs against mine. That's not a boast, it's a fact. Don't think for one second that, if you knock me out of one competition I won't get you back in another one somewhere down the line.

How did I celebrate my eleventh World Grand Prix title? With a pint of Guinness, of course – when in Dublin, you've got to go with the flow, haven't you? It's a fantastic country and the crowds are some of the most, er, passionate in the world. They can be a bit rowdy at times, but I love the Blarney Army. They enjoy the craic but they don't cross the line. The Emerald Isle will always be one of my favourite places to play darts. Even when I'm drawn against Brendan Dolan!

6

BARNEY

MY only consolation, after losing the World Championship final in a sudden-death finish against Raymond van Barneveld on New Year's Day 2007, was the explosion in the popularity of darts as a major televised sport that accompanied my defeat. We had enjoyed healthy viewing figures, climbing every year, until I met Barney in the last final to be played at the Circus Tavern in Purfleet. But that gripping finish, after I had literally thrown away a 3–0 lead, sent public interest through the roof – more than one million people tuned in on Sky, their biggest audience share for any sport outside Premier League football.

Maybe it was something to do with the bleak sporting landscape at the time – the England football team had come unstuck on penalties, as usual, at the World Cup six months earlier and in the Ashes we were heading for a 5–0 whitewash in Australia. Maybe people were craving a proper contest, or just a bit of sporting theatre beyond the ordinary. Sadly for me, but happily for the rude health of darts, Barney's fightback was perfect late-night drama to reel in a whole new generation of fans. For Raymond, it was arguably the high-water mark of a long-running rivalry, probably my longest-running duel in professional darts. And although we've had our ups and downs, culminating in one episode at the 2013 World Championship I would rather forget, our rivalry has never got in the way of an enduring respect for each other.

In any sport, you need a rival. It puts bums on seats, makes great TV and gives regulars something to talk about down your local pub. Nigel Benn and Chris Eubank would not have missed their rivalry for all the world, nor would Bjorn Borg and John McEnroe or Steve Ovett and Sebastian Coe. Liverpool v Manchester United in the Premier League, England v Australia for the Ashes, Muhammad Ali v Joe Frazier for the world heavyweight title . . . rivalry sells at the box office, and I don't mind a bit of needle in darts if it helps to pay the bills.

Back in the 1990s, my main rival at many of the big tournaments was Dennis 'The Menace' Priestley – except that Dennis is such a lovely bloke that I could never find it in my heart to consider him as the enemy. In fact, for around six years we pooled all our prize money, travelled the country together in a campervan and shared twin rooms in hotels to cut costs. To some opponents, Dennis might have been a menace because of his slow, ponderous style, but to me he will always be more of a soul-mate than a deadly rival. And he will always be in the record books as the first player to win both the British Darts Organisation and Professional Darts Corporation versions of the World Championship.

Around the time Dennis lost just a little bit of his sparkle, before he was diagnosed with prostate cancer in 2007, a big cuddly bear of a Dutchman was making a name for himself after winning the Lakeside world title two years running in 1998 and 1999. Despite his playing on the BDO circuit and my allegiance with the PDC, I had come across Barney a few times – notably at the British Classic in 1997 at Blackpool, where the atmosphere between the two organisations was icier than the North Pole – before our so-called Match of the Century at Wembley Conference Centre in 1999. That was a one-off game, played against the clock, for £100,000 in prize money: one hour, with the leader taking home £60,000 when the countdown reached zero and the runner-up receiving £40,000. Unofficially, it was a barometer to measure the strength of the two rival camps: the two-time BDO world champion, a big star in his native Holland, against yours truly, who had won seven world titles before the turn of the century.

From the outset, I must admit I was dismissive of Barney's chances. He has a lovely, languid throwing style, easy on the eye and wonderfully consistent, but I was in a rich vein of form, and in a two-horse race the bookies made him a distant third. The BDO did its best to make sure the contest never took place at all, fearing a win for the man from the 'dark' side in the PDC camp would be a feather in the cap of those who had formed a breakaway movement in 1993, which was originally known as the World Darts Council before adopting its modern PDC title. But Barney, good for him, insisted that it was a golden opportunity to make a big statement, claiming he had received torrents of emails from well-wishers in Holland who thought he would beat me easily. By the time commercial good sense held sway over politics, I was not hugely concerned about the money – I just wanted the chance to prove who was the best darts player in the world.

My old mate Sid Waddell wrote a piece in the official programme, warning me that 'hundreds of Dutch fans could make Wembley sound like Amsterdam when the fleet is in town', and there was plenty of orange in evidence when the two gladiators made their way on stage. But from the moment we toed the oche, Barney looked more rattled than a Patagonian's castanets. I don't know whether all the diplomatic manoeuvres behind the scenes had caught up with him, or if it was simply the enormity of the occasion that unsettled him. Ray was once a postman in The Hague, but he would have needed to shift sackloads of mail to make £60,000 in an hour in his old job. He had been feted with tickertape receptions and personal messages of congratulations from the royal family in Holland when he became a double world champion, but they didn't know much about me in his own country. They soon did.

After the first four legs went with the throw, I pulled away to lead 9–4 at the halfway stage and I probably broke his spirit with a 144 checkout to make it 10–6. When the clock ticked down to zero, I was leading 21–10 and my three-dart average of 103.40 was fully ten points better off than Barney's. At the time, I regarded it as the biggest win of my career – not for the money, which was nice, but for the prestige and the statement it made – but I was disappointed with van Barneveld's reaction afterwards. He sloped off through a side exit without giving a post-match interview to TV anchorman Eamonn Holmes. On my way out of the venue, I stumbled across a corporate function where most of the fans in attendance were decked in orange. I told them to go home and tell everyone in Holland who was the greatest player in the world. But I will always treasure the memory of my own tickertape shower when time ran out, and waving the Cross of St George on that Wembley stage.

Ever since that Match of the Century, I have always enjoyed playing Barney. There's always a frisson of excitement in the air, an edge to the contest that makes the sap rise in an old warrior but stops short of pure enmity. Down the years, I've had the better of our duels, but I still get excited whenever I'm playing him in the Premier League or any of the televised majors. Of course I wish I had beaten him in that sudden-death final in 2007, but I settled that score two years later at Alexandra Palace, where I beat Raymond 7–1 to win my fourteenth world title.

That was the night he walked on stage waving the Dutch flag, turning the final into England v Holland, which was his biggest mistake. He had built up a sizeable following among his Barney Army, and I did not expect to have all of a home crowd on my side by any stretch of the imagination. I don't know if he was waving that flag because his compatriot Robin van Persie, who was playing for Arsenal in those days, was supporting him in the audience, but it backfired on him. That little stunt turned the crowd against him, and as I waited at the top of the aisle ahead of my walk-on, the boos were drowning out the cheers for Barney. I was thinking to myself, 'Carry on waving that thing around, old son – it's not working for you, but it's doing wonders for me.' I was mindful of what had happened at the Circus Tavern, and I wanted to harness anything I could turn to my advantage. Raising the Dutch standard like that worked a treat. It was a spectacular own goal.

I had only dropped three sets on my way to the final, and to be honest Barney did well to make it four. I smashed him 7–1 with an average of 110.94, a record for the final. After letting a big lead slip in 2007, there was no way I was going to leave the door ajar for him this time, and I was right to be so clinical. Barney didn't play badly – only Dennis Priestley has ever lost in the final with a higher average than Ray's 101.18 that night. But did it feel good to turn him over? You bet it did. That made it 14–5 to me in world titles, but more importantly it cleansed the sudden-death heartbreak from my mind. I didn't need to have any more hang-ups about it after that performance.

Although I now considered Barney my biggest rival, I was also conscious that he was spending most of the year outside his own country, where his profile had increased dramatically over the previous decade. He had once had his own TV show and I was told that his picture hung in pubs next to football stars Marco van Basten, Dennis Bergkamp and Ruud Gullit. But sometimes, as I've discovered to my cost, there can be a sinister side to fame and celebrity. And in the year after I had beaten him in the World Championship final, I became aware that Barney was troubled by events away from darts. He was still idolised by crowds in Britain, especially the big crowds turning out on Thursday nights in the Premier League, but I sensed he was more comfortable playing on TV than he was offstage. Soon it became evident why he was distracted: back home in Holland, he was being blackmailed.

When a fellow player is being put through the wringer, and fears for his family's safety, rivalry takes a back seat and compassion takes over. When Barney was playing at the Grand Slam of Darts in Wolverhampton, a thirty-minute commute from the Potteries for me, I invited him to stay at Taylor Towers for a few days instead of being cooped up in a hotel. Although we don't exactly live in each other's pockets on the circuit, a change of pace, or a change of scenery, is often as good as a rest. I think Barney was relieved to be our house guest, with my wife making a fuss of him, when he could have spent a week in Wolverhampton feeling lonely and vulnerable.

The details of Barney's blackmail case are none of my business. Suffice it to say, some hoodlum was trying to extort 10,000 euros out of him, but I was careful to let him volunteer information rather than badger him to spill the beans. There was no doubt, however, that Raymond was at a low ebb, and it would have taken a heart of stone not to feel for him. I was just happy to help a fellow sportsman in his hour of need. As players, we all go through the same pressures and demanding schedules, and I could not stand by as a colleague on the circuit suffered without offering to intervene. Before the Grand Slam in November 2010, he gave an interview to the *Daily Mirror* that is pretty self-explanatory and needs no further comment from me:

> Tortured Raymond van Barneveld has thanked Phil 'The Power' Taylor for helping him through his blackmail terror . . . after a nightmare which left him fearing for his family's safety. Threats were made to post footage of him allegedly romping with a mistress on the internet or to hack into his computer and download child porn onto it.
>
> A 26-year-old Rotterdam man is due to be sentenced in court this week for attempting to extort £9,500 from van Barneveld – but the experience has left the five-times world champion a broken man who felt abandoned by fellow players to face a terrifying ordeal.

Only Taylor, the man he beat in a sudden-death finish at the 2007 PDC World Championship, has offered fans' favourite Barney meaningful support – and the experience has left him feeling shattered. Van Barneveld said: 'These past few months have been the worst of my life and I still don't know where it is all going to end. It has put a strain on my health, a strain on my marriage and I have had to cut down on my appearances in competitions to cope with it. Last year I was diagnosed as a diabetic, and when I went to the doctor for a check-up last month my blood sugar levels were still far too high, but I am not surprised because I've been trapped in this nightmare.'

Barney's ordeal began in February during the popular Premier League competition where he hit a nine-dart finish in Aberdeen. But he had no idea how quickly his life would unravel. He said: 'I was in Belfast when I started receiving a lot of crank calls because somebody had posted my cellphone number on the internet. At first they were just silly nuisance calls, but suddenly they became more sinister. One said he was going to hack into my computer, download child porn and destroy my reputation . . . and then came the blackmail . . . 'He told me, "Come to Rotterdam Zoo and pay 10,000 euros or we will post a sex tape of you and another woman on the internet." At first I ignored the calls, but they would not go away and they were very threatening. There were text messages saying, "We know where your children go to school" or "We saw your wife out shopping today" and their information was accurate. I was terrified they would kill my family.

'On another occasion, I was away playing darts and my wife was unsettled by a car parked outside our home. They began calling her to put pressure on her. When the threats are aimed at your wife and family, that is when you get scared, and I had to go to the police. Fortunately the police took it very seriously and they told me this guy had been calling me from a pre-paid cellphone. When they managed to trace him and make an arrest, I thought that it would all go away. But last weekend I was sat at home with my wife on the sofa and we received another threat. They said, "We have still got the tapes, you have twelve hours to make contact and pay up, the clock is ticking."

'I do not know why I have been singled out as a target for this blackmail. Of course, there has been no tape of me with another woman posted on the internet – if it existed, I'm sure it would have been made public by now. But we have the same saying in Holland as you do in the UK – there is no smoke without fire, and my wife believes there must be something to it. My marriage is almost in trouble and we have been through a tough time.'

Barney now feels more appreciated in Britain than in his own country, and during his blackmail terror he has been grateful for the support of his big rival Taylor. He added, 'I've been playing darts for twenty-six years and I thought I had made some good friends in that time, but only three players have taken the trouble to send me

> messages of support. My fellow Dutchmen, Vincent van der Voort and Co Stompe, have been kind, but the only other guy who has stuck up for me is Phil, which speaks volumes for him as a man. Last year, during the Grand Slam at Wolverhampton, he even invited me to stay at his house for a few days, and I cannot speak highly enough of him as a player and as a host.
>
> 'But at times over the past few months, I wish I had stayed a postman in The Hague. Of course it was special to win five world titles, but sometimes I wonder if it was all worth it, because out there on stage I have felt completely alone. Standing on the oche, you are always under huge pressure – but this has only increased my level of stress. You can't handle it, you can't live with yourself for putting the family under great strain and you want to take a year out, but it's not that simple. That would not make it go away – it might only suspend the problem for a year. I will have to think about hiring security guards, if not for me then for my family.
>
> 'And the damage has been done. Nobody in Holland believes in me any more – everyone seems to think there is a sex tape, and all the media have been giving their reaction on something that does not exist. There are people who think I should have paid him off, but where would it end if I did that?'

Can you imagine the strain Barney must have been under? It's a tribute to his mental strength that he is still competing at such a high level. The stress of something so awful would have pushed lesser men under. We are only human, and it's only right and proper that we should help each other out in times of trouble. Mind you, it only takes a tight game, with high stakes, for competitive instincts to take over again, and in December 2012 my World Championship semi-final against Barney boiled over moments after the winning dart.

Emotions run high when you are playing for a place in the final. As I've intimated earlier in this book, the semi-finals are often where you make your biggest push in a big tournament because they probably mark the frontier between success and disappointment. And by the time I had reached the last four at Ally Pally, I was riddled with man-flu. I don't know why, but I always fall ill around Christmas, and from now on I'm going to have a flu jab in October to make sure I don't rock up at the richest darts competition on earth feeling like death warmed up any more. On the night I beat Barney 6–4 to reach the final, I had been sucking energy sweets and lozenges like a kid in a sweet shop, and when I raced into a 5–1 lead I was bang on course for an early night: hot water bottle, Lemsip, lights out, lovely. Before the game, Barney had claimed he wasn't 'scared of [Phil Taylor] any more', but he was like a deer in the headlights when I closed out consecutive legs with 141 and 111 checkouts, and I assumed that would take care of business.

I should have remembered the 2007 final, though. Six years earlier, I had won nine of the first ten legs before

Barney came storming back. Now, blow me down, he was doing it again. I had missed two darts to win 6–1, yet half an hour later I was only 5–4 up and the tide was going out on me fast. Ray decorated his fightback with a fantastic 125 takeout – bullseye, 25, bullseye – and no two ways about it, I was rattled. Although I was knackered, and flagging fast, I managed to summon the strength and accuracy to take the tenth set and win 6–4. I don't mind admitting I was glad it didn't go to a decider because the momentum and the crowd were all with Barney, and there was only a sense of relief when I sank double 16 to book a date with another flying Dutchman, Michael van Gerwen, on New Year's Day.

After the obligatory fist-pump and outpouring of joy, bouncing across the stage like a beach ball on a sea breeze, I turned to observe the post-match formalities with Barney. Win or lose, you always shake hands as a mark of respect for what your opponent has gone through. We shook on it – no problem. But Barney, for some reason, would not let go. He pulled me around and then tried to embrace me, but instead of a warm hug he almost had me in a headlock. Let's get one thing straight: I'm sure that Barney was not trying to hurt me and that his intentions were based in sportsmanship, but he's a big, cuddly bear of a man, a gentle giant, and he's probably more powerful than he realises. When he was pulling me around, he was hurting me a bit – and when you are already laid low with a heavy cold, and your defences are low, the last thing you need is someone hauling you across the stage. I didn't like it and told him he was out of order. Although I don't remember doing so at the time, TV replays suggest that I used two words, in a seven-letter arrangement, which I should not have chuntered in public. Behind the stage, away from the all-seeing TV cameras, I told Ray, 'Listen, bud, we've always got on well and there's no bigger fan of you than me. We're not going to fall out over this.' When tournament director Tommy Cox told the papers, 'Nothing went on, so there's nothing to say,' I thought that was the end of it.

But when I woke up on New Year's Eve, still struggling with the flu and feeling crap, and switched on the TV, I was shocked by what I saw. The pictures of my little tiff with Barney didn't look great. If I was feeling lousy before, the replays made me feel even worse. I should have been buzzing after reaching another World Championship final, but instead I felt lower than a shipwreck on the seabed. On social media networks, the world and his dog were having their say – and most of the reaction was hostile towards me. I texted Barney to apologise if he thought I had over-reacted, and he promised to have a drink at the PDC Awards dinner at the Dorchester Hotel a few days later to put the whole thing behind us. He was very gracious and dignified, and our respect for each other as competitors and friends still transcends the heat of the moment on stage, which is the way it should be.

That was not the end of my soul-searching, though. The public backlash made me fearful that the crowd would turn against me in the final when I played Barney's compatriot Michael van Gerwen. Feeling sorry for myself, I threatened to retire. 'More than anything, I'm gutted and ashamed of myself,' I told the press. 'I will walk away tomorrow if people feel so much animosity towards me. Honestly, I will walk away because I feel very down, very low. This is cracking me up and doing my head in. I am scrutinised in everything I do and everything I say, I am plastered everywhere. I have a nice life, I have worked hard enough for it, but I have feelings, my family have feelings and I don't want my grandkids going through this.'

Barry Hearn, the PDC chairman, was on to me in a flash. He loves a bit of spice in the pot, and he told me in no uncertain terms that I was going nowhere. But the only way to win over the people who were critical of me following that incident with Barney was to make them proud of me again by winning a sixteenth world title. I came up with the right answer this time – although there was a different outcome when I next played against Barney in a major semi-final at the 2014 Premier League play-offs. More on that story later . . .

7

SLAM

November 2013

LITTLE did Adrian Lewis know, when he hit nineteen maximum 180s in the World Matchplay final against me and still lost 18–13, that our sequel at the Grand Slam of Darts four months later would set a new benchmark for quality.

Sometimes, when you get swept along by the moment, you feel there is no limit to how high you can raise the bar and how high you can drive your average. Rarely, if ever, do you find a match where both players push each other to new heights, like a pair of prize-fighters with neither prepared to back down. My Grand Slam semi-final against Lewis on 17 November 2013 was widely acclaimed by Sky Sports pundits and viewers as the greatest game of darts ever played, and I am not going to argue with the judges. They can't all be wrong. No disrespect to Robert Thornton, but when I beat him in the final, it was almost an anticlimax – not because I was sorry to get my hands on the winner's cheque for £100,000, but because the adrenalin rush of my titanic slinging match with Lewis was still subsiding.

Apart from the World Championship and Premier League, the Grand Slam is the most lucrative title on the circuit. Played over nine days at the Civic Hall in Wolverhampton – a compact venue where the crowd always feels on top of you (both in the stalls and the minstrel gallery on the upper tier) – I regard it as one of my happiest hunting grounds. It's also where I experimented by wearing glasses on stage for the first time in 2010, a trial I abandoned after being knocked out in the quarter-finals by Steve Beaton. I like the place because I can commute from the Potteries to Wolverhampton, and when the darts land where you want them to go, it's one of the best atmospheres you can experience in competition.

According to the statisticians, I had played Lewis fifty-four times before our semi-final on this Sunday afternoon – I had won forty-three times, Adrian ten and there was one draw – but if we live to play each other in another 1,000 games, we'll be hard-pushed to serve up a better one. For Adrian to average 110.99 over twenty-five legs, and lose 16–9, is a tribute to the quality of his darts. For him to contribute eighteen of the thirty-two maximums we shared – a record on the PDC circuit – speaks volumes for the way he fought fire with fire. And for the crowd to take it in turns to offer both of us voluble support shows how much both players' efforts were appreciated by the paying punters.

It only lasted fifty-two minutes, but that was long enough for Adrian and me to hit 180 a phenomenal thirty-two times between us – falling only one short of the world record shared by Ted Hankey and Chris Mason in their semi-final at the Lakeside in 2000. Poor old 'Jackpot' (I like Adrian's nickname, and the story behind it – he cleaned out a fruit machine in Las Vegas). His nineteen maximums against me in the 2013 World Matchplay final were not enough, and another eighteen were not enough this time. But in terms of two competitors firing on all cylinders, and sustained heavy scoring, it was the best game of darts I've ever been involved in.

To do it justice, I've had to watch a re-run of the whole match on the internet. When you are on stage, slugging it out like a pair of middleweights trading clusters of punches, you get carried away by the raw excitement. Adrian and I were often egging each other on, almost willing each other to raise the bar higher. It was magic, like a theme park ride where the louder you scream, the faster it goes. Sitting through the replay now, it still makes the pulse rate quicken. We've all watched action films where we know what happens in the end, but it doesn't spoil our enjoyment. Well, in this thriller Bruce Willis doesn't outsmart the bad guys in *Die Hard*, Clint Eastwood doesn't nab the serial killer in *Dirty Harry* and Daniel Radcliffe doesn't melt Lord Voldemort in one of the Harry Potter movies, but The Power corners his prey. Eventually. The best way for me to convey my sense of enjoyment as the vivid spectacle unfolded is to talk you through all twenty-five legs, one at a time. For sheer quality, if this wasn't the greatest game of darts that's ever been on TV, I would like to see a better one.

1–0: It always helps to settle the nerves if you pepper the treble 20 'lipstick' from the first dart. Three in a bed? That'll do nicely – and I'm straight out of the blocks with two 180s in my first three visits. Adrian does not take it lying down, replying with a 171 of his own, and although I make a meal of what should be a straightforward twelve-darter, I take out 44 on double 2 to break the throw. In the Sky Sports commentary box, Wayne Mardle thinks the tone is too friendly: 'They seem a bit pally-pally at the moment – I'm sure that's a Phil Taylor ploy to disarm Lewis.' People talk about mind games, but the best psychology of all in darts is to put your opponent under pressure from the off.

2–0: Another 180 puts me in charge of the leg and already Mardle is saying that I am 'scoring like a maniac'. It also raises the first chorus of 'There's only one Phil Taylor, one Phil Taylor, walking along, singing a song, walking in a Taylor wonderland' from the crowd. Can't say I mind it too much, but Lewis is up and running with his first 180 of the match, leaving me 84 to establish an early two-leg advantage. Bullseye does the trick, and after 24 darts I'm 2–0 up. But

Adrian is the type of player who can wipe out that kind of advantage in the blink of an eye, and I know he will come back at me. I don't have to wait long to be proved right.

2–1: Not that I was aware of it at the time but, as commentator Rod Studd observes, I am defending a 25-match winning streak on TV, closing in on my own world record of thirty consecutive wins in majors between 1999 and 2001. Now the crowd are booming, 'Lewis, Lewis' as Adrian hits his second 180 and gets off the mark on double 18 after 153 proves a checkout too far for me.

2–2: Adrian goes from the sublime to the ridiculous, following another 180 – our sixth of the match in barely three-and-a-half legs – with 24 on his next visit, a score that Studd jokingly derides as 'diabolical, shoddy'. (That's harsh – we work within such fine margins that occasionally you are going to play a duff hand. Nobody misses the big numbers deliberately, it's just the nature of sport.) I stay in touch with 177, switching downstairs to treble 19 when my first two darts leave the route to another 180 blocked, but after missing out on a 110 finish when double 15 goes astray, Adrian breaks back with double 10. There you go – I told you things could change quickly when he gets to work.

2–3: Going into the first break, we might look as if we're enjoying ourselves, and the banter is good-natured enough, but it's killing me that I'm behind after starting so well. Adrian knocks up 134 and 180 to put me under the pump, and by the time he edges ahead by taking out double 12, he is averaging 111.93 and it's abundantly clear that nothing short of full throttle will be good enough to beat him. It's vital that I win the next session.

3–3: A glass of water and a rub-down with a towel backstage, or a quick visit to the smallest room in the house, can often break your concentration or stifle the momentum of a contest. But there is no let-up in the heavy scoring as we resume where we left off, Lewis chalking up 140, 134 and 140 before he misses a shot at double 5 to go 4–2 up. I am grateful for the chance to level it up again after being left 48. Single 16, double 16 does the trick.

4–3: The crowd don't know which way to turn, and who can blame them? For the third time in seven legs, there is a break of throw, although Adrian is agitated when he misses two darts at double tops and I step in to take care of 84 in two darts.

5–3: More heavy scoring. When I win, one of my calling cards is to remove the board and sign it, but this one is in danger of being carried off on a stretcher. From my point of view, it should have been a twelve-darter as I open up with 180 and 140, but Adrian keeps me honest with a couple of 100-plus visits and, after missing doubles on 18 and 9, it's third time lucky and I'm on a roll after winning three legs in a row.

Another chorus of 'Walking in a Taylor wonderland' is music to my ears.

5–4: Another case of 'After you, Claude' – I pepper the lipstick again with another 180, only for Adrian to step up and return the compliment. You talk about keeping your opponent under pressure, but it's difficult to keep a good man down when he fires back at you within five seconds. And when Lewis has a tricky 87 to hold his throw, he makes it look easy: treble 17, double 18. Cheeky beggar – we used to rehearse that finish back in the day when we were practice partners.

5–5: At the second break, we are back where we started – all square. But the frustration of being pegged back is diluted by a leg of awesome scoring power, with Adrian hitting the twelfth 180 of the match, me replying with No.13 with the next throw and Lewis reeling off No.14 to complete the hat-trick. That's nine darts in a row hitting a target the size of a paper clip. Adrian is now laughing out loud at the perfect absurdity of our scoring, and I would have been laughing with him if I had nailed bullseye to maintain my two-leg advantage. As we walk off stage, Adrian puts an arm round my shoulder and kisses me on the head. As far as I'm concerned, the next time either of us puckers up, it will be to deliver the kiss of death in this contest!

6–5: So far, I'm averaging a healthy 109 and Adrian is threatening all kinds of records on 113. He's also leading 8–6 on the 180 count, although those stats don't take into account the times when I go 'downstairs' and score 177 or 174 by concentrating on treble 19. Wayne Mardle has already seen enough to call it a 'standard we've never seen before'. Right on cue, I produce a checkout which lives up to his billing. Although it's not easy to take out 167, there is less pressure on the big finishes because your opponent is expecting to get another throw – but treble 20, treble 19 and bullseye leaves Adrian shaking his head and gives me another break of serve.

6–6: Mardle is really going for it now in the commentary box. 'This is ridiculous,' he shrieks, as I trade 180s with Lewis again and leave 87 to reassert my authority, but my first dart hits treble 2 by mistake instead of treble 17. Adrian breaks back on double top, and referee George Noble steps in with a reminder to the crowd not to call out 'Miss!' when we are lining up game shot. We don't expect cathedral silence, but deliberate attempts to distract players are a no-no.

6–7: The lead changes hands again – this is getting serious. I land the eighteenth three-in-a-bed of the match, but Adrian is playing so well he is threatening my monopoly of the nine highest averages on TV. My record is 118.66 against Kevin Painter at the UK Open in 2010, but when Lewis hits 170 to leave himself with a single-dart finish on 32, I am nowhere near the required 137 checkout and he returns with double 16 to go in front for only the second time in thirteen legs.

7–7: Neither of us is giving an inch, and for the second time in five legs, there are three 180s in succession. It's no surprise that, after another machine-gun fire of improbably high scoring, the search for a winning double turns into an undignified scramble. I miss two darts at double 12, Adrian misses two chances at double 8 and eventually I restore parity on double 3. The expression on my face says I got away with it this time.

7–8: Radio Mardle is at it again. 'Oh, come on!' he protests, as I trade 180s with Adrian like we were shelling peas. Rod Studd is also impressed, calling our semi-final a 'tungsten fantasy happening in front of your very eyes'. He also shares the news that he is going to ring Mrs Studd and ask her to Sky+ the match so he can watch it all over again when he gets home. Adrian is in a jaunty mood as we go into the third break with little to separate two prize-fighters, neither of whom is prepared to back down. The tournament sponsors now make the contest an even-money bet, with both of us 10–11 to reach the final, and the stats in that third segment of the match are truly frightening. Lewis averaged 117.82 in those five legs.

8–8: There comes a time, in every long-course match, where you have to light the afterburners. So far, I've made little headway in seeing off an opponent who likes to play at a breakneck pace. Maybe I'm getting caught up in the whirlwind and rushing my throw a bit. Steady as she goes, I answer

Adrian's 180 with 137 and 134, taking out 42 in two darts to level the match again, and I'm grateful that my finishing has held up well – anything approaching a 50 per cent checkout rate usually takes some beating, and so far eight of my sixteen shots at a double have been on target.

9–8: George Noble has to give the crowd another ticking-off. 'Please give both players the respect they deserve and don't call out while they are throwing,' he reprimands them, before I take out 88 on bullseye and the momentum shifts once more. 'If you are not enjoying this, you have got something wrong with you – it's been spellbinding from dart one,' says Rod Studd on Sky.

10–8: Has Lewis cracked? After a near-miss with three-in-a-bed on treble 18, I miss a dart at double top for a 110 finish – but Adrian then wastes two shots at tops and I pinch another leg on double 5.

11–8: At last, I've got Lewis where I want him – on the back foot. For the first time there is clear blue sky between us after I produce my second monster checkout. In an eventful leg, I open up with the twenty-fifth 'maximum' of the match, only to squander the advantage with a truly pathetic 25 in my next visit (1, 5, 19). Nobody misses on purpose and, as I said earlier, you will get these horrid scores occasionally when you are dealing with fine margins and high pressure. I recover with 136 to leave us both on 160 – and I suspect the shoot-out may have broken Adrian's spirit. He misses double top for a grandstand finish, but I show him how it's done. He nods approvingly, then reaches for his glass of water and takes a good swig.

12–8: All that has been missing, from a game reaching for the stars, is a nine-darter – and when I ram my thirteenth and fourteenth 180s into the board for starters in the twentieth leg, a perfect set is on the cards. But my seventh dart wires treble 20 on the wrong side, and I am comfortably in front when double 16 extends my advantage at the fourth break. So far, The Power and Jackpot have shared twenty-eight maximums and our averages are now running at 110.45 and 111.53 respectively.

13–8: I sense, from his weary body language backstage, that Adrian will find it hard to come back now, and the resumption is relatively low-key. I knock out 96 in two darts – treble 20, double 18 – to show I'm not taking my foot off the pedal.

14–8: Just what the doctor ordered – an eleven-dart leg to keep my foot on Adrian's throat, in a manner of speaking, and now the winning post is veering into view. There is nothing wrong with my opponent's spirit as he knocks up 180, 121 and 140 in his three visits to the oche, but I'm pleased as punch with my 139, 177 and 140, which leave me 45 to hold the throw. Two darts later, the job's a good 'un.

15–8: From being 8–7 down, I reel off my eighth leg on the bounce. Once you gain some momentum in this format, it can be an unstoppable force. Less than twenty minutes after Lewis has been matching me blow-for-blow, I am now one leg away from delivering the knockout punch. To his eternal credit, he is still fighting, delivering yet another 180 (the thirtieth of the match). But I take out 65, despite hitting the bullseye with my first dart when I am looking for the outer bull, and double 4 takes me to within a leg of the final.

15–9: Adrian stops the rot. He deserves that, because my winning margin gives the false impression that it has been a comfortable ride. Double top keeps him in business – for now.

16–9: The final flourish sets a new record on the PDC circuit for 180s in a match. The privilege might have fallen to me, but I'm denied by a bounce-out and Adrian steps up to set the bar at thirty-two maximums, taking us past my sudden-death final against Raymond van Barneveld at the Circus Tavern in 2007 – a match where there were thirty-two more legs than this one. When the end comes, with my eighth break of throw, it's simple enough – 60 in two darts, finishing on double top. The warriors embrace, and we both know we've been involved in something special.

The final stats make awesome reading. Most impressive of all is that our combined averages (mine was 109.76, Adrian 110.99) represent the highest aggregate for any televised match. But my enduring memory is of the crowd, and how much they seemed to lap up the entertainment. It is easy to accuse fans of coming to darts for a booze-up and not paying close attention to the action, but the people who came to Wolverhampton on this Sunday afternoon were hooked. Adrian was gracious in defeat, shrugging his shoulders and saying in his post-match interview, 'To average 111 and lose . . . you can't do much about it, can you? I've just got to take it on the chin. We were just dragging each other along.'

You can say that again, bud. I kept hitting Lewis with everything I'd got, thinking his form would tail off or he would lose heart, but he just kept coming back. We got involved in a battle where we kept trading our best shots right to the end, and my seven-leg margin does not even begin to tell the tale of how well both of us played. Best of all, my old guru Eric Bristow had put £20 on Adrian to knock me out!

In the final later that evening, I found myself 5–0 up against Robert Thornton without even playing well. After that, winning my fifth Grand Slam title, and my fourth consecutive major championship win on TV, was a formality. Thornton's consolation prize transcended sport – during the tournament he had become a grandfather when his daughter gave birth to a son, named Robert after him. 'I can't wait to get home and hold him. It will be the proudest moment of my life,' he said. Good for you, mate. Some things in life are more important than winning darts matches . . . even the greatest match of all time.

8

GREATEST

ASKING a darts player to pick out the best five matches of his career is a bit like asking a bank cashier to pick out the crispiest £10 notes he's ever handled, or telling a farmer to nominate his favourite straws in the haystack – virtually impossible. By common consent, my 2013 Grand Slam semi-final against Adrian Lewis was the best match of my career, but there have been others that stick in the memory, for drama or quality, that would make a Greatest Hits album if I were a rock star.

If I was truly self-indulgent, I would include my first World Championship title on the list. But my 6–1 win against Eric Bristow in 1990 was more of a shock to bookies who had made me a 125–1 long shot than it was outstanding drama. I'm still embarrassed when I think of the morning after the traditional end-of-tournament dinner at the Lakeside, when the new world champion set off for home in a rattling old Austin Princess he had bought for £30 with holes in each door. If it was a surprise that I made it home in the old rust-bucket without any vital components falling off, I was genuinely touched to receive a personal letter from Sir Stanley Matthews, the wizard of the dribble himself, congratulating another local lad from the Potteries made good on his success.

So how do you select the top five games of my career? Names out of a hat? Bingo numbers? After twenty-five years, I'm spoilt for choice. The truth is, the public are the best judges, so this is not a definitive list. But I hope it jogs a few memories if you were there, or if you were watching on TV, when these games were unfolding. The Grand Slam classic aside, and with apologies to Noel Edmonds, who calls the biggest sums of money by the same name on *Deal Or No Deal*, these are my Power Five. They don't all have a happy ending!

1. PREMIER LEAGUE PLAY-OFFS FINAL v JAMES WADE, WEMBLEY, 2010

They call a nine-dart finish the perfect leg because it is the equivalent of a golfer's hole-in-one or a snooker player's 147 maximum break. To produce one on the floor in a qualifying tournament with rankings points at stake is incredibly satisfying. To deliver one in a televised major is magic. But let me tell you that to hit TWO nine-darters in the Premier League play-off final, and for those two legs ultimately to make the difference in a tight contest, is simply out of this world.

There was an unusual backdrop to my twin nine-darters against James Wade at Wembley Arena – and it wasn't just Stephen Fry doing a stint in the commentary box with Sid Waddell. The finals were delayed twenty-four hours by an almighty power cut, which wiped out large parts of the entire electricity grid in north-west London just hours before the curtain was due to go up on one of darts' biggest showpiece events on the Whitsun Bank Holiday Monday. I felt desperately sorry for the thousands of fans who had made a special effort to get there – many of them travelling long distances – only to be told that the show was postponed. I felt even more sorry for the PDC's long-serving master of ceremonies, John McDonald, when he had to venture outside the venue and tell the disappointed hordes that play had been abandoned for the night because the arena was without power. John served with the Parachute Regiment in his previous incarnation with the armed forces, and he knows a hostile environment when he sees one, but it was still bravery beyond the call of duty when he faced all those punters and asked for their understanding for the fact that their journeys had been wasted due to circumstances beyond anyone's control. Although there was an emergency generator in the venue, it had the capacity to keep all the lights on for only an hour – nowhere near long enough to play two semi-finals and a final – and throwing darts in pitch darkness, without knowing who or what they might be hitting, was never going to satisfy our friends in Health and Safety.

The play-offs were rescheduled for the following evening, which was a Tuesday night – not ideal for the paying public, nor for Sky TV, who found one of their biggest darts nights on the calendar competing for ratings with England's pre-World Cup friendly against Mexico in the national stadium next door. I suspect one reason why there were so many unhappy spectators when the original date was pushed back twenty-four hours is because they had bought tickets for the darts AND the football, planning their Bank Holiday weekend around the two events. The players were concerned that we would be competing for big prize money with only a few people dotted around Wembley Arena, and the grand finale to a fifteen-week competition would be submerged in anticlimax and farce. Everyone connected with the play-offs was astonished that around 3,000 ticket holders came back once the fuses in the Wembley sub-station had been fixed. Everyone connected with the play-offs that night remembers what happened next.

Wade was the defending champion, and he put up one hell of a fight. It says everything about his tenacity that I had to produce those two nine-darters, a feat I still rate as the greatest of my career, to beat him. The first was early in the contest, in only the second leg – 174, 180 and then 147, Ronnie O'Sullivan's favourite number. Treble 20, treble 17, double 18, bingo. But the second came at a critical stage when the final was deadlocked at 7–7, and it needed something special to separate the two rutting stags who wouldn't budge an inch. Fortunately, it was me who came up with the trump cards – 180, 180 and 141, which I wrapped up with treble 20, treble 19, double 12. I was so pleased that Sid, one of my closest friends, was on air to describe it. At the moment I made history as the first player to hit two perfect legs in the same game, his voice went up about three octaves and you could hear the excitement when that double 12 found its target and reserved our place in broadcast archives.

I had no idea until later that comic actor and all-round good egg Stephen Fry had been sitting at Sid's right hand in the commentary box, watching the drama unfold. I loved his comment afterwards that he had been 'like a pig in Chardonnay' in his privileged seat. And I was flattered that Fry turned down the chance to attend a film première in the West End, which Prince Charles was attending, to keep his date with Sid, who was darts royalty in his own right.

Also, I had no idea how many people would collar me about my two nine-darters weeks, months, years later. On a subsequent visit to London, I was standing outside my hotel on the Euston Road when a red double-decker bus came to a halt – even though I wasn't standing at a scheduled bus stop – and the driver leaned out of his cab to shout: 'Two nine-darters, Phil – nice one, mate!' Taxi drivers tooted their horns and gave me the thumbs-up, passers-by who stopped for autographs or a photo all seemed to mention the play-offs.

When I was voted runner-up in the BBC Sports Personality of the Year in 2010, I'm absolutely convinced my two nine-darters had more to do with it than any other single factor.

2. WORLD CHAMPIONSHIP FINAL v MIKE GREGORY, LAKESIDE, 1992

The first World Championship final to go down to a sudden-death leg was not the best I've ever played – but for sheer drama, it's up there with the most exciting. Even though it was nearly half my lifetime ago, it's amazing how many people still bring it up.

Not that I noticed at the time, but it was the first final in which neither John Lowe nor Eric Bristow had featured since the inaugural World Championship in 1978. By the time Gregory and I had frayed everyone's nerves, not least our own, we had set new standards of brinkmanship. When it went to a tie-break at 5–5 in sets and 5–5 in the decider, fortune smiled on me. Mike is probably one of the finest players never to win a world title – and he is probably still haunted, to this day, by the six darts he missed for the championship: two each at double 8, double top and double 10.

In terms of excitement, it was colossal. The match was full of big checkouts (I hit a 167 and Mike banked 161), and the lead changed hands more often than a deck of cards in a casino. From two sets up (3–0, 3–2) I found myself 2–3 down before we traded the next five sets to take it to the sudden-death climax. It made great television, and the £28,000 winner's share of the pot made all the drama worthwhile, but I dare say Gregory regards it as the final he lost more than the world title I won . . . and I wouldn't disagree with him. At 5–4 in the decider, I made a dog's dinner of my first throw – 26. Thanks for coming, Phil. And before I knew it, he had six darts to score 80 for the title, while I was miles away on 215. But after six shots for the crown, and six misses, I knew his mind was scrambled. He was snatching at his darts, pulling them one way and pushing them the other, and the tension got to him.

When people say you should play the board and not your opponent, that's nonsense. If you can get inside your rival's head, that's half the battle. But that nerve-jangling night at Frimley Green taught me a new adage: Don't get mad, don't get even . . . get lucky.

3. WORLD CHAMPIONSHIP FINAL v RAYMOND van BARNEVELD, CIRCUS TAVERN, 2007

Sometimes the best matches don't always evoke the happiest memories – but, as I've mentioned earlier this book, if there is such a thing as honour in defeat, I guess it happened in Purfleet on New Year's Day in 2007.

I'd had a good tournament, and enjoyed parking my Bentley outside the Circus Tavern, a venue that had been kind to me down the years, and when you go 3–0 up, over the best of thirteen sets, there should really be no

Chizzy rascal: Dave Chisnall knocked me out of the World Championship once, but I beat him here at the World Grand Prix in Dublin.

Best of enemies: My rivalry with Raymond van Barneveld has never got in the way of an enduring respect for each other.

Legend at work: Eric Bristow taught me how to be a winner.

Sudden death: Barney's moment of triumph at the Circus Tavern in 2007.

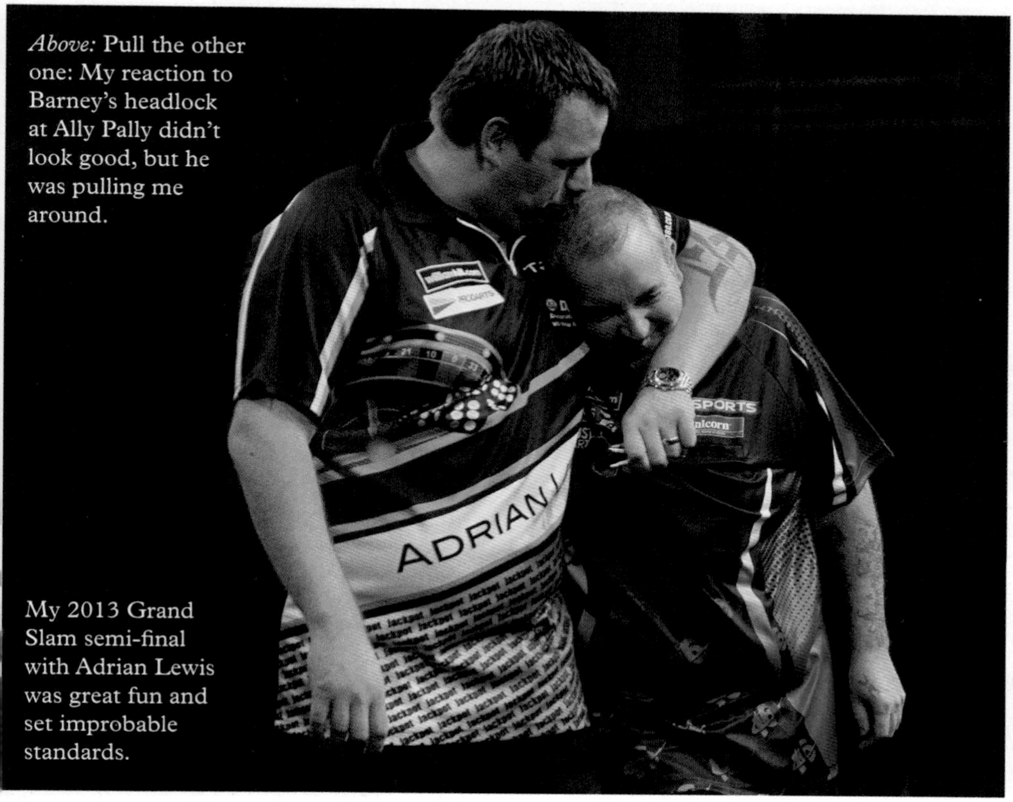

Above: Pull the other one: My reaction to Barney's headlock at Ally Pally didn't look good, but he was pulling me around.

My 2013 Grand Slam semi-final with Adrian Lewis was great fun and set improbable standards.

Above: James Wade is a fine player but cut a distracted figure at the Masters i Edinburgh.

Left: Heavy duty: It meant the world that I was first to lift the Sid Waddell Trophy by winning the 2013 World Championship. It weighs half a ton!

Left: Shake a leg if you're world champion: My comeback against Micl van Gerwen at Alexandra Palace in 20 was one of my best performances.

Below: Bully for you: Michael 'Bully Boy' Smith beat me fair and square at Alexandra Palace.

Double tops: Taylor, Van Gerwen and their shadows publicise the World Championship in a black London taxi.

Feeling the strain: On my way to defeat against Michael van Gerwen at Butlins in Minehead.

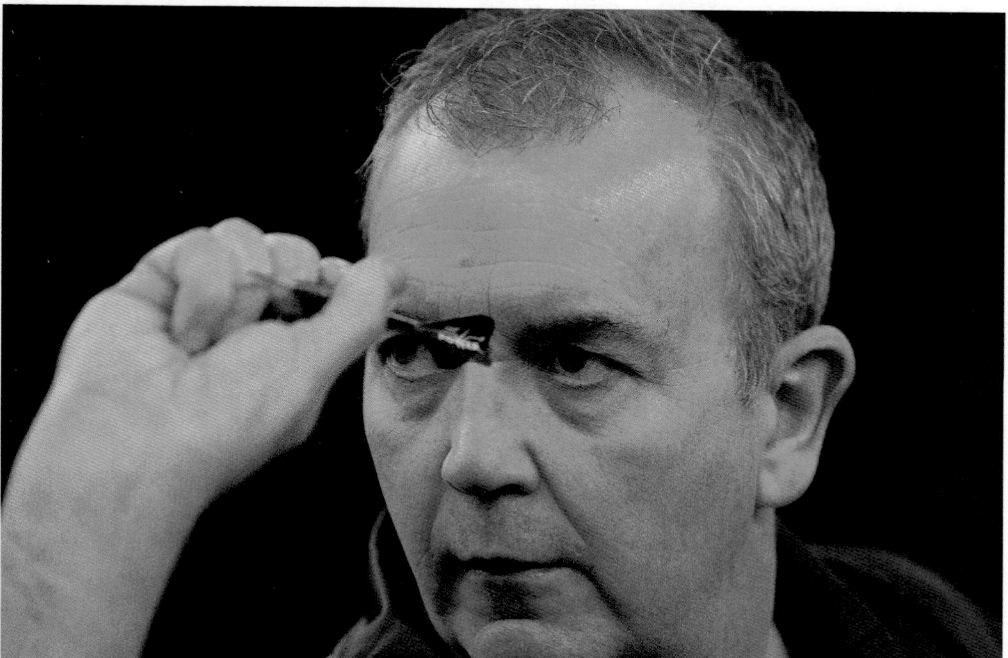

Running on empty: My shock defeat by Michael Smith at Alexandra Palace was a bitterly disappointing end to the year.

Sign here please: Target Darts managing director Garry Plummer (left) and Barry Hearn (right) witness my 'transfer' to a new set of arrows.

Above: Adrian Lewis beat me comfortably as I struggled in the early part of the Premier League campaign.

Face-off: Michael van Gerwen and I meet 24 hours before take-off in the Premier League at Liverpool. Little did I know what was coming next…

Left: Green machine: Michael van Gerwen on his way to a 7-0 whitewash, my heaviest-ever Premier League defeat.

Below: The loneliest walk: Retreating to the players' room in Liverpool after a horrid night on stage.

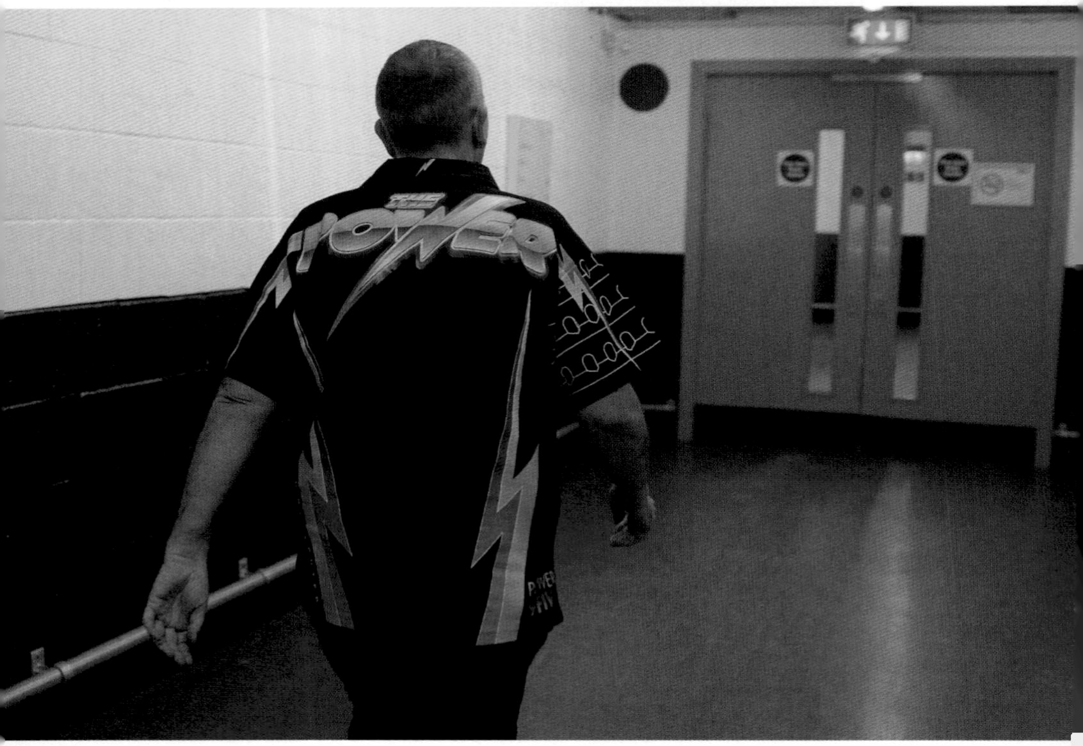

arguments. But the comfort zone can do strange things to a player's mindset, and I made the mistake of straying the wrong side of the line between confidence and complacency.

At 4–2 and 5–3 up, I never felt I was going to lose – until Barney fired off three sets on the bounce, and suddenly I was staring down the barrel. Before the sudden-death leg, we had a shot at the bull for the right to throw first, and my dart missed by a whisker. Raymond used my barrel as a target and, sure enough, his dart kissed mine on the way to bullseye. He gave me a knowing smile, the cheeky sod, and deep down I knew that might be a critical advantage. I was still well adrift when Barney missed a shot at double top, but he returned to clinch the deal and equal Eric Bristow's five world titles.

At the time, I said it was the greatest final I had ever been involved in – and if you leave aside the fact that I lost, it may still be true. From first dart to last, it must have been one of the longest televised matches in history. But if a genie of the lamp appeared and gave me one wish to turn a defeat into a victory, this is the one I would have chosen.

4. WORLD CHAMPIONSHIP SEMI-FINAL v ERIC BRISTOW, CIRCUS TAVERN, 1997

In the workplace, there is a saying that you should never teach a colleague to do your job better than you. Eric Bristow, my old master and sponsor, had conquered the demons of 'dartitis' to roll back the years and battle his way through to the World Championship semi-finals in Purfleet. The Crafty Cockney's resurgence was brilliant news for the sport, and the collision course that brought him head-to-head with the apprentice who was looking to equal his record of five world titles was a salesman's dream.

I'm not sure I enjoyed every aspect of the occasion – I remember feeling more battered than the cod in a chip shop by the time I had made it through the bawdy crowd on to the Circus Tavern stage – and at a conservative estimate, about 99 per cent of the crowd were braying for Eric. Once I had straightened my shirt and adjusted my barnet, which had been ruffled during the walk-on into a fashionably unkempt pulled-through-a-hedge-backwards look, I realised I was shaking like a leaf during the practice darts. And Eric, never knowingly short of conviction where plain cockiness would do, obviously fancied his chances. He had been telling everyone backstage that he was the only player who could stop me.

For seven sets we slugged it out until, with me leading 4–3 and 2–1 up in the eighth set, I needed double 4 to reach the final and Eric needed 141 – by no means a simple checkout – to stay alive. The old bugger made that holy trinity of darts look like three knocks at the door. The place erupted, and as a gesture of sportsmanship I held my right hand aloft to offer Eric a high-five. He slapped his palm into mine with such force that it actually hurt. I don't believe for one second that he meant any ill – he was simply carried away by his own bravado after such a stunning escape – but that high-five could not have stung me more if it had been a right-hander from Carl Froch. I thought, 'Right, you old bugger, you've had it now.' Sure enough, when the final set – where you have to win by two clear legs – was 4–3 in my favour, Eric missed a couple of darts at double 8 to make it all-square again. I made no mistake on double 2 to reach the final, where I would be playing for a first prize of £45,000, the biggest pot of gold in my career to date. I was so drained afterwards that I looked like the ghost that used to haunt my pub, the Cricketers Arms. Eric looked on the verge of tears – and it was the last time he came so close to the world title.

5. WORLD CHAMPIONSHIP FINAL v MICHAEL van GERWEN, ALEXANDRA PALACE, 2013

Back in 2008, when the PDC World Championship had switched to Ally Pally for the first time, I survived a major scare in the first round against an eighteen-year-old Dutch kid in a fluorescent green shirt called Michael van Gerwen. After Raymond van Barneveld, he was the next big thing to come out of Holland and he was widely tipped as a future star on our circuit. I scraped through 3–2, but only after Van Gerwen had missed two darts to send me packing at the first hurdle, and I knew he was destined for the top sooner or later.

In the final on New Year's Day 2013, Michael's star was in the ascendant. Three months earlier, he had just won his first PDC major, the World Grand Prix, and his rat-a-tat-tat delivery, firing off the darts like a Spaghetti Western gunslinger unloading in a shoot-out, was blowing people away. He had inflicted a first defeat in sixteen games on Adrian Lewis at Ally Pally in an epic quarter-final before holding off James Wade's gritty fightback in the last four (hitting a nine darter), and plenty of punters were backing him to topple an ageing grandad off his perch, too.

I laid down an early marker with a 170 finish in the opening leg, but Van Gerwen was not going to be intimidated that easily and he nicked the first set with a 140 finish of his own. Michael had come within a whisker of back-to-back nine-darters in his semi-final against Wade, and I soon found myself 2–0 down in sets. No sooner had I fought my way back to 2–2 than Michael surged ahead again at 4–2, and he missed a couple of shots to make it 5–2 – which was his biggest mistake. Galvanised by that moment of fortune, and determined to turn it into a turning point, I strung five sets together without reply, grinding him down and bullying him into snatching at his throw.

To win 7–4 against the form horse of the competition was incredibly satisfying, arguably the proudest night of my whole career. We had been on stage for 2 hours 18 minutes by the time I sank the winning dart on double 16, and I have never been so tired at the end of a game. One of the first people I saw backstage afterwards had the broadest grin of the lot – Eric Bristow had put a few bob on me to win 7–4, and he gave me a big kiss to thank me for making him richer. But in that World Championship, Michael was the best player I had come across. My only question mark against him was whether he had the willpower and single-mindedness to reach that level consistently.

9

FLIGHT

November 2013

KEEP Britain tidy? I thought I was only doing my bit to keep the stage clear of discarded litter at the Royal Highland Centre. But my housekeeping went down like a lead balloon with James Wade at the inaugural Coral Masters, a three-day event in Edinburgh – a straight knockout competition for the top sixteen in the PDC Order of Merit.

Any satisfaction at a job well done, and another £50,000 in the bank, was overshadowed by an innocuous incident in my semi-final against Wade, which led to his threatening to walk off stage and forfeit the match, basically giving up the ghost when he agreed to play on and, finally, heated words in the practice room afterwards.

The record books will say I beat Wade 10–1 in the semi-finals and then crushed Adrian Lewis, by the same margin, in the final. What they won't say is that James – whose courage in the face of mental illness has been no secret for several years – was in a bad place at the time, and that Adrian was ravaged by flu and running a temperature somewhere near maximum power on a standard microwave oven. Sometimes you have to play on, even when you feel lousier than a bad hangover, and it was Aidy's bad luck that it was his turn to try and perform when he was being consumed by an evil virus. But James is better, much better, than the poor sod who lost his rag that night in Scotland.

Early in the contest, one of the flights on Wade's darts broke and, after fiddling around with it for a couple of minutes (it may not have been so long, but I wasn't counting) he put the damaged flight on top of my darts case and fixed a new one to the empty barrel. I thought he had finished with it, so I swung round, lobbed it off the stage and told one of the lads sitting in the front row to catch it as a keepsake. James glared at me through his glasses and growled, 'I'll have that back – I needed that.' I could tell, from his tone of voice, that he was being serious – but as far as I was concerned, he was just being daft.

'What do you need that for?' I asked him. 'It's no good, it's bust. Come on, stop playing silly beggars.' But Wade was having none of it, and although he resumed the match, he was furious that I had disposed of his damaged and unwanted flight. After his demands to get it back fell on deaf ears, he started complaining to tournament director

Tommy Cox. He was threatening to walk off and forfeit the match, but Tommy was very firm and told him, in no uncertain terms, that he was to see the match through to its conclusion. James was playing with fire because he had only just served a four-tournament ban for bringing darts into disrepute, but he was in one of his darker moods and he did not hide his frustration.

Although he stayed on stage to the end, my win was little more than a charade. James went through the motions, and his impoverished three-dart average (73.99) told its own grievous story. I don't mind winning games by a big margin, but I don't like walkovers – especially against one of the best players never to win the world title, which is how highly I rate Wade. Backstage, it all kicked off in the players' bar adjacent to the practice room when I accused him of throwing in the towel. I had a go at him and told him to pull himself together – but, on reflection, that wasn't going to solve anything. When you have been through some of the things James has experienced, it's not quite as simple as that. Fortunately, the PDC security team was on hand to make sure it never became too animated, although it's fair to say that tempers were frayed and I was irritated.

James was still angry that I had thrown his flight into the crowd, but I told him, 'Look, if you chuck a flight away, pick another one out of your darts case and put it into your dart, then obviously you don't want the first one. Why are you so attached to that one flight when we all go through dozens of them every week?' I backed down before I could say something I would later regret. But I still maintain, to this day, that Tommy Cox was right to tell James to get back on that stage and do his job, which is to entertain people, when he was threatening to forfeit the game. And to tell the truth, James had been playing up a bit earlier in the tournament. When he beat Simon Whitlock the previous night, he celebrated by waving Simon off the stage, bouncing around like a kangaroo in the outback, pouring a glass of water over his head and throwing the empty beaker into the crowd.

He was up for it, and I thought I was going to be in for one hell of a game in the semi-finals. I don't know why he became so distracted by that one broken flight, but I didn't take any pleasure in beating him so convincingly. I like the fella, and I have James Wade to thank for some of my most memorable contests on TV, like the twin nine-darters in 2010 and the concluding leg of our 2008 World Matchplay final. Needing 132 to clinch my 18–9 win, my first dart landed in the outer bull and treble 19 left me a shot at bullseye to take the title: I had to move so far across the oche to squeeze the winning shot into the tightest of gaps that I was virtually standing on the south shore on Blackpool's promenade to deliver the winning arrow on the north shore.

Wade seems to bring out the best in me. Maybe that's why he complained that night in Edinburgh – he had probably just had enough of me. But don't get me wrong,

I have all the time in the world for him as a darts player. When he is in the zone, and he is hitting double tops for fun, he is a tremendous asset to the circuit. I know he did not see it at the time of his omission, but missing out on the Premier League in 2014 may work in his favour in the long term. I think he will come back with a new focus, a new desire to succeed – and I'll be one of the first to welcome his return when that happens. He's a good lad, and I just wish he realised how good he could be.

As for the Masters final against Lewis, that was one-way traffic as well. I don't blame Adrian that it turned out to be one-sided – he had edged a titanic battle with Raymond van Barneveld 10–9 in their semi, and I don't think there was much gas left in the tank when he found me lying in wait. Where I had a couple of hours to clear my head in the practice room, Aidy only had a few minutes to cool off. He was never going to live with me if I averaged 106, which would have been enough to win 95 per cent of major finals on television.

Adrian will understand when I say that I could not afford to be less than ruthless, even though I could see he was clearly struggling. In a strange way, opponents who are under the weather are dangerous because they play with no fear. They might be feeling rough, but they have nothing to lose, so you have to take them out. Sorry, but that's the way Bristow taught me to play. Do I wish I had beaten him 10–0? To be honest, yes. Did I begrudge Aidy the single leg he took off me when I was 9–0 in front? No way – like a valiant trooper he kept going, even though he was burning up under the TV lights and probably wanted nothing stronger to drink than a soluble aspirin.

One way or another, I won't forget that weekend in Scotland in a hurry. The locals turned out in big numbers to support a new event on the PDC circuit and, as I remarked to the assembled press afterwards, they dished out some stick to test our bottle. It's all part of the fun, but the next time I find an opponent's flight next to my darts case, I'll leave it to the cleaners.

10

NICKNAME

I'VE asked Robbie Williams, on several occasions, to write me a catchy new jingle as my walk-on music – but each time he comes back with the same answer: 'No way – because I'll never be able to top the one you've got already.' I've also asked Sky Sports a few times, as recently as early in 2014, if I could change my adoptive theme tune. Again, the answer is always the same: Not a chance.

Look, I've got nothing against Snap's monster No.1 hit 'The Power' from 1990, which has accompanied me on every walk to the stage for twenty years. It has been the one-hit soundtrack to my career, and sometimes – especially when I've been competing on stage – I go to bed with the distinctive synthesiser and vocals echoing round in my head, and I wake up hearing the same few bars next morning. It's become part of me, like my shadow. Friends tell me that my entrance, on a big night in the Premier League or at the World Championship, has the same sense of occasion as Chris Eubank strutting to the ring with

Tina Turner's 'Simply The Best' at full blast before one of his middleweight title fights. I wouldn't know about that – and, unlike Eubank, my walk-on is the prelude only to a game of darts, not to punching my opponent in the face.

I don't think Barry Hearn, the Professional Darts Corporation chairman, would let me change my 'Power' theme tune for all the tungsten in China, either. He says it makes every venue come alive, whether the crowd are cheering for me or willing me to fail. Thanks to Snap, more people call me The Power than Phil these days. I wonder how many of those people realise that I had already won three world titles, as plain old Phil Taylor, before my current moniker was bestowed on me by a Sky Sports floor manager? And I wonder how many people remember my original nickname, which commentary box legend Sid Waddell invented for me, although it never quite stuck?

As 'Crafty Cockney' Eric Bristow's apprentice, Sid thought it would be appropriate if my nickname reflected his influence on my career. And, given my upbringing in the Potteries, it kind of made sense when he started using The Crafty Potter as my soubriquet on air. I preferred that to Bobby George's alternative nickname for me, which was 'Eric's Sidekick'. I once had a T-shirt made with 'Eric's Sidekick' on the back, and paraded around in front of Bobby wearing it. I don't know whether he saw the funny side of it or not. And I still prefer the PDC governing body's official name to Bobby's alternative version of 'Phil's

Darts Club'. Bobby George was never going to be chairman of my fan club – he regarded me as one of the ringleaders when the PDC formed its breakaway from the British Darts Organisation, and any compliments he served my way were normally of the back-handed variety: ruthless, boring, clinical, that sort of 'compliment'. He used to run me down all the time, which is a pity. As the self-styled 'King of Darts', Bobby, in his cloak, crown and candelabra, was one of the sport's most flamboyant characters. I enjoyed his comment on my success when he said, 'Players like Phil come along once in a lifetime. It's just a pity he came along in my lifetime!'

Despite Sid's best efforts, the Crafty Potter nickname flickered but never really caught fire, until one night at the 1995 World Matchplay, when I was waiting to go on stage ahead of my first-round game with Canada's Gary Mawson. Directing operations behind the scenes with regimental efficiency was Sky's floor manager, Peter Judge, a model of professionalism who always scrubbed up well in a suit and tie. It was Judgey's job to make sure players were delivered to the top of their walk-on so that when it was our cue – lights, camera, action, march – the pre-match formalities went like clockwork. 'What's your nick-name?' asked Judge. I just gave him a blank look, a shrug of the shoulders, and replied, 'You tell me.' I have a fair idea that Judgey had already decided what the answer was. Some time earlier, I had given him a lift in my car and, climbing into the passenger seat, he had accidentally trodden on a plastic CD case in the footwell. It was 'The Power' by Snap.

Judge barked something into his walkie-talkie, and a few seconds later came the reply – which sounded like interference when your TV is on the blink, or when you are trying to tune the car radio – but the response was decisive. 'Ready, Phil? Our sound people have lined up that "Power" song, so from now on you are Phil "The Power" Taylor. Happy? Let's go,' said Judge. I didn't really have time to give it any consideration. Before the significance of Judge's inspired, if unilateral, decision had sunk in, I was walking on stage, shaking hands and getting my hair ruffled, to the strains of my new theme tune. As I prepared for take-off, I wasn't sure how it would go down, and I was thinking, 'Bloody hell, what have I done here?' But I need not have worried. The crowd at the Winter Gardens loved it, which only goes to prove that Judge knew what he was doing all along.

Peter Judge used to be in charge of Eubank's walk-on when Britain's former world champion boxer was in his pomp. Eubank could wind up a crowd with his strut and his carefully calculated posturing, which could upset the natives far more than a darts player's walk-on music, so I was happy to put myself in Judgey's hands. Over the years, in terms of public feedback, I've probably enjoyed 99 per cent goodwill and only 1 per cent negative reaction. I'm not going to complain about such a favourable ratio.

Nicknames can be a marketing man's dream. I used to be a bit jealous of American WWE wrestlers like The

Undertaker (also known to his family as Mark Calaway) and Mr Perfect (Curt Hennig) when I was trying to find the right one for myself. As it happens, we've already got a real-life undertaker on the PDC circuit – Nigel Heydon, a funeral director whose nickname reflects his occupation. We've got a Jackpot, a Machine, a Barney, a Mighty Mike, a Flying Scotsman, a Chizzy, a Thorn, a Snakebite, a Hammer and a Warrior.

But I'm lucky – Peter Judge trod on one of my CD cases, and the rest is history. Talk about putting your foot in it . . .

11

JACKPOT

I TREAT Adrian Lewis as if he were my own son. He is, without a shadow of a doubt, one of the most talented darts players on the planet. He plays the game at such a pace, and can make it look so easy, that I sometimes envy him.

When we play against each other and get into a shooting match as if we were knocking out nine-darters on the practice board, we are capable of producing some high-quality stuff like the epic Grand Slam semi-final in 2013. The World Matchplay final four months earlier wasn't bad, either. After winning back-to-back world titles in 2011 and 2012, Adrian is capable of winning several more if he puts his heart and soul into it. If I can't win a tournament, I always look out for Jackpot's results because I hold him in the same regard as my own flesh and blood – but it hasn't always been plain sailing between us.

Coming from Stoke-on-Trent – the capital of world darts – as both of us do, there are few secrets when promising young players appear on the scene. Word goes round the pubs like wildfire – and you don't need to look very far when one of these kids is winner of the British Teenage Open, as Adrian was in 2003. When he qualified for the UK Open the following year, it was already obvious that he was not some flash in the pan, and it was a matter of finding the right person to harness his talent and helping him to fulfil his potential. He found just the right man for the job. Me!

False modesty aside, I was pushing pennies over one night at Maureen Flowers' place (Maureen – or Goldfinger, as she was known – is the lady who used to be Eric Bristow's other half) when Adrian's mum and stepfather came to see me and asked if I would take him under my wing. I was thrilled to be asked, not least because it gave me the chance to do for another ambitious youngster what Eric had done for me. It was an opportunity for me to play a part in the development of a new generation. When darts runs in the family, perhaps it was no surprise that Lewis went on to become a two-time world champion by the time he was twenty-six. His mum, Yvonne, played for Staffordshire and she used to lend him £50 a week – a fair chunk of her wages as a care worker – so he could travel to tournaments. His father, a lad called Sammy Wright, also played for England. It's not my story to tell, but suffice to say Adrian's parents broke up and the first time he met his dad was when he knocked on Sammy's door, as a seventeen-year-old, to introduce himself. His mum and dad were later reconciled.

Adrian once described his personal life as 'an episode of *The Jeremy Kyle Show*' – I'm not qualified, or inclined, to comment about that, but I do know one thing: he's one hell of a darts player. It takes a special talent to decorate a first appearance in the World Championship final with a perfect nine-darter, as Aidy did against Gary Anderson in 2011. I had been knocked out of that championship by Mark Webster in the quarter-finals, but I made a special point of coming back to Alexandra Palace to support Adrian in the final because I know what a big hurdle it is to win your first world title. I did well to get a ticket – the previous night, patrons of the VIP seats included Prince Harry and his chums. Anderson had been in tremendous form, but Adrian held his nerve superbly to win 7–5, and I could not have been more proud if it was my own son being crowned world champion.

What happened next was hurtful for me and soured my relationship with Lewis for a while. In the aftermath of his triumph, Adrian told the assembled gentlemen of Fleet Street:

> A nine-darter in the World Championship final has never been done before, not even by Phil, so making that bit of history is a big thing for me. It's time to stop calling me Phil's protégé – all I've ever done is to practise with him, but I used to practise with my dad and nobody calls me

> his apprentice. How much of my success is down to Phil? He passed on a few tips, like going to bed early and telling me a few things I should be doing as a professional, but I had qualified for three tournaments on the circuit before I had even met him. For years I have lived with this thing about being his understudy, but since I beat him at the World Grand Prix three months ago he has not played as well as he can. I think that defeat hurt him more than any other because he had not lost on TV for years, and that's when I started believing I was the best. I don't know if I've broken his spell yet, but Phil will be back. We had a bit of a falling-out at the Grand Prix, but that was something and nothing. Every now and then we have a bit of a bitch-fight – and I'm the biggest bitch!

Adrian didn't know it at the time, but I was standing only a few feet away when he said those words. I thought those comments were very disrespectful – to suggest I had never done anything for him apart from telling him to go to bed early was not just dismissive, it was an insult. I was over the moon for the lad when he became world champion, and I didn't want to steal any of his limelight, but I thought he might have given me more than a couple of back-handed compliments by way of a name-check. For a few weeks I didn't say a word to him; in fact, I felt so let down that I told him to keep away from me.

Even if he thought I had contributed little to his success as a darts player, he failed to mention the fact that he had been living in one of my properties in Stoke and I had hardly been charging him any rent. I didn't just go around telling people I treated Adrian like my son – I was prepared to back it up with favourable terms between landlord and tenant. I wanted him to have a good life, I wanted to give him the preferential treatment that fathers give their sons. I had forgiven, and largely forgotten, what had happened at the Grand Prix in October 2010 – my first televised defeat to Lewis, where his keenness to beat me was almost tangible. In fact, after losing a tense semi-final 5–4, I lodged a formal complaint with the PDC about Adrian's conduct on stage that night.

If there is one thing worse than an ungracious winner, it's a bad loser. That's a reputation I have never been happy to cultivate. I didn't make my protest lightly on this occasion, and I would not rush to do it again, but somehow I needed to make my point. In a foul temper, I fired off an email listing my grievances, which included Adrian clicking his darts together as I was preparing to throw, stamping his feet and making the stage 'bounce', talking to himself while I was taking aim, and trying to accost me during an interval to protest his innocence after I had pulled him up about his gamesmanship.

Maybe it all sounds a little bit petty and none of those things in isolation is going to have the local constabulary knocking on your door to invite you down to the nick for an interview under caution. And people watching on TV must wonder how you can be put off by an opponent muttering in the background, a clicking sound over your shoulder, or feeling the stage vibrate under your feet when there are often thousands of fans in the arena singing at the top of their voices. But, trust me, it's bloody annoying. I suppose the nearest equivalent, in an everyday setting, is sitting on a train or an aeroplane when someone around you is playing music too loud on their iPod. The noise is intrusive, it drives you to distraction. Strangely enough, Adrian took exception to James Wade 'stamping' behind him in the final, which Wade won 6–3. And at the 2012 Players Championship finals, Lewis had another difference of opinion on stage with Richie Burnett about clicking darts, so these things were not a figment of my imagination. Other players notice them, too. As for Aidy talking to himself, I don't think it's a deliberate ploy to break his opponent's concentration, but sometimes he has tried to gee himself up by chuntering 'Come on, me' under his breath. My hearing may not be as good as it was, but I can still pick up on a Potteries accent at 100 paces, and if you're about to cock the trigger, especially on game shot, it can break the spell if you are trying to shut out all outside distractions.

But enough of short-lived grudges and cantankerous emails. The fundamental reason I was so reluctant to report Adrian in the first place is because I genuinely think the world of him. Just because we've had the odd spat doesn't mean we don't get on most of the time. I mean, there are occasions when I don't always like my own children's behaviour, but I still love them to bits. I do feel as though I have a lasting bond with Adrian, and I'll give you one example of it. During the first month of the 2014 Premier League campaign, when I was having a bad run (of which you will read more later) he was the one who did his best to lift my spirits. Every now and then, I would sense this big shadow over my shoulder and a familiar voice would be geeing me up: 'Come on, Phil, you've still got it. Come on, Phil!'

Some of these lads have spent a lifetime trying to beat me, and hating it when I win, but when I was struggling it was almost as if Adrian couldn't bear to see me lose, either. That was a touch of class, gratefully received by an old man going through a fallow period. Adrian drives around in a nice Jaguar these days, but it was nice that he could still remember the days when he would come round to my place on a pushbike for a practice session. Vincent van der Voort was another one who expressed genuine concern when my form dipped. He came up to me at one of the Pro Tour floor competitions and said, 'I hate it when you don't win because the money we can win by playing darts today is down to your achievements. Maybe I didn't like it when you beat me in the past – now I like it even less if you lose.' It was very humbling to hear a fellow professional talk like that. It put a smile on my face at a time when I needed it most.

Adrian also made me smile when he won his first World Championship – and more than half of his winnings went to the taxman. Poor sap, it was a harsh lesson for him to take a £200,000 cheque in one hand and write out another for £108,000 to the Inland Revenue to settle a tax bill. Who was it who said that the only three certainties in the human life cycle are birth, death and taxes? I guess it's all part of the growing-up process, and it reminded me of having my first winner's cheque in my hands for barely a minute before Eric Bristow took it off me as repayment for what you might call tuition fees.

I didn't know, until a long time after I first met him, that Adrian was once a goalkeeper on Crewe Alexandra's books, and by all accounts he looked the part until he broke his hand in five or six places. He supports Stoke City – I come from the other side of the tracks and follow Port Vale, although I've got no antipathy towards Stoke and I'm pleased they have enjoyed a few years of consolidation in the Premier League. Did you know Adrian once named his goldfish after Stoke striker Paul Peschisolido? (I'm not sure what the goldfish made of it.)

And, as I intimated earlier, the story behind Adrian's Jackpot nickname is a belter. After being knocked out in the first round of the 2005 Las Vegas Desert Classic at the famous MGM Grand, he went out in search of consolation from one of the estimated 198,000 slot machines on The Strip to top up his modest earnings. His trip took a turn for the better when he won the $75,000 jackpot on a one-armed bandit and went to collect his winnings from the cashier – only to be told that, under Nevada state law, he was too young to take home the loot since he was still six months short of his twenty-first birthday.

Some of the players seemed to find it funny, but I know Aidy was distraught. I was so pleased for him when those back-to-back world titles, worth £400,000 in prize money, gave him the last laugh. When he gets on a roll, he is still the most dangerous player out there on the circuit. I would be amazed if he did not go on to win more major titles.

12

DEITY

November 2013

BUTLINS holiday camps have always had a special place in my heart ever since my dad won £41 on the pools and took us on holiday for a week. I'm not sure what the Redcoats make of it now, but twice in three months the PDC bandwagon rolled into Billy Butlin's resort in Minehead, bringing thirsty hordes of customers in fancy dress – and one spectator who, for the second year running, came as he was. The trouble was that, to biblical observers, he looked like Jesus Christ.

I had been in rollicking good form going into the Players Championship finals, featuring the top 32 from the 2013 ProTour Order of Merit after rankings had been totted up from all Players Championship floor events, UK Open qualifiers and European Tour events. I was the reigning champion of the Grand Slam, World Grand Prix, World Matchplay, UK Open and, of course, I was holder of the world title itself going into the last televised tournament before I opened my defence of the crown at Alexandra Palace. This year, the playing distance had been reduced for the later rounds; instead of the semi-finals being the best of twenty-one legs and the final decided over twenty-five, the course was shortened to nineteen legs in the last four and the best of twenty-one in the final. The players didn't mind – over three days of competition, there was £250,000 of prize money in the pot, with £60,000 to the winner, not to mention a potential shot in the arm before we turned our attention to Ally Pally.

The previous year's Players Championship finals, at the same venue, had made headlines because the crowd paid more attention to an Australian electrician in the audience than the actual darts. With his long hair and well-stocked beard, you could make a case for Nathan Grindal bearing a passing resemblance to the son of God. I wouldn't know (I'm not a great student of religion, so please don't write in). All I know is that, in the 2012 final against Kim Huybrechts, I was more than once aware of a commotion among the 4,000 fans when they spotted Grindal. 'Stand up if you love Jesus,' they sang, which was absolutely fine. I've never had a problem with playing as a chorus of 'Stand up if you love the darts' fills the arena, so why would I complain if they tweaked the lyrics as a tribute to a 'saviour' in their midst?

For Huybrechts and me, the sideshow went a bit too far when 'Jesus' started moving around the auditorium and his 'disciples' followed suit. It was like that scene out of Monty Python's *Life Of Brian*, when Graham Chapman is wrongly identified as the Messiah and he is chased into the wilderness by his adoring flock. In 2012, Grindal was ejected from the hall and watched the end of my 13–6 win on a TV monitor elsewhere in the Butlins complex. Afterwards, when I was asked about the alternative entertainment going on in the crowd, I joked, 'If I ever see Jesus again, I'll crucify him myself.' In the papers, I read that Grindal was hurt by my throwaway remark, and he complained of the crowd 'bullying' him, picking on him because of his appearance and leaving him 'emotionally distraught'. My impression was that he rather enjoyed his celebrity – he certainly didn't mind when Huybrechts signed his programme 'To Jesus. Hard luck mate.'

But I was surprised to discover, after making the long haul down to North Devon for the 2013 tournament, that 'Jesus' had been barred from attending this time. I might add that he was not refused entry by the PDC, or at the insistence of any players. The decision was taken by the Butlins management, who feared his presence might be a disruptive influence again. I dare say they were probably anxious to run the show without any problems so the PDC would bring major tournaments back to the resort in future. Would you believe it? Jesus Christ refused admission to a night at the darts! Without straying into the realms of blasphemy, I did laugh when I noticed one commentator in an online chatroom speculating that his presence would have hit bar takings massively – because he would have kept turning the water into wine.

Background controversy over a false messiah aside, I could have few complaints about my progress to the final. Although I was not at my best in the first round against fair dinkum Geordie Paul Nicholson, I won 6–2 before stepping it up several gears against Peter 'Snakebite' Wright, who had enjoyed an excellent year on the floor, finishing third on the ProTour Order of Merit. Wright, one of only three players to average 100-plus in the first round (along with James Wade and Robert Thornton), was dangerous – but I put him away 9–3, averaging 107.85, before Raymond van Barneveld was on the receiving end of one of my best performances on TV all year. Barney was blown away 9–2 as I averaged 111.58 to book a date in the semi-finals with Justin Pipe, the former tree surgeon whose late development as a top ten player may have been due in part to his refusal to play in pubs as a youngster because the smoky atmosphere made his eyes water.

Pipe had suffered unimaginable distress in the summer of 2013, learning about the sudden death of his brother Mark just a couple of hours before he was due to play John Henderson on stage in Gibraltar. Out of respect for Henderson, Pipe concealed his tragic news from his opponent until after their match, which big Hendo won 6–4. That was typical of Pipe, who plays the game at a sedate pace from the Dennis Priestley school of hurrying, but he is a top professional with fantastic levels of concentration and he's a grafter who squeezes every drop from his talent. I was happy to see him off 10–4, lining up a collision with Michael van Gerwen in the final.

Since winning my sixteenth world title at Van Gerwen's expense at Alexandra Palace eleven months earlier, he had been the only man to beat me in the final of a televised major – at the Premier League play-offs. By now, it was clear that 'Mighty Mike' was not just a flash in the pan whose success at the 2012 World Grand Prix and in reaching a World Championship final was transitory; he was a serious contender on the world stage, and, along with Adrian Lewis, I regarded him as my biggest threat when trophies were being handed out. With the World Championship, where we would be the top two seeds, less than a fortnight away, here was an opportunity to lay down a little marker, to let MVG know the old grandad from the Potteries was still around . . . but I flunked it.

Leading 6–3, I was sitting pretty and good value to retain the Players Championship title I had won, in front of the 'Messiah' himself, the previous year. Then Van Gerwen produced one of those firestorms where he reels off several legs in a row, and something happened to me that I had never experienced before in twenty-five years of competing on TV. I lost seven consecutive legs, and I simply didn't have an answer to three 11-dart legs and a 110 finish. Finally I managed to apply the brakes in the seventeenth leg with a 177 and a checkout on double 16, a trusty old friend, but Michael's momentum was unstoppable. My form throughout 2013 had been so consistent that I was convinced I would take some stopping at Alexandra Palace – but here was a performance that said Van Gerwen was going to take some stopping too. As we checked out of our chalets, I believed the PDC World Championship was heading for another Taylor–Van Gerwen final, and in a conciliatory mood, in true biblical fashion, I even offered Nathan Grindal an olive branch.

Call it seasonal goodwill, if you like – after all, Jesus effectively invented Christmas – but I intervened by asking the PDC and their security associates not to ban our friend from the World Championship. The *Daily Mirror* picked up on it, reheating our stand-off with Nathan under the memorable headline 'One Hundred and Deity', and I pleaded for common sense to prevail on all sides.

Every year we get people dressed up as Superman, Batman and Spiderman coming to watch darts, and punters in fancy dress undoubtedly add to the colour and fantastic atmosphere of the occasion. I told the PDC there was no reason why we should not admit a bloke who happened to look like Jesus – as long as he behaved himself along with all the other superheroes. If Clark Kent, Bruce Wayne or Peter Parker misbehave, they get thrown out; the same rules apply to our friend 'Jesus'. As players we love performing in front of big crowds having a good time because it makes us feel like rock stars, but it is important that we are not distracted by exhibitionists or sideshows in the audience. Ultimately, we are playing for big money and our livelihoods up on that stage. It's our workplace, and spectators would not like it if guests came to their offices or factories and made such a fuss that they were unable to do their jobs properly. All we ask, as professionals, is that fans allow us to produce our best form.

I have no idea whatsoever whether Nathan Grindal and his holy alter ego, One Hundred and Deity, made it to Ally Pally for the 2014 PDC World Championships. Sadly, I was not in the competition long enough to find out.

13

TURKEY

December 2013

THERE are only two words to describe my physical and mental state going into the 2014 PDC World Championship at Alexandra Palace – absolutely knackered. According to my birth certificate I was fifty-three years old, but I felt about 100. And at least you get a telegram from the Queen when you reach a century.

The only memory I will take from being knocked out in the second round, after going into the competition as favourite to win my seventeenth world title, is the feeling of total desolation and emptiness. For more than an hour, I stayed in the players' bar downstairs, staring at the floor and unable to face the world. Most people have to wait until Boxing Day for their first helping of cold turkey at Christmas, but I got mine a week before the rest of the country had even basted their poor birds. Not for the first time, but never more vividly, I felt like an old man with

Old Father Time tapping him on the shoulder. Down the years, Christmas has been kind to me. More often than not, I've had the later stages of a world championship to concentrate my mind. This time, it was as limp as the jokes inside a cracker.

When prize money at the top end of darts has gone through the roof since I started playing the game professionally, it seems a bit ungracious to complain about the demands of our schedule. After all, world champions now earn ten times what I first banked in 1990. Despite economists saying we have been through two recessions during my career, darts has been up there among the biggest inflation-busters of them all, so please do not interpret my observations on the tournament roster as sour grapes. But it can't be right when the leading players turn up for the biggest fortnight on the calendar feeling shattered. Would Usain Bolt have been able to win Olympic sprint gold medals, and set world records along the way, if he had been flogged into the ground before settling into the blocks? Not likely – his preparation was tailored towards peaking on the big occasion.

In darts, we are not athletes like Bolt – and we have the waistlines to prove it. But you need a certain staying power, and by that I mean high levels of durability and concentration, to sustain consistent accuracy on the oche when you are under the fierce glare of TV lights. I once had a sauna built in my house and used it as part of my preparation for majors because it was the nearest thing to replicating the intense heat of being on stage. If you are feeling under the weather, or you are not ready for the feeling of being gently microwaved for up to two-and-a-half hours (in extreme cases), you simply melt on live television. It was a masterpiece of bad timing that I headed for Ally Pally with my batteries running low.

Barely twelve hours after I had lost against Michael van Gerwen in the Players Championship finals 200 miles away in Minehead, MVG and myself found ourselves in London, watching the World Championship draw live. There's always a heightened sense of anticipation when the draw is made – people work out who's in your half of the draw and start plotting your route to the final – and I must admit I was happy enough when the names came out of the hat. Your worst nightmare, in the first round of a World Championship, is a dangerous wild card among the unseeded players, like John Henderson and Dean Winstanley in this year's case. Experts looked at the way the cards had fallen and pronounced 'It will be another Taylor–Van Gerwen final' . . . if only it were that simple.

My first-round draw was the proverbial hiding to nothing. I would face the winner of the preliminary-round tie between Ian Moss, a handy player I had come across on the ProTour circuit, and Rob Szabo, a relative 'unknown' from New Zealand. Immediately I found myself dredging my brain: I was fairly certain I had come across Rob before, probably at a World Cup tournament, but I knew he had not beaten me before. (Don't worry, I would have remembered him if I had lost against him, even if it had been twenty years earlier – he would have been a marked man.) Michael, on the other hand, knew exactly who he would be playing – Austrian dark horse Zoran Lerchbacher – but, on paper, his prospective route to the final would be hazardous: Gary Anderson in the third round, Raymond van Barneveld in the quarter-finals and Adrian Lewis in the semis all lay in wait if it went with the formbook.

Of course, you should never count your chickens unless your name is Colonel Sanders and you're in charge of the KFC franchise and, looking back, I guess I was tempting fate when I rented an apartment in Finchley, just ten minutes from Alexandra Palace, for the duration of the tournament for £500 a week. In previous years I had been worn down by the drag of commuting from Staffordshire to London; this time, I was happy to have my own base, my own space, just a couple of miles along the North Circular. On days when I wasn't competing, I could practise for a couple of hours, go shopping at Brent Cross or go and watch a film. It seemed like the sensible option when I was feeling so tired.

Determined to do everything right, with nothing rushed, I came down the night before my first-round tie, checked into the flat and pictured myself spending Christmas there, with a bung-in-the-oven chicken curry, a party hat and my feet up in front of the telly. A much better option than a soulless hotel room, it was a home from home, and I even decorated it with a few strands of tinsel to make the place feel festive. I felt I was ready – knackered, yes, but as well prepared as I could be – and headed for Alexandra Palace without any hang-ups or superstitions about facing Szabo on Friday the 13th. I would have had a more comfortable night if I had been doing a neighbourhood watch shift on Elm Street or sharing a lift with Freddy Krueger himself.

Because I have won sixteen world titles, a lot of people think I walk into Ally Pally with the swagger of a bloke who owns the place. In fact, my record there is not brilliant. Yes, I have lifted the trophy three times after beating Barney, Simon Whitlock and Van Gerwen in the final, but I also came unstuck there against Wayne Mardle, Mark Webster and Dave Chisnall – the first two in quarter-finals and against Chizzy in the second round. Don't assume, for a minute, that I pulled up outside the players' entrance with the ebullient confidence of a man who thought it was going to be a piece of cake.

When you walk into the Palace, you are immediately struck by the size of the place. It's easy for even the biggest ego to be swallowed up and drowned by the high ceilings and soaring brickwork. And the stage itself is absolutely massive. It's a never-ending platform and somewhere, in the middle of it, is a dartboard. At the 2012 championship, James Wade's semi-final with Adrian Lewis was interrupted for half an hour by draughts of air wafting across the stage and making the darts wobble in mid-flight. It's remarkable that this is the only occasion when play has been halted by gusts of wind – it must be virtually impossible to keep such a huge venue airtight. Every time I set foot in the place, my admiration for the PDC's air conditioning department grows.

I don't like waiting backstage in the practice room at a world championship without knowing who I am going to be playing. Under the competition format, sixteen qualifiers are drawn to face each other in a preliminary round, over the best of seven legs, with the winner playing later the same night in the first round. Even when you are ranked No.1 in the world and you are overwhelming favourite to make the second round, it's nice to have a level playing field, and there is little doubt in my mind that Szabo – who edged his sudden-death qualifier 4–3 against Moss – had got any nerves out of his system by the time he returned to the stage to play me.

A builder by trade, and an easy-going Kiwi by nature, Rob will be the first to admit his preliminary-round game was no classic. Neither player's average made it to 80, which is understandable if, like Szabo, you are playing on TV for the first time and you are not used to performing in front of the fancy dress corps in high spirits with the Christmas party season in full swing. But, sure enough, when the time came for his tilt at a giant-killing, Rob's stage fright had disappeared – and I was the one who looked more nervous than a turkey on Bernard Matthews' farm. Excuse the poultry analogies, but I played like a headless chicken.

It may have been something to do with the late start – the winning dart didn't land until 11.10 p.m., or chucking-out time by most people's watches – but I felt sleepy and lethargic . . . and I got the fright of my life. At 250–1 on with title sponsors Ladbrokes, I'm told I was the heaviest favourite in history for a darts match, virtually unbackable at the bookies. In other words, if you put £250 on me to win, you would get £251 back. Now that's what I call driving a hard bargain. Those odds suggested that Szabo should not only be whitewashed but he would be lucky to get a dart at a double to win a leg.

To be honest, if his first match of the night had been against me, and he had been a bag of nerves because he had never played on a stage the size of a basketball court before, I suspect it might have turned out that way. But Rob had got rid of all his butterflies against Moss earlier that night, and by the time he was back on the oche, he had nothing to lose. Take nothing away from the lad, he was fearless and in the first set he played brilliantly, knocking out finishes of 128 on the bullseye and 105 on double top to put the cat among the pigeons or, to be nearer the mark, he put the fox among the headless chickens. I lost the opening set 3–1, and I was shitting myself.

I was rattled to such an extent that Rob broke my throw in the opening leg of the second set, and now the unthinkable was possible. I was a set and a break of serve down in a contest that was the best of five sets. To put it into context, if every subsequent leg had gone with the throw,

I was heading out of the World Championship at the first hurdle – and into sporting legend for all the wrong reasons. I didn't want to follow Mike Tyson, knocked out by no-hoper James 'Buster' Douglas in 1990 – the year I won my first world title – into the record books among the biggest upsets of all time. I didn't want to be a giant slayed by a minnow. If I had gone out that night, against a chap who was a 2,000–1 long shot to win the title, I might have been tempted to retire there and then.

More by willpower than stunning accuracy, I managed to pull out of my nosedive in the nick of time. Maybe it was a case of my game improving from embarrassing to respectable, maybe Rob scented a huge upset and suddenly felt the pressure, maybe it was a combination of the two, but I put together eight legs in a row to take control of the match. I suspect his spirit was broken by my consecutive checkouts of 115 and 114, which turned the second set in my favour, but I was happy to get out of there with my dignity just about intact. 'I've never tried so hard to win in all my life,' I told the wise men of Sky Sports afterwards. 'I wish it had been a boxing match so I could have banged him out with one punch and got out of there. I was all over the place – at one stage my head was gone, I didn't know what I was doing.'

Grateful to still be in the competition, I retired to my rented bachelor pad in Finchley to count my blessings and settle in for a long weekend of practising and chilling out in front of the box. On the Sunday night I watched Andy

Murray crowned BBC Sports Personality of the Year – deservedly so after ending Britain's long wait for a Wimbledon men's singles champion – and British Lions full-back Leigh Halfpenny was runner-up. Four years earlier, that had been me finishing second in the nation's leading sports opinion poll, and I think it scared the living daylights out of the BBC. It was a major wake-up call for them when a darts player who makes 99 per cent of his competitive appearances on Sky Sports made the podium in their showpiece review of the sporting year. Even if I win the next four world championships, and fire a hat-trick of nine-dart finishes in each one, I doubt if I will ever make their Sports Personality shortlist again.

I remember Tottenham manager André Villas-Boas got the sack that weekend after losing five-zip at home to Liverpool – and the reason I can recall it is because I was probably the only person in North London who was feeling lousier than AVB ten days before Christmas. I don't know if it was just a seasonal bug, the collection of symptoms now known as 'man-flu' (I'm not sure how it differs from woman-flu) or a valiant attempt to contract bubonic plague in the twenty-first century, but I felt chuffing awful. You have to be careful what medicines you take because players on the PDC circuit are subject to the same anti-doping regulations as Olympic athletes, and some common cold remedies contain banned substances on the World Anti Doping Agency's no-go list. It's bad enough having to drop your trousers and pee into a bottle in front of a stranger with a clipboard – imagine how terrible it would be if you got a letter in the post adding a doping ban to the humiliation just because your nasal spray contained a tiny drop of something on WADA's blacklist.

Feeling sorry for myself, and patched up with medication in soluble, capsule and syrup form, I did my best to get ready for a second-round date with 23-year-old Michael Smith, nicknamed 'Bully Boy' because of his fondness for checking out on the bullseye, on the second Friday of the tournament. Like Dave Chisnall, who had knocked me out in the second round at Ally Pally two years earlier, Smith comes from St Helens – but even though I was ravaged by man-flu and felt fatigued, I wasn't unduly worried about lightning striking twice. On the other hand, let's be clear about one thing: I did not underestimate Michael Smith or take him lightly. As Gary Anderson's protégé, I knew he would be well-prepared, and he had not won the youth World Championship by accident. Smith is a proper player in his own right.

Once again the bookies did their best to give the impression that it was more of a walkover than a contest, making me a modest 1–80 to reach the last sixteen. No pressure there. And I made a decent enough start, taking the first leg against the throw with a 156 checkout. That should have been the catalyst for Michael's confidence to sink, and when I reeled off the first set without missing a double, I must admit I fancied an early night with a cup of Lemsip. But in the second set, that clinical finishing deserted me, and I can't explain why. If I was remotely inclined to be cocky about my flying start, any complacency was knocked out of me by the fifth leg of the match, which scraped the bottom of the barrel. We were both down to shooting for double 1, or the 'madhouse' as it is sometimes known, and it was like a pair of blindfolded party-goers trying to pin the tail on a donkey. Between us, we traded fifteen shots at a double before Michael put us out of our misery.

Three times I went a set up, and three times Michael pegged me back as my darts lurched from mediocre to pub standard. By the time it went to a deciding seventh set, I was bored with my own performance – and struggling to stay awake. Michael was throwing more consistently than me, he was playing better than me. No excuses about a cold virus, or staying up way beyond my normal bedtime, can cover for that simple acknowledgement. When the best-of-seven-sets tie came down to a decider, he had more gas left in the tank than an old man longing to hit the sack. One of us had to win it by two clear legs, and Michael was the only one who ever looked like doing it. When he sank the winning dart at around a quarter to midnight, he was a deserving winner. One of my idiosyncrasies in victory is to sign the board; after pulling off his upset – on the bullseye, of course – Michael kissed it.

I shuffled off the stage feeling shell-shocked and in a trance like a zombie. How could I have played so badly for six sets after the first one had gone utterly to plan? In the players' bar, down two flights of stairs from the West

Hall auditorium, I looked like death warmed up and just stared at the floor. I didn't want to face anyone and I didn't want to speak to anyone in case I said something I might later regret. In a comforting touch of class, I heard Anderson telling his triumphant apprentice, 'Don't go shouting your mouth off – make sure you give that man the respect he deserves.' Gary can be a feisty competitor, especially if there isn't a machine or a barista dispensing a decent cup of coffee to his liking, but he is a class act. I've seen young players bouncing off the walls and rubbing your face in it when they win, but it speaks volumes for Anderson that he was as concerned for a beaten top seed as he was delighted for the impressive young man he mentored.

As for Michael, he is a genuinely nice kid. I've given a lot of these young lads some real bashings in the past, and as the old saying goes, it's no good dishing it out if you can't take it. He was a model of diplomacy afterwards, saying, 'When I lost the first set 3–0 I was thinking, "Uh-oh, I'm going to get battered here – twelve legs in a row, please don't embarrass yourself." But Phil wasn't on his game in the second set, and when I won that leg which went on forever I suddenly found myself daring to think it could be my night.' Good on you, kid – I was disappointed for Michael when he went out to Peter Wright in the third round.

There were four people called Smith in the main draw – enough to form a band who've sold more albums than we've baked oatcakes in the Potteries – but heaven knows I was miserable now. Rather presumptuously, I had taken out a short-term tenancy in my flat for three weeks, but there was nothing going on but the rent in North London after I had bombed out of the World Championship. As I mentioned earlier, for an hour I could not bring myself to leave the scene of the accident. There were still five days before Christmas, and I was already out of the biggest tournament on the calendar, which still had another twelve days to run. I hate losing – it's never sat easily with me. I can understand why the greatest football manager of our time, Sir Alex Ferguson, could be so frosty when his team lost because he was used to winning. It was all he had ever known. I hate losing because I feel like I'm letting down my sponsors, the companies who pay good money to have their emblems on my shirt or their darts in my hand. Blue-chip firms don't pay top dollar to see me get knocked out in the second round, they want to be associated with winners who are at the top of their game on the big occasion.

When Ally Pally was almost deserted, and the coast was clear for me to make a melancholy exit through the back door, it was the loneliest walk in the world down the covered stairway outside, where players and officials habitually nip out for a crafty fag. I couldn't bear to switch on the car radio for the short drive back to Finchley. I knew sports desk bulletins on the graveyard shift would only remind me of the shock result. It was a thoroughly miserable journey, the longest ten minutes I can remember among the thousands and thousands of miles I clock up every year. It was horrible.

Having taken my medicine, both from the chemist and from Michael Smith, I could not let the disappointment pass without registering a mild protest afterwards. Late nights and old men are not often compatible in professional sport, and I had made my feelings known at earlier world championships about the schedules getting later and later, but until now I've had the feeling my observations have fallen on deaf ears. At the risk of being accused of sour grapes – and let me repeat, Michael beat me fair and square on the night – I need to get this off my chest.

Name me another sport where the world No.1 takes to the stage, or walks on court, or tees off, at 10.20 p.m. at night and his/her match finishes at nearly midnight. How often has Rafa Nadal sealed victory on Centre Court after the last Tube home from Wimbledon? When was the last time you saw Tiger Woods sink the winning putt as the clock ticked round towards the enchanted hour? I know Steve Davis and Dennis Taylor's famous black ball snooker final in 1985 went deep into the night shift, but that was an exceptional battle of willpower between two sportsmen who went to the very last ball of the very last frame. My game against Smith was always scheduled to catch the last hour of Sky Sports' coverage – I had no say in the matter.

Maybe I should take it as a compliment that Sky want to screen my games at the back end of their programmes to catch their peak audience, but on 20 December 2013 they weren't due to go off the air from Alexandra Palace until midnight. As a shareholder in the PDC, perhaps I should exercise my democratic right to demand a bigger say in the matter, but the bottom line is that a 53-year-old grandfather with twenty-five years of professional darts on the clock is not always going to produce his best form at that time of night because he is knackered. In the Premier League, we get it right: games rarely go on much beyond 10 p.m., but the punters still get their value for money, Sky still pull in the viewers and the players are invariably at the peak of their powers. I've spoken to PDC tournament director Tommy Cox about this several times before, and I'll keep talking to him until we get some form of resolution. I understand that big viewing figures attract bigger revenues, and that increased income filters down to the players. Yes, we like playing for bigger prize money. Yes, we like playing in front of big crowds at the Palace and on TV. But the load needs to be spread more evenly among the top ten, twelve and twenty in the rankings. Midnight finishes are miles too late for me. I can't do it any more. Sometimes it screws me up into the following day, especially if the drug testers are in town and you don't get to bed until two or three in the morning. We are not athletes, but the stamina required to keep winning is increasing.

Eric Bristow, bless him, noticed the sympathy – or sycophancy – for the beaten champion. 'Look at them all,' he told me. 'When you beat them every week, they hate your guts. As soon as they start liking you, it means you are no good.' Good old Eric, you can always rely on him to tell it like it is. No bullshit. He's got more bottle than Mike Tyson.

The world doesn't stop turning when you get knocked out of the World Championship before Christmas, but it feels like the end of the world. I went home and switched off the mobile phone to make sure nobody could get hold of me. The worst thing I ever did was to buy a mobile phone. You know how to prepare properly, but you are not allowed to prepare properly if the bloody thing is ringing every five minutes and somebody else wants their pound of flesh. I've never been alone since I had a mobile, but there is always somebody in the world who is worse off than you, so spare a thought for the poor sod who piled £100,000 on me to win, at odds of 40–1 on, the night I lost against Smith. And that Christmas dinner of chicken curry for one, in my Finchley hideaway, never happened. I packed up, went home and we had a big Sunday roast with the grandkids jumping all over me afterwards until I fell asleep in my armchair.

I'm afraid I could not be arsed to watch the rest of the World Championship on TV. If I switched on the box and there was some darts on the telly, I could only bear to watch it for a couple of minutes if there was a decent film on another channel. I would just look at whoever was playing and think 'I beat him last month', or 'I knocked him out last year' or 'I could beat him standing on my head.' Jealous? You bet I was. When Van Gerwen beat Wright 7–4 in the final on New Year's Day, I was tucked up in bed when the winning dart landed. Once I had finished sulking, there is no question that Michael was a worthy champion and Peter was a deserving runner-up. They were the only two players in the competition who had posted two 100-plus averages on their way to the final.

But I am not going to deny I was riddled with envy. For just about the whole of 2013, I had had a cracking year, consistently playing some of the best darts of my life, but the whole thing had come crashing down when it mattered most. And, worst of all, Van Gerwen's maiden world title meant that he took over the mantle as No.1 in the world rankings, ending my six-year run at the top of the charts. Michael was only nine months old when I had won my first world title, and there was much talk in the press that MVG's triumph marked the end of an era. Losing my World Championship was bad enough. To lose the No.1 ranking with it was a real body blow. I felt like a man who had lost his wallet and his ego. Yet in a strange way, my serving of cold turkey at Alexandra Palace gave me a fresh incentive as we rang in the New Year. I had proved the doubters wrong time and again in the past – now I had a clear target for 2014. I wanted to be No.1 again.

14

DETOX

January 2014

No wonder I had been feeling so tired and running out of gas. I was a fat bastard, creeping back up towards my heaviest weight – which at one point in my career was nudging 20 stone. I don't want to die of a heart attack before I'm sixty. One of the things that has always frightened me is the thought of earning all this money from my career and not living long enough to enjoy the fruits of my labours. I've always hated the common, and cheap, perception that darts players are all fat, lazy, unsociable, alcoholic and inactive. And although it may not always have been evident, especially when I had to wear XXXL shirts, I have always been conscious of my weight. As a thirteen-year-old I was teased at school for being portly, which prompted me to take up weight training. And at various stages of my career I had been on health 'kicks', losing 5 stone in 2001 during a phase when I used to go to the gym every day with my wife. Then, in 2012, the year before I won my sixteenth world title, I had walked off stage during a tournament in the Shetland Isles when drunken abuse from the crowd, which included vicious jibes about my weight, were simply too vile to ignore. One of the reasons I made a stand was that I had lost around 3 stone in six months from an ample starting point of 17 stone 11lb after following a fitness and healthy eating plan devised by nutritionist Laura Church.

But the weight had crept back up again during 2013, and after my shock defeat at the World Championship, I decided drastic readings on the bathroom scales called for drastic remedies. Losing to Michael Smith had not just been a case of a few arrows missing their target – I had to find a way of making myself fitter, and feeling healthier, if I was going to get that No.1 spot back.

I had come across Jason Vale, the celebrity lifestyle coach and motivational speaker also known as The Juice Master, socially in recent years and knew he had a retreat in Portugal that was ideal for an overweight darts player looking for a New Year detox plan. I had been there before, in high summer, when I took up swimming and spent my days bobbing up and down in the pool or relaxing in the jacuzzi. I had seen Jason talking about his juice diet on Alan Titchmarsh's TV chat show, and by the time I contacted him later, I was convinced his juice-only plan was well worth a try. I had a month to take stock, to take on board a new regime where the first priority was getting the right vitamins and nutrients into my system, so I could come back in February feeling revitalised and ready to take on the rigours of a fifteen-week Premier League campaign.

There were no short cuts, no calling in favours from a mate. I booked my stay at the Juicy Oasis, in Portugal's Vale do Serrao, on the internet after sending Jason an email to ask if there was any availability. He said there was a room free from the second week of January if I wanted it. I couldn't get to the airport fast enough. People make New Year resolutions without seeing them through, but I was deadly serious. If I didn't get myself in shape, I wasn't going to win a hill of beans. I wanted to be 100 per cent match-fit and properly rested for the Premier League. At my age, rest is as important as practice – going to bed at 3.30 a.m. after a 200-mile drive home through the graveyard shift is nobody's recipe for success.

Whereas the healthier lifestyle prescribed by Laura had been based mainly around exercise, Jason the Juice Master's plan contained two fundamental elements: juice (no surprises there) and lots of walking – around 10 to 12 miles a day, usually all in one go. The retreat is set in a range of hills, with a river winding down through the valley below, and the peace was just bliss. No phone calls, no long treks up the motorway and filling up with crap at service stations en route. You just live on juices, and if you stick to Jason's plan you get a salad every Saturday as a reward. I loved it – especially the visitors who paid £2,500 for a specialist detox and spent the week moaning about how much they craved a burger, and how they couldn't wait to pig out on a half-pounder at Lisbon airport on the way home! You've got to laugh, haven't you?

I did take my dartboard with me, but in the three weeks I was away, I hardly practised at all – maybe for forty-five minutes, but only once or twice – and the internet connections were poor, so I didn't spend much time on the iPad either. And there was no television, no mind-numbing drivel to fritter away whole days at a time. Now I know how Ricky Hatton felt when he went into a training camp before he fought Floyd Mayweather or Manny Pacquiao. I was going to bed at nine o'clock every evening, and if I woke up in the middle of the night, I just turned the light on, read for twenty minutes and nodded off again.

Scott McArthur, a mate of mine who is a qualified juice therapist, came over to Portugal and at first light every morning, around 7.30 a.m., we would hit the road for two to three hours before breakfast. Then it was juice for breakfast, lunch and dinner (more about the varieties on the Juicy Oasis menu later) and the rest of the day was about relaxing. I did a lot of reading, including Novak Djokovic's autobiography, and I could feel the pounds falling off me. Suddenly trousers that had been snug were roomier, shirts that used to cling to my torso were flapping in the breeze, and I just felt better in myself.

Barry Hearn was not happy about me disappearing into the back end of Portugal for an unscheduled spell of recuperation, and gave me a real ticking-off, but I told him,

'Tough luck – it's my life, I've got a long, difficult year ahead of me and this is the way I'm going to do it.' Like I said, this was not an exercise in personal vanity. I was not a millionaire socialite spending a bit of pocket money because I was bored: I was not very well and if I was going to compete for the major prizes in 2014, I needed to get away and sort myself out. I needed to do it out of self-respect, but also out of respect for my sponsors, the people who pay to come and watch me play and the punters who back me in the betting shops. Suddenly, my own health had become far more important than winning titles. And as far as I was concerned, one was not going to be possible without the other.

Although I would have stuck to the detox programme religiously if I had been at the Juicy Oasis by myself, I was glad of Scott's company. He is not a nutty professor whose faith in juicing is one of these dietary fads with no scientific merit. Back in 2007, he needed major surgery after a bad accident in his kitchen resulted in thirty-three metal staples inserted from his chest down to his pelvis. Doctors who warned him he would need to stay in hospital for at least two weeks were amazed at his rapid recovery from the operation and discharged him after six days. The secret of his rapid recovery? Drinking up to 2 litres of liquidised spinach and greens. Effectively, it healed his body from the inside out.

Apparently, what Scott calls natural juice therapy has been around, in some shape or form, for centuries. I don't pretend to understand all the science involved, but freshly extracted juices from fruit and vegetables can provide the body with an ideal balance of all the vitamins, minerals, carbohydrates and anti-oxidants it needs. From high blood pressure to heart disease, from gout to dermatology issues, from being overweight to feeling lethargic, Scott reckons he can help just about any condition. All I know is that, after three weeks of juicing up in Portugal, I felt better than I had for months.

When the pressures and demands of staying at the top wear you down, you can understand why Stephen Hendry quit after winning seven world snooker titles, even when a lot of the players and people around him felt he had another few left in him. I was reaching an age where I could easily have opted for putting on my slippers and settling for the quiet life. I needed the boost of Jason and Scott's juice cocktails to give me fresh vitality, a jump-start to give my flat battery new life. I knew that, on its own, putting avocado and wheatgrass in a blender wasn't going to make my darts pin the target any better, but my detox early in 2014 undoubtedly made me feel happier in my own skin.

Everyone thinks money makes you happy. Trust me, it doesn't. Good health is the most direct route to happiness. You can spend £1 million on a palatial house with all mod cons and all the latest interior designs, but once you shut the door it just becomes your home. One man's conservatory is another man's bird cage. We didn't have hot water or electricity when I was a kid, but we were happy because my mum and dad raised their family as best as they could. And you can drive the flashiest motor around town, like top footballers these days, but the speed limit is the same whether you drive a Bentley or an old banger. I bought a villa on Tenerife, but my car out there is a knackered old Fiat I bought for buttons and spent a bit of time doing up. Even now, I don't think it would make it to the top of Mount Teide, where a lot of Tour de France cyclists do their altitude training every winter, and if it did make it to the summit there would be smoke coming out from under the bonnet. But it's my set of wheels, and I don't worry about what it can't do: I'm more grateful for where it can take me.

Losing my world title in such a limp fashion made me do a lot of soul-searching about various aspects of my life, and going to Portugal was a bold opening statement in the fight to regain my status as market leader in darts. I cannot do justice to the treatment by going through every ingredient of every juice; instead I will let Scott tell you a bit about juicing, what it has done for me and, dare I suggest, what it might do for you . . .

We all knew Phil had remarkable willpower – because you don't win sixteen world titles by waking up one morning and deciding you're going to be the greatest darts player who ever lived. But when you are living in a lovely place, and you have achieved everything it is possible to achieve in your profession, it's easy to give in to temptation when you fancy a burger or a kebab.

He has the mental capacity to win major championships under massive pressure because he is Phil Taylor, but when it comes down to a big change in your lifestyle – which is what natural juice therapy is – you have to want to do it. He knew, instinctively, he had to get away from home life, the demands on his time, the rat race, and make juices and exercise the main focal points of his life for three weeks. That's a hell of a long time to stay so disciplined when most people only do it for seven days at a time. Phil went for full-on detox, a very intense period of purging his system of all the refined foods, additives, chemicals and crap that were making him feel lousy, and he gave his digestive system a rest.

There is no magic ingredient like moondust that makes you feel better – but a juice containing avocado, apple and ginger is one of Phil's favourites. It gives him a lift with its anti-histamine and anti-inflammatory qualities, but instead of a shot of caffeine, which the body has to absorb, he gets a healthy kick-start from the nutrients of the juice naturally. For breakfast he might have wheatgrass, which has pro-biotic properties, with a bit of pineapple to sweeten it, plus lime, avocado and dark greens, maybe spinach. It's a meal in a glass, and two juices a day are full of enzymes that make you feel you've satisfied your appetite – which is why juice diets go hand-in-hand with weight loss.

When I first worked with Phil, I would go up to his

house and take my juicer with me. He bought one for himself, but increasingly he found it became a pain in the backside to buy the stuff in, chop up the ingredients and prepare two or three juices every day because it was not compatible with the demands of his job. So I used to pop in once or twice a week, make up a few days' worth at a time, pop them in the freezer and he could take out one or two the night before, to let them defrost, so he could enjoy them next day. He is sleeping better, feeling better when he gets up in the morning, feeling less tired during the day and generally more alert because he has replaced the toxins and chemically manipulated foods you get in takeaways or microwave dinners with all the vitamins and minerals he needs.

I suspect that what Phil really wants to do, now he has spent twenty-five years at the top, is to supplement winning darts matches with good health so he can enjoy his success into old age. A high-level juice diet sounds hippified, if there is such a word, but most people's digestive systems are overburdened from years of eating food – and yet we wonder why diabetes in Britain is at an all-time high and why we are suffering from arthritis at fifty. Now Phil has got the 'buzz' from this health kick, he wants to stay ahead of the game. There is a wonderful quote from American fitness and nutritional expert Jack LaLanne (he lived to be ninety-six, so he knew what he was talking about), who said, 'Exercise is king and nutrition is queen: together you have a kingdom.' In a nutshell, that's what Phil has tried to do with his life since he spent those three weeks in Portugal at Jason Vale's resort. He was tired of waking up after nine hours' sleep feeling sluggish because his body was struggling to break down all the sugars, stimulants and toxic substances he had been putting into his system.

At fifty-three, Phil decided to get a grip of life and keep the diseases and ailments that can take root in middle age at arm's length. After six months, he had lost around four stone and looked so well that he was probably feeling as if he could reverse the ageing process. Do I think he will win a seventeenth world title? Yes, I believe he will do it – the young guns chasing him are fantastic, but if he transfers the willpower of his juicing regime to the board, I have no doubt there is another world championship there for him.

Before I sign off, I had better tell you why I ended up in intensive care . . . I used to do a bit of work as a DJ, and after getting home a bit drunk one night, I felt peckish and started to cook myself some minted lamb chops. I had an accident with a kitchen knife, which is how I ended up with a chest wound that came within one millimetre of puncturing my heart. I was on my own in a new-build apartment and had to phone for the ambulance myself while trying to stem the blood loss with duct tape and kitchen towels. I was lucky to escape with my life – and now that juicing has become a mainstream way of helping people to lead fitter, more active lives, I'm privileged to be working with an achiever of Phil Taylor's stature, and I'm privileged to count him as a friend.

Scott is the bloke who recommended a film called *Fat, Sick and Nearly Dead* to me. It's a documentary about Joe Cross, an Australian fella who observes a sixty-day juice fast to regain his health. Following his diet, the guy loses 100lb (7 stone) and discontinues all the medications he used to take before he discovered juicing. None of us likes to think we have too much in common with Joe Cross, but I didn't want to wait until I was diagnosed as diabetic, or suffered a serious medical episode, to find out.

Barry Hearn, my manager, did not want me to take a whole month off early in 2014, but he was in favour of my conversion to vegetarianism, in a manner of speaking, when he realised how good I felt, and how much healthier I looked, on my return from Jason Vale's juicing spa. I had made a fresh start, in every sense, by the time I flew home early in February. If I had not got my long-term health under control, at least I had applied the brakes. Now for turning over a new leaf in the day job – armed with a different set of weapons . . .

15

TARGET

February 2014

SAT behind a desk, pen hovering over the dotted line, fixed smile for the cameras, I felt like a footballer completing a big-money transfer. So this is what it was like for Gareth Bale when he signed for Real Madrid, or Cristiano Ronaldo when he joined Manchester United. Well, maybe not, but it felt like a red-letter day in my life, and I was as nervous as a kitten. After seventeen years with Unicorn, I was changing my darts manufacturer, having landed a five-year deal with Target. As far as I'm concerned, this contract will see me through to the end of my playing career. To sign another one would take me beyond my sixtieth birthday, and I would have to be mad to carry on at an age where I should be looking forward to a free bus pass.

I have only happy memories of my long association with Unicorn, especially when they took me on a VIP trip to China back in 2000 and I serenaded the crowd, karaoke-style, with my renderings of 'My Way', 'Mack The Knife' and 'Danny Boy'. They took me to the Great Wall of China, the Forbidden City, and made me feel like I owned the Imperial Palace itself. But during a brief hiatus in my association with Barry Hearn as player and agent/manager, there was a small vacuum in my contractual arrangements with Unicorn and I began to wonder if they had forgotten about me. I would argue that I didn't leave them – in football terms, it would probably go down as parting by mutual consent, with some parts of the consent more mutual than others. But in that little window of opportunity, several darts companies approached me and the first one I talked to was Target Darts, based in Harlow.

As soon as I met Garry Plummer, their managing director, I liked the fella and his ideas straightaway – it certainly wasn't just about the money – and after reaching a crossroads in my career, where I was looking at my health regime and other ways to improve my performance, I decided the time was right for a change of weapon. Footballers change their boots, cricketers change their bats, tennis players try different racquets – so why shouldn't a darts player experiment with new equipment if he believes it can improve his game by just 0.1 per cent? Let's make it clear from the outset: this was not a vanity project. Down the years, I had always been prepared to try new shoes, wearing glasses, different shirts, new diets and alternative sleeping patterns to try and squeeze every last drop from the well.

It would be no exaggeration to say I was reinventing myself. Michael van Gerwen had overtaken the old Phil Taylor as World No.1, so it was time to find out if he could live with the new, improved 'Power'. As far as I was concerned, I had nothing to lose.

Garry's knowledge and enthusiasm was infectious. He wanted to launch my own range of Power 9Five darts, using Target's hi-tech pixel grip technology with blue titanium nitride highlights. The 95 per cent tungsten barrels with steel tips would be made to my personal specifications – 41 mm long, 7.85mm wide. From the first time I spoke to him, I knew I would not need to negotiate seriously with anyone else. A bad workman blames his tools, and I knew Target's bespoke spears would not fly into the treble 20 bed by themselves without a steady arm to direct them. For Target and Taylor to make their alliance work, I would have to be more dedicated and professional than ever. But there was no getting away from the harsh truth: changing my darts at this stage of my life was a gamble, and I would have to make it work.

We wanted to make exact replicas of the darts I use in matchplay so the punters could share my throwing experience, if there is such a marketing term. You can buy replica football shirts, bats as used by Test cricketers and tennis racquets as used by top players at Grand Slam tournaments, so why not share the technology that goes into a set of arrows? At around £65 a set, top-of-the-range Power 9Fives look the part, feel the part and, yes, cost the part. But from the moment I signed for Target, at the Victory Services Club near Marble Arch on Monday, 3 February 2014, they were flying off the shelves.

I was saddened to hear later that Unicorn, with whom I had known only cordial relations, were threatening legal action against Target because they claimed ownership of the Power trademark. I don't know whether their claim holds water under legal scrutiny, but as I explained in the earlier chapter about nicknames, if anyone holds the intellectual rights to my 'Power' soubriquet, it should be former Sky floor manager Peter Judge. All that interested me was getting to know my new darts in the same way that Rory McIlroy had made the acquaintance of new golf clubs after changing manufacturer a few months earlier.

At the launch, I told the media there might be teething troubles and it might take me a few weeks to get used to my new ammunition – just as Rory did not pull up any trees immediately after putting his new sticks to the test in a competitive environment. Those words would soon come back to haunt me, but I regarded this moment as an important step towards a fresh start: a slimmer, healthier figure unleashing brand new weapons at the Premier League.

Fans with an eye on technical aspects of the game often ask me what I regard as the most critical aspect of the darts in your hand – and without a shadow of a doubt, it's the grip. People say you can throw any dart and the result will be the same, but that's cobblers. If I walked on stage with a set of cocktail sticks instead of custom-designed barrels and stems, I might hit the board but I wouldn't be the best player in the world. For me, it's all about the grip. If your fingers are not comfortable when you are lining up a shot, you've got little hope of landing it in the right bed when you let the dart go. It's a never-ending process because you are always experimenting with tiny adjustments, but essentially the design remains the same. I used to change my darts every match because the pixels would become chipped if one dart used the other as a 'stacker' and kissed the barrel on its way into the bed, but my new hardware doesn't nick or scratch so easily.

The art of perfecting the best barrel is simply a case of trial and error, like a Michelin-starred chef adding only a pinch of salt or a few grains of seasoning to make his soup just the way he likes it. Sometimes, almost on a whim, you can borrow someone else's darts to see if it makes any difference to the flight path or the way they lie in the board. At the World Cup in June 2014, when I wasn't firing on all cylinders in the first round, Adrian Lewis marched into the practice room and said, 'It's not you, it's the darts – have a go with these.' Aidy, whose tungsten is also supplied by Target, loaned me his stems and, hey presto, instead of lying in the bed at an angle, blocking the path of other darts, they went in straight as a dye.

As for weight of dart, mine are 29 grams, but there is no hard and fast rule that dictates that one size fits all

– it's simply a question of personal preference. Some players like tickling the board with a feather duster, others ram their spears into the cork like warriors at Rorke's Drift. I do not think the quality or accuracy of your darts is necessarily improved if you have to make an Olympian effort to release each one, like tossing the caber at the Highland Games. If I wanted to start breaking records again, I needed to take all these factors seriously.

At the press conference called to mark my 'transfer' to Target, I admitted it was make-or-break, a calculated gamble. I was well aware there might be fluctuations in my form, as per McIlroy's change of golf clubs. I was well aware there would be some people willing me to fail. And at the launch, I said to Garry Plummer, 'I know you are over the moon, but this might be the worst thing you ever do.' I reminded him what record producer Pete Waterman had once told me about the growth of his business in the 1980s, when I was starting out. Pete used to have twenty people working for him in a compact but successful operation – and then along came Kylie Minogue, and millions of records later, his life was never the same again. He had to employ 100 people to keep up with the explosion of sales and transformation of his marketing department.

'I should be so lucky,' said Garry. Within hours, his wish would be fulfilled. The Target website crashed because it was inundated with enquiries from potential customers, and one of his biggest online clients shifted more sets of darts from the new Power range in two days than he had expected to sell in a month.

Has there been any jealousy from other players about the financial success of my signing for Target? Not one bit – they know how it works. They know the trickledown effect from one commercial deal stands to benefit them all in the long run. Stephen Bunting, the new BDO Lakeside world champion who had announced his switch to the PDC circuit only days earlier, came down to the Victory Services Club and we had a nice chat about the new earning power at his disposal.

It's not every day of the week that a sportsman signs a long contract that will take him up to the end of his competitive career. That Monday morning in the West End felt like the dawn of a brave new era. Now all I needed to do was to make the darts land where I wanted them to go . . .

16

WHITEWASH

February 2014

THREE days after changing my darts came my first public workout with them – the opening night of the Premier League in Liverpool. I didn't expect to make the earth move after basically taking a month off, but instead of causing an earthquake I got caught in a landslide.

For the first time in my entire life – and I sincerely hope it will be the last – I was whitewashed on live TV, thrashed 7–0 by Michael van Gerwen, the man from whom I had hoped to recapture the No.1 ranking. Disaster is a word too often used in sport, so it's important to keep the result in some perspective. A disaster is when your father, or son, goes off to serve his country in a war and never comes home. A disaster is a tsunami, a famine, a flood, but not a darts match. Even when you lose 7–0. But that annihilation at the Echo Arena on Merseyside, in front of 8,000 fans and a big audience on Sky Sports, was more than a defeat. It was like a dagger through my heart.

There are lots of excuses I could trot out, but the bottom line is that Michael played better than me. He played like a world champion. Much as it felt good to wake up in the morning after eight hours' sleep without still feeling tired, thanks to my detox in Portugal, the truth is that I was rusty in terms of competing. If I had been a footballer, you would have said I was physically fit after being out for a month, but I was not yet match-fit.

Although I only had time to practise with my new arrows for a couple of days before heading to Liverpool, there was certainly no blame attached to the darts. Out of the ten players who went on stage that night, there were only three whose match averages were better than my 99.45 against Van Gerwen – Gary Anderson lost 7–2 to Raymond van Barneveld despite averaging 100.71, Barney posted an impressive 108.52 . . . and MVG started the campaign with an ominous 109.59. I could have played out of my skin and it might not have been enough to win. Just as Adrian Lewis performed brilliantly against me in the 2013 World Matchplay final and Grand Slam semi-final and still lost them both, I had to take it on the chin.

Of course, there are easier starts to a Premier League season than walking into a firestorm of Van Gerwen's arrows. But in 2011, I had suffered an 8–2 defeat at the hands of Lewis on the opening night, and I recovered to reach the semi-finals (where Aidy beat me again). It was nothing new for opponents to pull out their 'A' game against me, and Van Gerwen had certainly done that. No arguments, no quibbles. Confidence-wise, I had felt fine: I was obviously mindful of my new darts, and I would have liked a bit longer to prepare with them, but in practice everything had been lovely. They were going in nice and straight.

But Michael was still riding the crest of a wave after lifting the Sid Waddell Trophy at Alexandra Palace five weeks earlier, and everything he touched was still turning to gold. I should have been full of admiration for the way he cleaned me out, but as each leg went his way, the same two words went through my mind over and over again: 'Jammy bugger'. If it was sheer opportunism when he took the first leg against the throw – one of my favourite methods to demoralise an opponent – a 121 checkout to make it 2–0, a direct hit on double 16 and another on double 8 (when I had been a whisker away from a morale-boosting twelve-darter) were all hard to take. It would have been nice to avert the clean sweep, but when I made a mess of taking down 48 in the seventh leg, I knew it was not going to happen.

It was all over in just thirteen minutes. Apparently, you could have got odds of 66–1 with tournament sponsors Betway on Michael to win by a 7–0 wipeout. Stunned, I walked off stage in a daze to be told it was only the fourth whitewash in Premier League history. I can't remember my reaction verbatim, but it was along the lines of, 'Oh, thanks for telling me that. I feel better already.'

Of course, there was nothing streaky about the way Van Gerwen beat me up that night. When he's on song, he's a genius. But on the basis of my overall performance, I still think 7–0 was a harsh commentary. Yes, I was losing each leg, but I was losing most of them by tiny fractions. When I was missing, I was usually missing to the left. It was like driving a new car – the engine, the gearbox, the brakes were all technically fine, but on the road it handled a bit differently. In the fine margins that often separate winners and runners-up in elite sport, I thought only a 1 per cent adjustment would be needed.

In a long campaign lasting fifteen weeks it's not the end of the world if you lose your first match in the Premier League. And whenever disappointment rears its head, you only have to wait until the following Thursday night to get it out of your system. But on the other hand, you also know that if you start with three defeats on the bounce, there's a real danger that you can get cut adrift – and the following week, in Bournemouth, the fixture 'computer' handed me another tough assignment against my old chum Lewis. Brilliant – there are no easy games in the Premier League, as the cliché goes, but for starters I had landed the two players either side of me in the world rankings.

This time, I produced the second-highest average on the night, but Lewis produced the best, and his 7–3 win left me anchored to the bottom of the table. I tried to put a brave face on it, but the doubts were now creeping in like shadows at nightfall. Being the good chap he is, Aidy hated me not playing well. As much as he wanted the points, and wanted to beat me, he kept saying, 'Come on, Phil, come on, Phil' – as if he wanted another tear-up like our semi-final in Wolverhampton three months earlier.

But when Peter Wright inflicted my third consecutive defeat in Belfast on 20 February, even though my 101.03 average was better than his, I was shitting myself. I thought I was going to come last. For the first time since making major changes on and off the oche in 2014, I wondered if all the hassle was worth it. I had thrown little strops before, like reversing my decision to quit in 2004, within days of winning my eleventh world title, but this was killing me. If it had not been for my daughter being on the payroll – Lisa, my eldest, is now my PA who looks after my diary – and my feeling responsible for helping her to pay the mortgage, I might have cut my losses there and then. Blood is thicker than water, and when it came to the crunch, I didn't want to leave anyone in my family worse off because I'd jacked it all in. It was sorely tempting to retire, to settle for the quiet life without the pressure of competing live on TV every week, and call it a day at fifty-three. It was only that responsibility to all the people around me that was keeping me going.

In the commentary boxes and on the internet, the 'experts' were having a field day. Most of the critical analysis was based around my weight loss, and whether it was affecting my balance at the moment I released the darts. I had been here before, eleven years earlier, after losing the 2003 World Championship final 7–6 against John Part, when I shed 4 stone in three months. There had been talk of sudden weight loss affecting the fluids behind the eyes – I thought it was garbage, although my pals Eric Bristow and Sid Waddell both told me there might be an element of truth in it. Nobody said there was anything wrong with going on a crash diet, or the pressure of fluids in my eye sockets, when I had won 7–0 in the final twelve months earlier, but Sid reckoned I was slimming down too quickly. He was entitled to his opinion, even if I didn't agree with him.

This time, Wayne Mardle was leading the bandwagon on Sky Sports, and he was straight on the front foot after my rout by Van Gerwen in Liverpool. 'The fact that Michael got the better of him the last time they met, in the Players Championship final . . . Phil may have been thinking about that. Then Phil went into the world championships, where he played poorly, Michael went on to win and now Phil was playing the world champion. It's only my opinion, but losing as much weight as he did in six or seven weeks is no good. His darts were weak.'

In *UK Darts Magazine*, sports scientist Paul Gillings, head of the Darts Performance Centre in Hampshire, agreed: 'Because Phil has lost so much weight, his arms will naturally be in a different position when he is throwing. Their weight affects the force of the throw, and their movement (through the air) too. The combination of his weight loss, new darts and Van Gerwen becoming world champion could very well have affected Phil's physiology and made him over-think.'

In fairness, Wayne and his fellow commentators can only talk about what they see, or what they know about. When I lost those first three games of the 2014 Premier League season, it was easy to blame it on my detox or the new darts. Yes, I had lost a fair bit of timber and, yes, it was bound to take me a few weeks to get used to the new tungsten in my hand. But the truth is that other things were going on in my personal life that were bound to be a distraction, and I was determined not to advertise them.

Some of the best darts I played in the early weeks of 2014 had come immediately after my stint of juicing, walking 10 miles a day and the weight falling off. There were nine-darters in practice, a pair of nine-darters on the same day at the UK Open qualifying rounds, one of them in the final against Adrian Lewis, and a ten-darter in a Players Championship event in Crawley after missing a shot at double 18 for a perfect leg. There wasn't a lot wrong with my game on those occasions, although it did not go unnoticed that I was producing my best form in floor events and not in televised majors. And after spending most of 2012 on a fitness kick, when I dropped two shirt sizes, I also played some good stuff.

But I'm not going to deny it. By the time I headed to Glasgow's SSE Hydro for a bottom-of-the-table dogfight with Simon Whitlock on 27 February, I was desperate for a win. It had been seventy-six days since my last win on TV – in the first round at Alexandra Palace – and although I wasn't depressed enough to look up whether I had ever gone longer without a victory on stage this century, that scrambled 3–1 win against Rob Szabo felt like a lifetime ago. Salvation arrived in the nick of time, and after a convincing 7–3 win (average 104.82), my frustrations came spilling out after eleven weeks of unprecedented frustration. Not for the first time in my career, I admitted I had considered quitting. But this time, I was not bluffing.

'If I can't put it together in the next twelve months, I will finish,' I said in my post-match interview. 'It would break my heart, but if I can't do the nine-darters, what's the point of carrying on? I've been trying everything to get it right, I've been beating myself up and there's a lot of pressure off me for now. I've changed darts, lost weight, altered my stance and tried different stems, but the real problem has been between my ears. I've had a mental block, but I'll sort it out.'

On paper, my stats against Whitlock looked tasty enough. In a moment of self-deprecation, I dismissed them as 'rubbish', although I wasn't complaining about a 78 per cent checkout strike rate. And it was nice to finish with a flourish, taking out 82 with two darts: bullseye, double 16. I was just relieved to get that first-night whitewash out of my system and haul myself off the bottom of the Premier League after losing four consecutive games on TV. I had dished out a few beatings in my time, but being on the receiving end of annihilation was no fun, and I never want to go through an experience like that again.

17

VIKING

ON the same night that I suffered a crushing defeat against Michael van Gerwen on the first day of term in the Premier League, 55 miles up the coast in Blackpool an old friend was making his comeback in front of the TV cameras after eight years.

Andy 'The Viking' Fordham, who won the Lakeside world title in 2004, had not competed on stage in Britain since the awful night he had been rushed to hospital from Frimley Green, minutes before he was due to play Simon Whitlock in the BDO version of the championship, in January 2007. Later, he revealed doctors had drained 18 litres of fluid from around his lungs. No wonder he was struggling to breathe – it must have been a frightening experience for Andy and his family.

I was pleased to see The Viking back in business in the BDO World Trophy at the famous Blackpool Tower ballroom, even if his comeback was short-lived and he was beaten 6–2 by 2014 Lakeside runner-up Alan Norris. He is the proverbial larger-than-life character, and I hope we have not seen the last of the big man in major tournaments, but Fordham's return to televised orbit allowed me briefly to forget my own problems and jogged my memory about our one-off challenge match, promoted as The Showdown, at the Circus Tavern in November 2004.

Like my Match of the Century against Raymond van Barneveld at Wembley in 1999, it was a rare collision between the reigning world champions from either side of the great darts divide. I was flying the flag for the Professional Darts Corporation, Andy was standard-bearer for the British Darts Organisation – and there was £100,000 prize money at stake for the first darts match in history to be shown on a pay-per-view basis on Sky Box Office. I don't agree with the concept of pay-per-view myself, at least not in darts, although one million subscribers stumped up £9.95 a pop to watch The Showdown, and you can't argue with market forces of such vast persuasion.

As far as I was concerned, there were two primary motives for me to take the game seriously: I wanted to pocket the lion's share of the prize fund (£60,000 to the winner), and I wanted to maintain the PDC's bragging rights over the BDO. Relations between the two organisations had remained, shall we say, strained since I beat Barney against the clock at Wembley. I knew that if I lost against Andy, the BDO would jump all over us and we would never hear the end of it. This time, the format was the best of thirteen sets, the same distance as a World

Championship final and a long shift by any yardstick – too long for Andy, as it turned out.

The warm-up act wasn't bad: Eric Bristow and John Lowe, who met in three world championship finals in the 1980s, rolled back the years and rekindled their rivalry. Eric won 6–1, and I was rather flattered that the man who had given my career such a big helping hand when I was starting out was now my support act! Next up was Wayne Mardle, the local boy from Essex, who was cruising against Dutchman Roland Scholten until Mardle turned from 'Hawaii 501' (because of his colourful shirts) to Hawaii five-oh-dear and lost 6–5. Then it was showtime – a game modestly billed as the biggest darts match in history. No pressure on the two players, then.

Eric added his uniquely brash smattering of hype to the contest by predicting, 'The only way Andy is going to stop Phil is with a baseball bat.' And although there was no trash-talking between the two rivals, I did sense a boxing-style build-up. It may not have been Ali and Foreman's famous Rumble in the Jungle, nor Benn and Eubank's rematch on Judgement Night, but there was a pay-per-view audience, the Tavern – where I had won eight world titles in a row from 1995 to 2002 – was banged out and there was more than money at stake. I'm just glad there wasn't a weigh-in. That would not have been a pretty sight.

For the occasion, I shaved a pair of lightning bolts into my hair; I seem to recall Andy passed a fitness test on the broken wrist he had suffered earlier that year and he was cleared to play after a check-up, although I was no size zero myself in those days. In other pre-match admin, Fordham was asked to wear trousers and shoes instead of tracksuit bottoms and trainers, which had become his preferred attire on stage. The PDC dress code is pretty strict – long, dark trousers, dark shoes, collared shirts with sleeves, with all sponsors' logos to be checked and cleared by the tournament director.

Before we went on stage, Andy had been on the practice boards for a couple of hours, downing bottles of Pils for Dutch courage. I never had him down as a guy who would practise for hours at a time. He was more the type of player who achieved what he did on instinct, and he was brilliant at doing that. But there was no shortage of support for The Viking as he ambled on stage to the strains of 'I'm Too Sexy For My Shirt' and weighing in at something close to 30 stone. I took one look at him and wondered if he would be able to handle the heat of those fierce TV lights. Outside, it was cold enough in late November just inside the M25 at Purfleet, but in the Circus Tavern it was 100 degrees Fahrenheit on stage. Commentator Sid Waddell meant no offence, I'm sure, when he came up with one of his classic one-liners to describe Andy perspiring heavily in the febrile atmosphere. He said Fordham was 'sweating like a hippo in a power shower'.

I won the opening set 3–0, but Andy settled down and he was well in the game until, at 4–2 up, I noticed he didn't just look shattered any more. He looked ill. I can remember toeing the oche and hearing this voice behind me saying, 'I don't feel very well.' When I turned round, the poor fella was gasping for breath and Fordham told me he thought he was going to pass out. After I had won the seventh set, we both requested a break, (I don't think one was scheduled in the TV advertising slots) and we never returned to complete the match.

First and foremost, I was concerned about Andy's health. Some like it hot, but it was really cooking that night and he simply could not stand the heat. I felt for the people who had paid good money to watch on pay-per-view and for those who made the effort to come and see it live. And in fairness, nobody was more gutted than Andy Fordham, but it was the right decision for him to retire at 5–2 down. Barry Hearn, who had promoted the event with his usual panache, explained to TV subscribers: 'Sometimes a fighter has to be saved from himself in the boxing ring, and Andy Fordham has got to be saved from himself tonight. He is not well – to go back out again now would be a huge risk to his personal health.'

For what it's worth, I believe I would have, in any case, gone on to win the match if it had gone the distance. In the last set before we were forced to call a halt, I had knocked off checkouts of 121 and 124. They would have broken a lion's heart, and I don't think there would have been any way back for Andy. But that wasn't my concern at the time – because I was genuinely frightened. As Fordham received medical attention backstage, I was shaken up. 'In the seventh set, Andy said he couldn't breathe properly and that was that,' I told the larger-than-usual press corps. 'Andy's size has got a lot to do with it. He's a big lad and it's very, very hot down there. It's 100 degrees plus and I think it's taken its toll on him. I was actually worried he was not going to pull through – I turned round and thought, "Crikey, I'm going to kill him here." Andy knows he's got to do something about his weight. He's told me he's going to appear on Celebrity Fit Club, and that might be the boost he needs. As a friend, I've told him he needs to drop the weight, he's got to do it. If he doesn't, it will kill him.'

After Andy's health problems in 2007 – he spent a month in hospital after collapsing at the Lakeside, and then suffered a mild stroke within hours of being discharged – I was delighted that he lost nearly half his body weight – he went down to something like 16 stone and he looked much better for it. In 2009, he joined the PDC circuit, but he found the competition ruthless and in his first year, I'm told he only won about £800 in prize money at Players Championship events and on the European Pro Tour. He will always be a big draw, wherever he plays, because of his tremendous performance to win the Lakeside world title in 2004, but a lot of players who join the PDC don't realise how hard it is to earn a living there. Even when you make it to the Premier League, the PDC pay for your hotel on the Wednesday night – it is a competition rule that we have to be in the host city twenty-four hours before every round – but if you stay over beyond the Thursday night, it comes out of your own pocket. And travel to each venue is at the players' expense, too. When the Premier League comes to Belfast, we have to pay our own air fares across the water. I bet you didn't know that, did you? It's not all horse-drawn carriages and being carried through the streets on sedan chairs in this job, is it?

As for Andy Fordham, I wish him all the best. He gave me a run for my money in The Showdown until he was forced to stop playing. I'm just grateful that, ten years on, he was still motivated to keep chasing rainbows and trying to recapture former glories. But he will know, being only a couple of years younger than me, that it gets harder to reach your top form and break records when you get older. If I had any misgivings about The Showdown and its forerunner five years earlier, the Match of the Century against Barney, it was nice to win them both. I thought they were both great adverts for the sport. These days, the best way of settling arguments between the PDC and BDO is the Grand Slam of Darts in Wolverhampton, where players from both organisations take part. In its first seven years, only one champion – Scott Waites in 2010 – was affiliated to the BDO. Modesty forbids me from reminding you who won it five times out of those first seven.

One man's Grand Slam is another man's Showdown, but either way it's better to solve these things in meaningful competition. John 'Boy' Walton, the Lakeside world champion in 2001, was offered the chance to play me in a one-off match, but he said he would rather play me down at his local pub in front of the open fireplace. I doubt if there would be a lot of money in it for either of us, but that's John for you. A top player on his day, and a nice bloke who would never make a soap opera out of a drama.

Talking of soap operas, at least Andy Fordham's success earned him worldwide recognition. The Aussies took him to their hearts, and when the fur started flying on one episode of *Neighbours*, I believe his name appeared in a line of the script: 'Who do you think you are – Andy "The Viking" Fordham?' I settled for a cameo appearance on *Coronation Street* in February 2009, as a character called Disco Dave from the Flying Horse pub darts team who give the Rovers Return a good hiding in their own boozer. My mum was dead chuffed – she has been a Corrie addict since the days of Ena Sharples. It was a huge honour to be asked – I even broke into my preparations for the 2009 World Championship to film my scenes.

Normally, I clear the decks and nothing is allowed to interfere with my preparations for the World Championship, but my short-lived career in soap opera acting didn't do me too much harm: I went on to beat Barney 7–1 with the highest average to date in the final. And on the cobbles, after scoring 180 in the Rovers Return, I even win the leg by taking out 76 on the bull. Disco Dave . . . that lad's got potential.

18

FORTUNE

February 2014

THERE will always be a tinge of sadness about my clan's success on *All-Star Family Fortunes*, and making a £10,000 donation to the Donna Louise Hospice after winning through to the 'big money' final round, because it was the last time my wife Yvonne and I appeared in public as a married couple. The show was recorded in late 2013, and by the time it went on air about two months later, on 16 February 2014, we had agreed to call it a day and file for divorce. It is a sad fact of life that couples break up every day of the week. For the sake of our extended family, I am not going to sling mud or rake over old coals here. We had simply drifted apart.

One thing I will say about Yvonne, without being patronising, is this: she looked great on *Family Fortunes*. And it was smashing to be part of a family show that has almost become a national institution down the years on ITV.

Along with our eldest daughter, Lisa, son Chris and my cousin, Wayne Walker, we made a great team – good enough to beat TV presenter Julia Bradbury and her family team. We may not have won the £30,000 jackpot, but we flew the flag for the Potteries and we had a good laugh.

Let me assure you that it's a thousand times more difficult to play the game in the glare of TV cameras, and in front of a live audience, than it is shouting answers at the telly in your living room. In that final round, where you get fifteen seconds to answer five questions with basically the first thing that enters your head, it's more nerve-racking than a shot at double top to win the World Championship. For those of you who know the format, Wayne and I scored 133 points from our ten questions combined – well short of the 200 required to win £10,000 and nowhere near enough to find the top answers from each survey, but it's not easy when your mouth is dry and your brain is fried. Poor old Wayne copped a bit of grief afterwards when he was asked to name a female relative and his mind just went completely blank.

When the programme was shown, the stick was merciless. People told our Wayne he was the worst player who's ever been on the show. When I watched it, sharing every second as he stumbled over that question about female relatives, I thought he was going to give our Auntie Lil as the answer! Laugh all you like, but there was no shame in our final family fortune of £5,370. I had hoped to present the Donna Louise Hospice with at least ten grand if we won, so I offered to top up our prize fund to £10,000 out of my own pocket. It's a fantastic local charity, and I felt a little solidarity with such a good cause was the least we could do.

It would not be my last donation to the Donna Louise fund before the winter was out, but behind the smiles and banter of a light-hearted game show, there were breaking hearts. After twenty-five years, my marriage was on the way out. I repeat, I will not be playing the blame game because I have too much respect for Yvonne, our four kids and the fact that we've spent the lion's share of our lives together. In a nutshell, we got together on one of the disco nights down at the Sneyd Arms in Tunstall in 1977, when *Saturday Night Fever* was all the rage and I went out on the pull in a three-piece white suit, just like John Travolta in the hit movie. I think Yvonne was more impressed with the battered, corroded Hillman Imp in which I gave her a lift home than with my fashion sense, but we were soon going steady and it probably helped that her mum and dad had a dartboard in the house, just as we did, although it would be another eight years before I took my darts seriously.

Although we finally got married in 1988, we already had two kids at that point; two more would follow within four years of tying the knot at Hanley register office on 9 April 1988. We had been together for thirty-four years as a couple, twenty-three of them married, when we announced our separation in March 2011. Three months earlier, I had been voted runner-up in the BBC Sports Personality of the Year poll, an unbelievable 'lightbulb' moment for darts as a sport. That night, I said I was the 'happiest man on the planet' and I wish it had been true. In reality, my private life was under stress. When my daughter, Natalie, went into labour and gave birth to her little boy, Jack, nine weeks prematurely just before Christmas in 2010, all domestic arguments were put on hold. The well-being of mother and baby was our only priority. Yvonne was up at the hospital virtually non-stop for seventy-two hours after the birth – a heroic shift – and I only got about two hours' sleep in four days because it was a very worrying time. The medical emergency brought us closer together for a while.

It wasn't an ideal preparation for that year's World Championship. I played rubbish against Gary Mawson in the first round – not surprising after little sleep and even less practice – and my win against Per Laursen in the next round was lukewarm, too. I had a bit of a pop at Sky commentators Sid Waddell and Stuart Pyke for jumping on the bandwagon and criticising my performance without acknowledging the reasons for it. I don't expect special favours from experts on the air, but the Sky lads all knew what had been going on behind the scenes with me in the build-up and I felt they should have tempered their comments a bit. As it happened, after beating Peter Wright 4–1 in the third round, there was little gas left in the tank after Christmas, and I was well-beaten in the quarter-finals by Mark Webster, the qualified plumber who had won a world title at the Lakeside.

Ten weeks later, Yvonne and I revealed we were separating. It was not a 'snap' decision, and neither of us rushed into it lightly, but for a while I moved out of the marital home and into my own place on the eastern side of Stoke. I put out a statement through the PDC, conceding, 'Our relationship has become strained. We bicker a lot and the years of me being on the road have taken their toll. We have stayed together a long while for the sake of the kids. We still love each other, but we need space. We need to live our lives separately and see what happens. You never know, when the dust settles we might get back together.'

And that, to all intents, is how it panned out. There was no instant rebound, but in a strange way history repeated itself. For eighteen months, I worked closely with fitness instructor and nutritionist Laura Church – people who didn't know the facts put two and two together to make nine and decided we were a live-in couple – but she was definitely a good influence on my lifestyle and eating habits. I called Laura 'The Sergeant Major' because she pushed me so hard to get fit, and she devised a fantastic diet to help me keep the weight off. In 2012, I lost almost 5 stone – and it was all recorded in a documentary, *Fit Britain*, on the Active Channel.

Towards the end of that year, Natalie went into labour prematurely again – little Lola had breathing difficulties when she was born, although thankfully she recovered well and she is right as rain now – and inevitably it brought us closer together again as a family, including me and Yvonne. As was the case with Jack's birth, medical drama was a force for unity and, for a while, we got along well again, culminating in my sixteenth world title on New Year's Day in 2013. But nothing is forever, especially if you take it for granted, and when the arguments started again in the months that followed, the writing was on the wall.

When I look back at the year 2014, among other things I will remember it as the year I got divorced. I can't say it was an enjoyable experience, going to court on 11 July 2014 and having every aspect of my finances scrutinised. The lawyers wanted to know what every cheque was for, and whether I had any secret reserves of money hidden away, but their forensic digging was in vain. I was never going to play silly games with my fortune. If the curtain was going to fall on a quarter of a century of marriage, I saw no point in making things worse by trying to pull the wool over a county court judge's eyes. It's sad when such a big part of your life reaches the end of the road, but nobody could accuse me or Yvonne of cutting and running at the first sign of trouble. We gave our marriage every chance.

Regrettably, it was not even public knowledge that Yvonne and I were splitting up for good before the Taylor family's privacy was compromised by a woeful piece of tabloid fiction on 2 March 2014. Days earlier, I had moved out of the marital home again and back into the same property on the outskirts of Stoke where I had parked when Yvonne and I had first separated three years before. Somebody who is not as clever as he thought decided I had moved in with Laura Church, and the *Sunday Mirror* ran a baseless story under the headline, 'Darts ace bounces back out to fitness lover after marriage reconciliation fails.' I knew nothing about it until my daughter, Lisa, rang me up on the day it appeared, sounding anxious and asking, 'Dad, where are you?' I had no idea why she was so agitated. 'I'm at home – where else?' I replied. 'So you're not in Kent, then,' said Lisa, who thought I must have been in hiding down by the Medway, where Laura is based.

At first, I thought it was all a poor joke and tried to laugh it off. But at a time when there were already enough sensitivities on the line, with divorce proceedings under way and my kids emotionally vulnerable, my faint amusement soon turned to anger. For starters, although I was still in touch with Laura, she had long since hooked up with a boyfriend and I didn't want their relationship to be damaged by lies. I was also struggling to get a foothold in the Premier League, and this was a distraction I could well have done without. I asked Matt Porter, the PDC chief executive, to sound out contacts in the media who might be able to shed some light on the mystery and resolved to seek legal redress.

Before we could even fire off a solicitor's letter, however, the story was picked up by the *Daily Mail* website and recycled as fact. Nobody called me, or anybody at the PDC, as far as I can make out, to check whether the yarn had any credibility. An untrue story on a computer screen is just as hurtful as an untrue story in a newspaper – why don't people check their facts? I have always enjoyed a good rapport with the lads who cover darts for national newspapers and I regard them as mates, but I won't stand back and allow poorly informed reporters I've never met to play fast and loose with the truth. Once somebody chased me for a response after I had been spotted sloping off to the supermarket with an attractive brunette half my age. It was my own daughter.

At least the Donna Louise Trust was richer for the experience. As well as an apology, the two news organisations involved were invited to settle legal costs with £15,000 in donations to the charity. And Laura's new fella saw the funny side, too. When the kettle boils now, he shouts up the stairs, 'Do you want a cup of tea, Phil?'

For the sake of everyone around me, I hope the finality of divorce will mean that nobody can get hurt any more by people using my so-called celebrity as a chance to make a fast buck.

And whatever the future holds for Yvonne, I wish her every happiness.

19

UNITED

March 2014

JUST when I thought things couldn't get any worse, I scraped the bottom of the barrel (no pun intended) when I was knocked out of the UK Open in my first match of the tournament. Back at Butlins in Minehead, where the wheels had started to come off three months earlier in the Players Championship final against Michael van Gerwen, I was drawn to face youngster Aden Kirk, ranked No.137 in the world, when I joined the competition at the third-round stage. In football terms, it was like Manchester United playing a club in the relegation zone of the Conference North, in the sixth division of English football's pyramid. Not even my beloved Port Vale have been down that low in my lifetime. And, of course, it was an absolute banker. United could never lose against Stalybridge Celtic or Harrogate Railway in the FA Cup, could they? It would be the biggest Cup shock of all time if that happened.

But in my wretched sequence of hard-luck stories and defeats that broke all the wrong kinds of record, it was my misfortune to be on the wrong end of the biggest upset in the history of knockout darts – at least, that's what the papers said. I didn't see it that way myself at the time, and I still refuse to perceive it as a 'giant-killing' because that demeans Kirk as a player and diminishes how well he played on the night.

Yet there was a viable comparison between my winter of discontent and the fortunes of a certain football club at Old Trafford who were suffering a torrid season for the first time in twenty-five years. My results in 2014 were so poor that I feared I was turning into the Manchester United of darts. I was having sleepless nights, tortured by my worst run of form since United's early days under Sir Alex Ferguson, going back to before I had won my first world title. Losing four of my first five games in the Premier League, including that unique 7–0 whitewash by Van Gerwen, had left me dicing with relegation from a competition I had won six times in nine years. And in the cold light of day, it was a fact – a hard, cruel, awful fact – that in twenty-four years since my first World Championship, Kirk was the lowest-ranked player to beat me in a televised major.

The UK Open is considered to be the FA Cup of darts because amateurs can qualify and the big guns normally join the draw at the third-round stage. Undeniably, my 9–7 defeat against Kirk was a new low. I should have had enough experience to beat him standing on one leg – the lad had never even played on TV before and I found out afterwards he had won only £650 in prize money on the PDC circuit in 2013.

I sloped out of Minehead next morning a broken man. The old adage says that form is temporary but class is permanent, yet my ghastly run of poor form was beginning to feel nearer never-ending than temporary. Kirk took his chances when I faltered – and good for him, that's what you are supposed to do in professional sport. But I played like a pub ringer that night. My average was 86.53, lower than I can ever remember on TV. It was doing my head in. Any benefits from the healthy juice diet, complete rest and escape from ringing telephones on my detox in Portugal had been replaced, for now, by waking nightmares and wondering where it was all going to end. I wasn't sleeping right, often waking up in the middle of the night, sitting bolt upright and wondering how the hell I was going to break the cycle of bad results.

As I told the *Daily Mirror*:

> You lie awake at two, three, four in the morning, thinking about every aspect of your game. From stems, flights, barrels, footwear, eyesight, posture, diet . . . you name it, I've gone through it all a thousand times, mostly when the rest of the country is fast asleep. I've never had a run like it in my whole career, and it's only human nature to wonder if this is the end of an era. But last year, I was playing the

> best darts of my life. I haven't become a bad player overnight, and I'm not going to turn my back on the circuit at the first sign of trouble. I'll take the comparisons with Manchester United as a compliment. Yes, my form has been patchy this year, a bit like United . . . or maybe Port Vale. But my sponsors have been fantastic, they have backed me all the way. I'm still playing only 50 per cent at my best and 50 per cent rubbish, but when I get it right, it's still as good as new – a bit like Ryan Giggs!

Twice in three months I had come to Minehead, and each time – for different reasons – I did not leave with a holiday camp spring in my step. I had played like a man struggling with the flu, but in truth there were no excuses. I was just plain terrible. I was throwing darts with the confidence of a player suffering from a virus, but I didn't need any plink-plink-fizz or medicine to make me feel better, because my problems were all upstairs, between the ears.

Mentally, I was exhausted and I was powerless to stop the fatigue consuming me. Behind the mask I wore in public, I was being increasingly distracted by personal issues. As I have already explained, my marriage was heading for the divorce courts. But there were other matters, which were too delicate to share with you, occupying my time and attention away from the oche. Amid the busy schedule – going from one competition on a Thursday night to another in Minehead twenty-four hours later – there never seemed to be any time to put things right. I was still getting to know my new darts, tweaking a few things with the stem and my stance, but I was trapped in a cycle of losing matches and there was no slack in the schedule to go home for a few days, rest up properly and solve any problems on the practice board.

The 'experts' were having a field day at my expense. Not for the first time in recent years, the grapevine was humming with talk of The Power running out of voltage and the end of an era. In fairness, after being knocked out in Minehead, I had lost five of my last six games on TV: against Michael Smith at Alexandra Palace, against Michael van Gerwen, Adrian Lewis, Peter Wright and Gary Anderson in the Premier League, and now against Aden Kirk in the UK Open. Now it was official: that sequence was the worst run of my professional career, and I won't lie. It was chewing me up inside like never before.

When you have enjoyed more than twenty years of winning, still the best habit in sport, defeat hits you harder because it is such an alien experience. Suddenly, taxi drivers who used to wind down the window and shout 'Nice one, Phil' if they had been watching me win on TV the night before, were now giving me stick. 'Got your arse kicked again, mate' was one comment that stuck in my craw. I felt like taking note of that particular driver's badge number and reporting him to the police, but that would just make me look like a sore loser. For the first time, I wasn't just dealing with a blip in terms of form: I was in a crisis.

Fellow pros remained largely supportive. Without wishing

to sound too self-important, they know I've set the standard for others to follow. They know prize money has increased by more than 1,000 per cent at the World Championship since I won my first one. And they know a sixteen-times world champion who is struggling when they see one. If I was physically shattered at the end of 2013, and needed that three-week break in Portugal to give my body a rest, now I was all over the place mentally, and it was showing in the way I was scattering my darts across the board.

At times like this, you wish the schedule was not so jam-packed. My personal opinion is that we are reaching a tipping point where standards will not rise any further, and may suffer, if there are too many tournaments shoe-horned into the calendar and the intensity of competition takes its toll on the players. And, again without wanting to moan too much about my lot, the PDC will always turn to me if they need to promote one of their shows. If it's the Premier League finals, they want me in a cable car over the Greenwich peninsula; if it's the Gibraltar Trophy, they want me to do a photoshoot up the Rock; and if it's the World Matchplay, I know someone will want to drag me off to the Pleasure Beach, the Golden Mile or up the Tower for some holiday snaps. I understand that we need to promote our sport, I understand we need to be salesmen to help with ticket sales and TV ratings. But when the PDC need a face to publicise their product, I feel like Italian footballer Mario Balotelli: why always me?

20

PANIC

March 2014

I HAVE never been diagnosed with clinical depression, nor have I ever been prescribed antidepressants by my doctor. But looking back to March 2014, when my form was at an all-time low, I think I was depressed. Darts – namely the pressures and the demands that come with being me – probably had something to do with it, but increasingly I was also being weighed down and preoccupied with personal issues.

Out of respect for fellow sportsmen who have genuine mental health issues (James Wade, for one, has been diagnosed as bipolar) I have to be careful not to be too glib about depression because it is a serious condition. But I have learned to gauge my mood swings, and there were definitely times early in 2014 when they were swinging too low for me to dismiss them as simply getting out of bed on the wrong side.

I had been to some pretty dark places before – I contemplated suicide after being convicted of assaulting two women by a Scottish court in May 2001 – and had thought about it many times since. But in the past, I had always been able to put my troubles to one side when I went on stage. Playing darts had always been a release from the stresses of everyday life. Not any more. I was beginning to feel there was no escape from the demands on my time. Now, playing badly in public and struggling in private, I felt like crying out for help. I have rarely felt the need to hire a psychologist, a hypnotist or seek 'alternative' medical consultants to improve my performance or unclutter my mind, but it might not be such a bad idea as long as you see the right person. The England football team took a psychologist, Dr Steve Peters, with them to the World Cup, and I know he has previously worked with British cyclists and my snooker pal Ronnie O'Sullivan. These people are all high achievers – they don't mess about with hocus-pocus if there is nothing in it for them. When my form has wobbled in the past, I have always been pretty good at working out for myself where the problem lies – with one exception.

Shortly after I lost the sudden-death World Championship final against Raymond van Barneveld at the Circus Tavern in 2007, I did consult a psychologist for a while, and was initially enthusiastic about his ideas. He got me to listen to tapes of crowd noise, to imagine I was right there in the heat of battle, and to put on my favourite Oasis CD at full blast before I went on stage – just like Stuart Pearce used to listen to punk rock before he walked out to play for England – to put me in the mood for a contest. And he would encourage me to meditate, or visualise the moment when I was lining up the winning double to clinch a world title. But it didn't do me any good at all.

At the time I decided to knock it on the head I was rather dismissive of psychologists, and made that clear in an interview I gave to the *Guardian*, saying, 'I wouldn't bother with it. They tell you things you already know. You can't teach people to win – it's in your bloodstream. You've either got it, or you haven't.' But if I was approached about psychology or psychoanalysis again now, I would be more open-minded about looking more closely at the psychological side of my preparation, since it was this that was clearly at fault during the first three months of 2014.

Back in the twentieth century, there was a stigma attached to sportsmen who sought help from psychologists. They were perceived as weak – if you needed support from outside influences, you were pigeon-holed as being 'flaky' and, in a team sport, you were not worthy of your place. Now it's a very different story. Everyone seems to be doing it. Would I turn to help from a 'shrink' if I decided outside help was necessary? Yes, I would. In fact, I would hire a zookeeper if I thought it would make the doubles go straight in the bed. If anyone recommended a well-qualified professional who could help me reach the top again, I would be foolish to ignore them. As the old saying goes, don't knock it until you've tried it.

They say that with mental hang-ups, the first step towards curing any problem is to admit it, so I'm not going to duck the issue. I was in trouble, and after losing five matches out of six on TV, I knew where the problem lay. It was my mindset. My mind was in a bad place and negative thoughts were taking over.

As I mentioned previously, I had always been a confident performer on the stage. In the workplace, I had always been able to play darts with an air of assurance. In times of trouble, I had always regarded the game as an oasis of calm. Even in my darkest hour of 2001, after that court case, I had summoned the mental strength to put on a brave face and show the world I wasn't finished by going out and winning my tenth world title three months later. But now I was in the grip of a horrible run, I was unable to separate personal issues with my performances on stage. I was suffering from what I would describe as panic attacks.

I don't use that phrase lightly, but the evidence was there for all to see when I was on stage. At Alexandra Palace, I led Michael Smith 3–2 in a best-of-seven-sets and blew it. In the Premier League, I didn't get out of the starting blocks against Michael van Gerwen and got wiped out 7–0, and at the Players Championship finals Van Gerwen had reeled off another seven legs without reply. I never used to suffer from these mental blocks, but there was no use in denying there was a problem. Van Gerwen is a nice lad, I practise with him sometimes and I could still beat him when we were backstage or out of the public eye. I could beat him before breakfast, lunch and dinner. On the practice board I was still the best player in the world. I was completing nine-darters for fun. All the party tricks we do at exhibition nights were in good working order. But up there, on that stage, in front of thousands of fans, the TV cameras and the whole world, something wasn't right. Where I used to walk on stage and regard it as my turf, my territory, I could no longer flick the switch.

Some of the lads used to ask me what was my secret to winning so many titles. I would tell them that having four kids was a good way to focus the mind. You had to put food on the table, shoes on their feet, see them off to school and put £1 under their pillows when they lost a tooth. When you were on stage, you weren't just doing it to put a nice, fat cheque in the bank and let the taxman help himself to 40 per cent of it – you were doing it to provide your family with a decent upbringing. And when the adrenaline was pumping, you raised your game and you would punish your opponent every time he left the door ajar for you. But now, when the adrenaline was pumping and my heartbeat was pounding, it wasn't about the excitement of winning a duel: my pulse was racing because I was crapping myself.

I did say earlier that I'd rarely felt the need to hire a hypnotist, but apparently, I have already practised hypnosis without even knowing it. I can't remember anyone dangling a stopwatch in front of my eyes, telling me I feel very sleepy, clicking their fingers and then waking up to find I was in a deep trance. But Elliott Wald, a hypnosis expert who has appeared on TV, says on his website that I'm a perfect example of a darts player who uses hypnosis. 'Ever noticed how he drags past both eyes before throwing? That's because he is setting off a post-hypnotic suggestion that allows him to see a plumbline from the target to his darts,' says Wald. Really? I can't honestly say that any of my sixteen world titles, to the best of my knowledge, were down to any post-hypnotic sensations. But I might have to tap into Wald's methods if, as he says, he can help players to get past those stumbling blocks where tight legs go the other way.

> Hypnosis can help you when you should be beating this player, but you are not, and your tone of voice – and whole body posture – is full of self-doubt. You can't shift those negative thought patterns, your average starts to drop, and the next time you play darts, you already have that negative, self-fulfilling prophecy deep inside: You know you can take him out if you were on form, but somehow you can't seem to switch it on. You can't find your natural rhythm, you snatch at the darts.

I'm really not sure how Elliott Wald thinks I've already been hypnotised, but without even knowing it, he just about diagnosed my troubles to the letter. I was convinced my career was not in terminal decline, but those panic attacks, that negative mindset, the death throes of my marriage, were all taking their toll. The next couple of months would provide compelling evidence, one way or another, of whether I could throw off the shackles – and the time was fast approaching for a reunion with Van Gerwen in the Premier League. Another whitewash was simply unthinkable. If there was a repeat of my 7–0 defeat on the opening night in Liverpool, it would kill me . . .

21

REVIVAL

March 2014

SALVATION, at last. The worst sequence of defeats on TV in my career came to an end at the Capital FM Arena in Nottingham on 13 March 2014. And without wishing to sound churlish, it was about bloody time.

It wasn't the prettiest game of darts I've ever played, nor the highest-scoring, but I got over the line. Just. From 3–1 up against Dave Chisnall, including a nice 122 finish for a twelve-dart leg, I could never quite shake him off. Chizzy was like a letter from the taxman – you think you've dealt with it, and then another one drops through the letterbox – and I had to hold my nerve, in the face of two 180s, to go 6–5 up and guarantee myself at least a point. Even then, Chisnall missed a shot at the bullseye to claim a draw and there was only relief, rather than euphoria, when I managed to take out double 16 for a nervy, unconvincing 7–5 win. 'I'm in a position I've never been in before, and I've got to come out fighting,' was my post-match verdict to the media. 'This is a cruel game, and it's a very lonely place up on that stage. If you're not firing on all cylinders, the nerves start jangling and negative things start going through your mind. For me to stay at the top, I've got to work twice as hard as everyone else, but I'm getting there.'

Still in the bottom two, it was too early to talk about a revival. But world super-middleweight champion Carl Froch made an appearance on stage in his home town that night, having just agreed a huge rematch with George Groves at Wembley. Maybe I was inspired by 'The Cobra' and his never-say-die spirit, because he knows better than anyone how to fight his way out of a tight corner. I've been a fan ever since he was miles behind on the judges' cards and still summoned the willpower to knock out Jermain Taylor, in his own back yard in the States, in the last thirty seconds of the final round in 2009. As I drove away from Nottingham, I made a mental note to check the diary and see if I was free to watch Froch–Groves II on 31 May.

Two wins out of six sounds a whole lot better than four defeats out of five, and the next stop in the Premier League was a new venue on the roster – and, more importantly, a chance for me to escape the relegation zone.

Leeds city centre is great for a night out if you can find your way round the one-way system. Somewhere just off the Loop Road (aptly named because it drives you round the bend), is the First Direct Arena, where we played in front of the biggest live audience in darts history. Some 11,000 fans turned out to watch the seventh round of fixtures, and they made one hell of a racket. I don't know if they came to see a burial, but I knew another defeat would leave me marooned in the relegation zone and in serious danger of being eliminated from the competition on Judgement Night in Cardiff two weeks later. This time my opponent was Wes Newton, who was also flirting with the wrong end of the table. In football, they would have called it a six-pointer; for me, it was the point of no return. No denials, I was as nervous as a turkey on Christmas Eve, but unlike the previous week, when I had lived on my nerves against Chisnall, I left my troubles at the stage door, producing easily my most accomplished performance of 2014, crushing The Warrior 7–1 and moving out of the bottom two. After six weeks of tunnelling through darkness, it was like surfacing into daylight. The stats don't always tell the full story, but on this occasion they didn't lie. My average of 106.91 was my best on TV for four months, and across the eight legs I sprinkled four 180s, which kept the crowd happy.

I've never felt so relieved in all my life – not so much for myself, but out of eternal gratitude that my sponsors had finally got something to show for their investment. I am never happy when companies pay me good money to advertise their products and all they get in return is an old man losing at darts. I had been trying to get every aspect of my preparation right, and there had been no shortage of application, but sometimes you need to back up all your good intentions with results. Here, at last, was some proof that I could still deliver the goods when the pressure was at its most intense. If I had lost against Newton – a doughty, determined competitor who had worked hard to get into the world's top ten – that might have been the death knell for my Premier League campaign. Instead, it felt like the kiss of life.

Knowing I had rematches coming up against Michael van Gerwen and Adrian Lewis, who had both given me a hiding in the first two weeks, it was vital to get some points on the board. But the rot had stopped, and at this point it is only right that I pay special tribute to Garry Plummer, the managing director of Target Darts, whose patience had been biblical. For weeks, he had indulged every one of my suggestions about tiny adjustments to the grip and stem of my arrows. All the chopping and changing was not a diva being awkward, it was a perfectionist whose performances had strayed from the route towards perfection. I call Garry 'The Genius' because every time I asked him for the slightest technical tweak, his mechanical engineers would go back to the workshop in Harlow and come back with the adjustments I requested.

Two consecutive wins – one of them scrappy, the other convincing – had given my season a belated lift-off. Now, all of a sudden, I was looking up the table towards a place in the top four, which would earn me a ticket to the play-offs, instead of looking over my shoulder and missing the cut for the first time in ten Premier League campaigns. The next four weeks would be a test of my mini-revival, though: Raymond van Barneveld, whose career was enjoying a resurrection of its own, was next up for me in Dublin, where I was looking to preserve one of sport's longest-running unbeaten runs in a head-to-head rivalry. In eighteen matches against Barney in the Premier League, I had never lost – sixteen wins, two draws – and I had no intention of letting it slip at the O2 arena in the Irish Republic.

Personal vendettas don't pay the bills, though. Winning streaks against one player don't put bread in the toaster. The bottom line, in front of another noisy crowd, was that a 6–6 draw was enough to guarantee I would not be relegated on Judgement Night. It was a cracking match where the final averages did not do justice to the see-saw drama, but in the end I was happy enough with a point. Barney took out 160, then broke my throw after I missed three darts at a double and followed up with a 121 finish to go from 2–1 down to 4–2 up. When it went with the throw in the next two legs, to leave me trailing 5–3, it looked as if that eighteen-match run was going to fall by the wayside. But Raymond seemed to lose his nerve, or his concentration, and missed out on a couple of doubles himself to let me back in the contest at 5–5 and the eleventh leg was one of the best I could remember all year. The Irish crowd were raising the roof, sensing a nine-darter, when Barney started with consecutive 180s, and I did well to stay with him.

Offer any top pro 137, 125 and 180 from their first nine darts, and they will take it. That's what I came up with, but Barney put me under such pressure that I had to take out 59 for a twelve-darter to make certain of at least a point. Fortunately, double 10 did the trick, and, although I was slightly annoyed to miss the boat in the final leg, at least I had the consolation of being unbeaten in three weeks and, in many ways, it felt like a win because I was guaranteed a place in the second half of the campaign. Barney said, 'It was a great battle and there's no disappointment. After being 5–3 up and then 6–5 down, I thought I had blown it. There were a lot of nerves out there, but I'm happy with a point against the best player in the world.'

Flattery gets you everywhere, but it was nice to hear Barney talking about me like that. For most of 2014, I had not played like the best player in the world – and probably not like the best player in my street – but we have twenty-one world titles between us, and that enduring respect between old rivals should always take precedence in the heat of battle. I've had my share of dramatic nights playing against Raymond, and this was one of them. Now I could see a path to the top four, and a possible shot at my seventh Premier League title, which was unthinkable a month into the tournament.

With Simon Whitlock already ousted from the top eight, there was one more relegation spot to be filled on Judgement Night in Cardiff on 3 April, and I was heartily glad it could not be me. Safely insulated in the top six, I headed for Wales through red mist – not an explosion of foul temper, but a Saharan sandstorm that had turned much of the UK into a cloud of smog – to face Robert Thornton, and a 7–4 win (average 102.48) was good enough to lift me into fifth place. But could I break into that top four? The run-up to Easter would prove my own version of Amen Corner with those back-to-back games against Lewis and Van Gerwen.

I didn't quite make it to the promised land of the play-off places on 10 April at Sheffield's Motorpoint Arena. Aidy has handed me one or two thrashings I would prefer to forget in the Premier League, so I'm sure he won't mind me admitting it was immensely satisfying to beat him 7–4 on the night – even if it cost my pal his place in the top four. As a contest, it was nowhere near the high standards we had set in the Grand Slam semi-finals five months earlier. It would take something very special to top that one. But it was not without its twists and turns, Lewis breaking throw to go 3–2 up when I missed a crucial dart in the fifth leg before Aidy wired a shot at double 10 to go 5–3 up and I checked out with 102 to level the match at 4–4.

In professional sport, the margins between disappointment and jubilation can be tiny. In darts, they often amount to the width of a wire on the board. In the first half of the match, I was clipping the wires like an electrician, usually on the wrong side of the bed, but from 4–2 down I strung together five legs on the trot. The Sky Sports commentators were saying I was back to my old self, but the truth is that fortune was kind to me that night. I only got away from Aidy by breaking serve in the tenth leg with a 180 that was as timely as it was overdue. The 102 finish and that 180 were massive because Adrian was putting me under pressure in every leg. The difference between winning and losing on this occasion, ultimately, was a couple of legs where I delivered when it mattered.

Now came the acid test – not that I was prepared to concede any ground to Van Gerwen, who was next in the firing line in Aberdeen on the night before Good Friday, in the build-up. Asked whether I was apprehensive about facing the man who had demolished me 7–0 ten weeks earlier, I presented a stiff upper lip and summoned all the defiance I could muster. 'I haven't got to get ready to face Michael van Gerwen,' I protested. 'He's got to get ready to face me. We have seventeen world titles between us, and I've got sixteen of them. Don't worry – I'll prepare properly, I'll be ready. They are all scared of me now, they're all running scared. Even Michael. There are no thoughts of revenge. It's just about winning the game if I can, and if I get the chance to beat him 7–0, I will take it.'

It would be a travesty if I wasn't nominated for an Oscar, or a BAFTA, for such brass neck. Van Gerwen had only lost once, against Barney, in the competition all year. He was the reigning Premier League champion, the reigning world champion, he was playing fantastic darts and I had more front than Blackpool to suggest he should fear playing me after my frightful start to the season. I don't know if anyone fell for my world-class bullshit, but it turned out lovely in Aberdeen. Second on stage – no hanging around half the night in the players' suite – I moved into the top four for the first time in 2014 with a 7–4 win.

I like Aberdeen. Sometimes I've had a rough ride from crowds in Scotland, but they love their darts and in 2012 I hit a nine-darter in the Premier League against Kevin Painter in the granite city – 180, 174 and 147 on double 18. I was delighted with the win, delighted with the two points, delighted to move into fourth place and more than happy with my 106.30 average. For once, it was good to transfer my form on the practice board into the arena. I had started the Premier League with five defeats in six matches, now I had strung together five wins and a draw from my next six. All of a sudden, I was the bookies' second favourite behind Michael to win the competition outright. But there was little time to wallow in the satisfaction of recovering from rock-bottom in the table to fourth, with four weeks to climb higher if possible, because we were off to the Maritim Hotel in Berlin, a short hop from the Brandenburg Gate, for the German Masters. A three-day tournament, played over the Easter weekend, with a £20,000 winner's cheque from a 48-man field at the end of Unter den Linden is not to be sniffed at.

I played all right. In fact, I did better than all right – I won my first broadcasted title in five months. I had enjoyed some success on the floor in Pro Tour events, beating Adrian Lewis 6–2 in a UK Open qualifying tournament final in Wigan on 9 February and Ian White 6–0 at a Players Championship event in Crawley on 23 March, but there is a greater sense of occasion when you are playing on TV. And what should have made the German Masters title extra special is that, for the second time in four days, I beat Van Gerwen. But my jubilation was tempered. Although it should have been a breakthrough moment in a difficult year, I didn't really feel I had turned a corner.

As much as I wanted to keep my personal life separate from the professional demands of playing darts, my impending divorce from Yvonne was now irrevocable and it is hard to excel in the workplace when there are family matters occupying your mind. In the past, there had been times when the oche was an escape from life's slings and arrows. But now, when I let go of each dart, there were a thousand things running through my mind. Whatever the critics and comedians may say about us being athletes, there is no doubt you need a clear head to play darts properly. In that context, winning £20,000 in Berlin was one of my best achievements – but it was not a solution to the domestic matters that were crowding in on me.

On a sporting level, the weekend was obviously a great success. I whitewashed Sweden's Magnus Caris in my first game before taking on the whole of St Helens over the next three rounds. I saw off Dave Chisnall 6–3, beat Michael Smith 6–0 with a 109.98 average – my best of the year – and defeated Stephen Bunting 6–3 in the last four to book a swift reunion with Van Gerwen in the final. Happily, I saved some of my best darts for Mighty Mike again, opening up an early 3–1 lead with a twelve-dart leg and the treble 19 bed serving me particularly well with scores of 177 and 174. I recovered well from a blip when I missed a shot at tops to maintain my advantage and Van Gerwen broke back to level the match, but I finished with legs of thirteen, eleven and thirteen darts – just the sort of consistency that had deserted me for too much of 2014. My third 180 of the final and double 16 sealed the deal. 'I think beating Michael in Aberdeen got into his head a little bit,' I told pdc.tv afterwards. 'He's been blowing people away, and maybe he's started to think about the game instead of just playing on instinct. He brings out the best in everybody now, and I'm going to have a big push this year to try and get back above Michael as number one in the world.'

Brave words, but behind the smile of the German Masters champion there was the sadness of a man whose private life was dragging him down. I couldn't wait to get home and have a cup of tea with my mum.

22

BOTTLED

May 2014

ON paper, to go unbeaten for the last eleven matches of the Premier League campaign – after losing four of my first five games – was a decent effort. And to qualify for the play-offs was no mean achievement after that shocking start. But the truth is that I made desperately hard work of it. When Usain Bolt finishes an Olympic sprint, he is beating his chest and showing off to the crowd, not crawling over the line on his hands and knees and grateful to qualify for the final in third place. After beating Michael van Gerwen twice in four days, I should have been flying, confidence restored, ready to take on the world again. It says much for my state of mind that I drew three of my next four games, and went into the final night of the league campaign needing at least a point to reach the end-of-term party at the O2 arena.

Against Gary Anderson, in Manchester, I was 3–1 ahead

but had to settle for a draw. My 106.65 average was more than eight points better than Gary's 98.01, which tells you everything about the quality of my finishing that night. But the following week, at Birmingham's National Indoor Arena – where I have always seemed to do well – it was my turn to play twice in one night. Three points from those two matches, against Raymond van Barneveld and Dave Chisnall, was a satisfactory outcome in as much as it lifted me into third place. But the old Phil Taylor would never have settled for anything less than two wins. My old guru Eric Bristow would have had me on toast for breakfast if I thought I had done enough by drawing 6–6 with Barney and beating Chizzy 7–2. He would never have given me a moment's peace about the point that got away, and that was an accurate reflection of where I was with my form.

Yes, I had improved a lot since those dark, depressing nights at Ally Pally, Liverpool and Minehead in my winter of despair. But in the past, at my best, I had always been ruthless, relentless, cut-throat when I got an opportunity. Now those traits were missing, and I seemed to be putting myself under pressure all the time. Against Barney, I had to come from 5–3 down to scramble a draw and extend my unbeaten run against him in the Premier League to twenty matches. I cannot claim I deserved anything more – my average of 95.69 was my lowest of the campaign. I got nervous because I was fighting for my life, Barney had been flying and I knew it was going to be a tight affair.

Fortunately, when I went back on stage later that night, I was more relaxed and, dare I say it, more ruthless.

Clinical efficiency deserted me again a week later in Newcastle, however. Knowing a win against Peter 'Snakebite' Wright would guarantee my place in the play-offs, I missed the boat and had to settle for yet another 6–6 draw. It was tense, exciting stuff – both of us averaged a shade in excess of 100 and the lead kept changing hands like a juggler's props. Wright, whose sculpted hairstyles and kaleidoscopic outfits have brought a dash of colour to the PDC circuit, was in the Premier League on merit after reaching the World Championship final and consistent results in 2013 that had singled him out as the rising star of darts. He broke my serve immediately, but I took out the next three legs, culminating in a 120 checkout that should have cleared my path to the O2.

Not for the first time, I did not finish off an opponent who was on the back foot. For a couple of legs I was sloppy, if not actually negligent, and all of a sudden I was 4–3 down before I took out 65 to level it up again and then produced an eleven-darter, and a sound finish on tops, to move 6–5 ahead. The dramatic final leg did not leave me in the best of moods. Wright, pausing to conduct the crowd between his second and third darts, narrowly missed out on a 150 finish. After nailing treble 20 with his first shot, he surprised the commentators by heading over to treble 18 with his next dart, leaving 36 for a brilliant checkout. He wasn't far off-target, but now it was my turn: three darts to take out 62 and book my play-off place with a week to spare. It would have been nice to get the job done and spend a day on the beach in Brighton, with a knotted handkerchief on my head and my backside parked on a deckchair, ahead of the final round of matches – but it wasn't to be.

Leaving myself a shot at double 16 to clinch the deal, it landed a couple of millimetres the wrong side of the wire, in the single bed, and Wright returned to hit double 9 at the first attempt to share the spoils. A lot of people thought I was upset by Peter's antics in that final leg, namely goading the crowd and playing to the gallery. In fact, I had no problem with it. If that's the way he chooses to play the game, by showboating between important shots, that's his choice. I would not go down that route myself, mainly because it would break my concentration, but if my body language at the end of that match was hangdog and grumpy, it's only because I missed a great chance to win, so let's clear that one up. I was far less impressed with my own lack of killer instinct that night than with anything Peter did on stage.

Down in Brighton, the equation was simple. Two Dutchmen, Barney and Van Gerwen, had already qualified as the top two and, after fifteen weeks of jostling for position, there were three of us chasing the last two play-off spots: me, Anderson and Wright. If I won my final game, against Robert Thornton, I would be going to the finals; anything less would leave it in the lap of the gods. It was, as Sir Alex Ferguson once put it, squeaky bum time. Not just squeaky, but twitchy, twitchy, twitchy. Anderson kept his side of the bargain, beating Van Barneveld 7–4, and now it was my turn. Typically, I turned plain sailing into choppy waters and made heavy weather of it.

I wasted three darts to win the opening leg against the throw, got lucky when Thornton missed bullseye by a squeak to break for a 3–1 lead and, even when I pulled away into a 6–3 lead, I blew two darts at double top to win it 7–3. If I said I wasn't worried when 'The Thorn' clawed his way back to 6–5, I would be lying. And in the final leg, I did my best to squander a substantial lead by missing two more darts for the match on double 16. When Robert, who was miles adrift, suddenly piled on the pressure by hitting 180 to leave himself on 104, I knew it was now or never. Double 8 came up trumps and the relief was massive.

'Normally I would not be happy with finishing third in the table,' I conceded afterwards. 'But after losing four of my first five games, I'll settle for that. When I was missing those doubles, I was even thinking to myself that a draw might have to be good enough tonight. Everyone wrote me off a few weeks ago, and they had every right. I was struggling big-time. But I knew I would come good in the end.'

The Premier League play-off format pits the league winner against fourth place in the semi-finals, with second and third contesting the other match. So in the last four I was facing Barney – who had never beaten me in twenty

Premier League meetings, remember, and a man who had lost all six of his semi-final appearances in this competition. Immediately, I was troubled by the law of averages. Somewhere along the line, at some point, Barney was going to break those spells – and at the O2, he had a chance to break two for the price of one. I wasn't going to take anything for granted.

I summoned Scott McArthur to administer a refresher course of juice therapy, switched off the mobile phone and resolved to get every last detail of my preparation spot-on. No late nights, no junk food, not a single naughty thing – not even a biscuit with a cup of tea. In the 2013 final against Michael van Gerwen, I had been going well until I hit a wall and ran out of steam, losing 10–7 where it could easily have gone the other way. This time I was going to make sure my energy levels remained high.

On the eve of the play-offs, the four semi-finalists did their pre-match publicity for sponsors Betway at their London headquarters. I was happy enough with the keynote of my propaganda ahead of facing Barney, which would be the second semi on stage in front of more than 10,000 fans. 'If I can get inside his head, put him under pressure and make him think, "Here we go again", I could find myself in the final,' I told the gentlemen of the press. By establishing an early lead, I felt Raymond would get that sinking feeling and lose belief that he could break that twenty-match winless streak. In theory, it was a decent game plan. Satisfied that I had expertly planted a few seeds of doubt in his mind, I opted for a spot of local sightseeing after lunch instead of shutting myself away in a soulless hotel room and took a look around the Cutty Sark, which is now permanently docked in Greenwich. Since I enjoy the odd cup of tea myself, I thought the least I could do was to pay tribute to one of the sturdy vessels that used to make long-haul trips to China, around the treacherous Cape of Good Hope, so we could put the kettle on.

When it was time to bring my Premier League campaign to the boil, though, it turned out to be an absolute disaster – a criminal waste of three months fighting my way back into form. For five legs, it all went according to plan. I put Barney under the pump early on, racing into a 4–1 lead and, frankly, it should have been 5–1. Barney was like a rabbit caught in the headlamps and I fancied my chances big-time of turning my eleven-match unbeaten run in the Premier League into a dozen. But then the magic ingredient, ruthlessness, deserted me again and my game disintegrated in a way I had never experienced before in thirty years of playing darts from pub level upwards.

I missed six darts – not two, three, four or five, but six – to go 5–2 ahead, and one of those panic attacks that had visited me earlier in the year resurfaced. For no obvious reason, except my wayward darts leaving the door wide open, Barney sensed an opportunity to turn the match on its head and churned out five legs in a row to make it

6–4. Suddenly, in a best-of-fifteen-legs format, I had no margin for error, and although I managed to stop the rot and reduce the deficit in the eleventh leg, the momentum had shifted irresistibly. Van Barneveld clinched his 8–5 win with an eleven-dart leg to set up an all-Dutch final against Michael van Gerwen and went on to claim the £150,000 jackpot with a 10–6 triumph.

I was so furious that I needed half an hour to calm down after coming off stage so I didn't say anything to the media I would later regret. But I was brutally honest after letting Barney lay three jinxes for the price of one – his first-ever Premier League win against me in twenty-one meetings, his first semi-final win in seven attempts and the first time he had beaten me in a televised major since the UK Open in 2008. 'I was pathetic,' said the broken-hearted old fossil to the newspaper lads in the bowels of the O2:

> Maybe it was an achievement to reach the play-offs after losing four of my first five games of the league season, but I had a massive chance to reach the final and I blew it. This is not some Mickey Mouse competition, this is the Premier League – the biggest prize in darts after the World Championship – and you don't pass up the chance to win it lightly. I only hit five doubles out of nineteen tonight, and all those missed chances are doing my head in. I can't make excuses, I bottled it. I missed those six darts at a double and my head was gone. In my head, I was thinking

> I should be 5–0 up and it completely threw me. I've been through something here that I've never been through before in my career and I hate myself for it.

I hoped I would calm down overnight, but I woke up still raging inside at the golden chance I had let slip. The competition might be stiffer, and there are probably more lads capable of winning the big prizes, but the players are not miles better than they were ten years ago. Barney didn't blow me away by hitting me with nine- and ten-darters or a 120 average. He took advantage of an opponent who let it slip, and I was driving myself doo-lally just thinking about it. Only three games in the whole 2014 Premier League season had been won with a lower average than Raymond's 92.27 going rate in our semi-final. On the other hand, if I'm being honest, then hand on heart I struggled that night because I had been struggling for a while.

Over the last six months, I had found little air pockets of form where I could still turn it on, hit the big numbers, hit my doubles, sustain the big averages and convince myself that everything in the garden was lovely. But the harsh reality of my Premier League campaign, and the crushing anticlimax that ended it, is that if you are not mentally right, you are going to struggle.

There are lots of people worse off than me, and for a bloke who used to make ceramic toilet handles for a living, I can't have too many complaints. My mum, bless her, has to live with rheumatoid arthritis. Getting close to recapturing your best form as a darts player but not quite making it back to the top of the mountain doesn't really come close, does it?

23

BARRY

May 2014

BARRY Hearn and I have made a pact – to retire on the same day. It may happen in four years, when he turns seventy and my contract with the Professional Darts Corporation runs down, or we may both soldier on for longer, but it's a gentlemen's agreement – and I happen to think we will abide by it. So the day I pack my dartboard away in the attic, and put my darts case in the top drawer, Barry will fold away his spreadsheets, forsake his briefcase and retire to spend more time with the carp in his favourite fishing lake. Pretty much since the turn of the century, Barry has looked after my financial contracts and investments, and I would trust him with my life.

One day back in 2000, I was sat at home when the phone rang. The voice on the line had a southern twang, but it sounded familiar. 'Barry Hearn here. I'm going to be your manager,' he blustered. 'Oh, really? When's that going to happen?' I replied. 'Tomorrow,' said Barry. 'Let's have a chat. Don't worry, I'll sort it all out.'

And that, more or less, is how one of sport's greatest promoters came to look after my business affairs. No messing about, no small talk, no beating about the bush. We just cut the crap, shook hands and got on with our lives. I don't remember ever signing a contract with Barry, and in any case we don't really need one. He's an accountant by trade and numbers are the tools of his profession. I've never needed to ask where the money is – because there has been plenty coming into my bank account for a long time.

One of the best things that ever happened to darts as a sport was Barry accepting an invitation, in 2001, to become chairman of the Professional Darts Corporation (PDC). He had changed the face of snooker since becoming the manager of a fresh-faced young prospect called Steve Davis in 1976, and guiding him to six world titles. He had also been at the vanguard of a golden age for British boxing, staging a colossal series of world title fights involving Nigel Benn, Chris Eubank, Michael Watson and Steve Collins. Anyone who can cut a deal with Don King and Frank Warren, and stage a rematch between Benn and Eubank at Old Trafford in front of 42,000 fans, must have formidable bargaining power. It is fair to say that I have not gone hungry since I hooked up with Barry. His guiding principle has never changed: 'You make a few quid for me, and I'll make a lot for you.' That arrangement suits me fine.

Since Barry got involved with the PDC, prize money and TV ratings for darts have gone through the roof. That is a tribute to his salesman's patter, and no figure better illustrates the financial muscle he has brought to our sport than the difference between my first pay cheque as a world champion in 1990 and my last one twenty-three years later. It had gone up from £24,000 to £200,000, and the winner at Ally Pally now rakes in a cool quarter of a million. Barry's deals with Sky Sports and headline sponsors have been the driving force behind darts' acceleration to levels way beyond the Bank of England's rate of inflation.

Until I shook hands with Barry, Tommy Cox had been my manager. We are still great friends and look out for each other as mates do, but Tommy already has a lot on his plate these days as PDC tournament director and I just sensed that Barry was better placed to develop my career and, yes, increase my earning power. I have a fantastic rapport with Barry – I can phone him at any time, day or night, wherever he is in the world and I regard him more as a friend than a business associate. One of his other sporting investments, until he sold the club in July 2014, was as chairman of his beloved football club, Leyton Orient, a post he held for nineteen years. More by chance than design, I happened to be in London two months earlier and accepted a seat in the directors' box at one of the greatest nights of his reign, when Orient won their League One play-off semi-final against Peterborough and booked their place in the final at Wembley.

Daddy dearest: A kiss from daughter Natalie during the walk-on at Ally Pally. My kids and grandchildren are the reasons I keep playing.

Frustration: This game can drive you mad sometimes – my expression says it all as a double goes astray in Cardiff.

Stage fright: By the time I was knocked out of the UK Open by Aden Kirk I was suffering from panic attacks in an environment where I had always prospered.

Andy 'The Viking' Fordham's success was cut short by serious illness. I hope he makes it back to the top.

1bove: Record
›reakers: The
argest crowd
n darts history
urned out to
vatch us in the
?remier League
ıt Leeds.

Right: Sign of
:he times: Peter
Snakebite'
Wright signs
:he board in
Newcastle – his
ıair sculptures
ınd colourful
›utfits are works
·f art.

Bottled it: Wondering where it all went wrong after losing my unbeaten record against Barney in the Premier League.

The Boss: Barry Hearn has been one of sport's greatest salesmen. As my manager, I trust him so much we don't even have a contract.

Miss you, buddy: Sid Waddell was not just the voice of darts, he was an irreplaceable friend.

Winter Gardens, Blackpool: An evocative and stylish venue, one of my happiest hunting grounds.

Second best: Adrian Lewis and I put on a brave face after losing the World Cup final against Holland. Raymond van Barneveld and Michael van Gerwen were unstoppable that night.

Gary Anderson, a fantastic player and class act. Our World Matchplay semi-final in 2014 was a classic.

Michael van Gerwen was in tears after our World Matchplay final, but we will have some fantastic battles in the future.

The Genius and The Power: Target boss Garry Plummer shares my triumph at the 2014 World Matchplay.

There you go. I told you it was coming: I picked out my chum Bob Glenn in the crowd after landing a nine-darter in Blackpool.

Nobody was more pleased by my fleeting appearance on *Coronation Street*, as a darts player called 'Disco Dave', than my mum. She never misses an episode.

Behind the smiles, when the Taylor clan appeared on ITV's *All-Star Family Fortunes* in February 2014, was personal sadness. With me on the winning team, left to right, are Yvonne, daughter Lisa, son Chris and my cousin Wayne.

High fives: Grandsons Matthew and Nathan share my joy after the 2014 World Matchplay final in Blackpool.

The directors' box at the Matchroom Stadium is more like a presidential balcony, a mezzanine level above the main block of seats. I must admit I got swept along in the euphoria that night. The place was really rocking. Leyton Orient chief executive Matt Porter, who stood down from his role in the summer of 2014 although he continues in the same capacity (very capably, I might add) for the PDC, reckons it was the best atmosphere he had ever known in more than twenty years as a supporter or administrator at the club, which is saying something when you consider Orient held Arsenal to a 1–1 draw in the FA Cup with a last-minute equaliser in 2011.

When it was all over, after a heart-stopping finish where 'The Posh' missed a great chance to force extra time, fans invaded the pitch, gathered below the presidential gantry and called for Barry to lead the singing. 'Chairman, chairman, give us a song,' they exhorted. Quick as a flash, Barry played to the gallery. 'East, east, east London,' he bellowed, pumping his fist with each syllable, and the masses below responded in kind. It was a brilliant night – Barry told me the only game that had brought him as much joy as chairman was the day Orient won promotion, on the final day of the season, at Oxford in 2006.

Unfortunately, I could not be at Wembley for their play-off final against Rotherham, which ended in a heart-breaking penalty shoot-out defeat. I had intended to make a weekend of it and take in a show at a West End theatre on the Saturday night before going to the match on the Sunday, but I was on grandad duty in the Potteries, and family comes first. I did, however, make it to Wembley the following weekend, on 31 May, among the record 80,000 crowd for the Carl Froch–George Groves rematch – another commercial triumph for the Hearn dynasty. This one was primarily the work of Barry's son, Eddie, a real chip off the old block if ever there was one.

The pay-per-view figures were fantastic, the stadium was full and the walk-on entrances were something else. In darts, we only have to march about 40 yards, escorted by security and the walk-on girls, to reach the stage: the walk from Groves' dressing room was so long that he hopped on a double-decker bus at one point. It was a great occasion, and I was grateful that Barry got me tickets with a decent view in amongst the crowd, but from the moment I pitched up at Wembley with my mate Bob Glenn, it was almost as if I was topping the bill. Every step of the way, punters recognised me, asked me for autographs or a picture on their mobile phones.

Of course, public recognition is a great compliment and please don't think I am moaning about it, because without it I would still be working in a ceramics factory. But even Bob, my driver, said, 'I never knew it was like this for you – I've never seen it like this before.' As I go about my everyday life, it's nothing new for people to stop me in the street. That goes with the territory, and if Joe Public is courteous and civil towards me, the least I can do is give ten seconds of my time in return – but the Froch–Groves fight was on a different level altogether.

We were sat by Andy Goldstein, the talkSPORT radio broadcaster and TV presenter, and he will vouch for how often the punters came calling. Even during the fight, between rounds, it didn't stop. Celebrity and recognition are fine, but sometimes people can smother you with good intentions and goodwill. That's what was happening to me that night – they were killing me with kindness. It reached the stage where, after the seventh round, it looked as if the fight was going the distance, so I turned to Bob and said, 'Let's get out of here, nip back to the hotel and watch the last few rounds on the box.' So we sneaked down the aisle, out of the concourse and on to Wembley Way when we heard an almighty roar as we walked down the ramp.

It was pretty obvious someone had been knocked out because, seconds later, we looked over our shoulders and there were thousands of people streaming out of the stadium. For just a few moments, we had gone maybe 150 yards without being stopped. We had had Wembley Way to ourselves because 80,000 people with tickets were all inside, but now we were like a couple of cowboys being chased by a swarm of Indians, and we legged it back to the car as fast as we could to make a quick getaway. Later on that evening, Bob and I caught up with replays of Froch's knockout punch – right on the button, goodnight George – and reflected on the irony of it all. We had made a special effort to attend one of the biggest sporting events of the year, thanks to Barry Hearn and son, and yet when the plot unfolded in a dramatic climax, we had missed the punchline. Just my luck, but I have no complaints. It was my decision to cut and run early, but I hope you can understand why I did it.

Much as I would have liked to stay to the end, I was pleased for Barry that another branch of the family business had enjoyed such a big success. It was just another example of everything his Matchroom empire touches turning to gold. Or at least a concerto of ringing cash tills. At sixty-six, I've never met anyone with as much energy, enthusiasm or an eye for a deal as him. When he had a heart attack, a year or so before he became my manager, he only resented it because he might miss Orient winning promotion if it killed him before the end of the football season! Since then, if anything, he has become even more of a workaholic than he was before. If you get out of bed at 7 a.m. and try to catch him on the phone before breakfast, the chances are he will have been in the gym for an hour already. Like I said, his energy and his knack for spotting a business opportunity, or a promotional deal, is legendary.

Do we ever fall out? No, although sometimes he'll be giving me a little pep talk and I'll ask him, 'Are you telling me off?' He will say, 'Yes, I am, you no-good little bastard, but don't tell me you're sorry or I'll come up to Stoke-on-Trent and kick you up the arse.' He's also very good at sifting through ideas and working out which ones he's tried before and which ones have the potential to make him a few bob. Once or twice I've suggested things – probably some form of merchandise – and he'll reply, 'Nope – I'm not having that because I tried it thirty years ago. It didn't work then and it won't work now.' But he's a real hustler, absolutely brilliant at picking up the phone and, ten minutes of conversation later, he's cut another deal. He will ring up a watchmaker and say, 'I've got lads who are on TV for fifty hours this week – why aren't they wearing your timepieces?'

If you don't agree with Barry – like having a boxer miles ahead on points when the judges' scorecards all have it going the other way – he is always right, even when he is wrong, because he regards controversy or polarised opinions as a potential gap in the market for a rematch or a grudge match. But one thing I can say about him, hand on heart, is that he has never given me a bollocking when I've played badly. Not once has he ever told me, 'You played crap last night' if I've lost a match I should have won. He will only say, 'What's the point in being upset? There's another tournament next week, let's show 'em what you're made of.' He knows I only play to win because, when Eric Bristow is your role model, ruthlessness pays the bills.

Losing became more of a habit in the first half of 2014 than previous years, but Barry doesn't bother with reading the riot act. His attitude is that losing a darts match isn't the end of the world, so there's no point in getting upset when it happens. He's always the first with a handshake when things go well, and the first to draw a line under any disappointments. Down the years, I have done well out of him – and he hasn't done badly out of me. I like the fact that we work without a contract.

There are only a handful of people who would stop whatever they were doing, and drop everything, to help me if I was in a tight corner, even if it was the middle of the night on the other side of the world. Barry Hearn is one of those people. He has bent over backwards to keep my career going forwards. It's been a year of upheaval, on and off the oche, but, as I keep telling him, 'Let's get this year out of the way and things will improve.'

I believe my old form will come back. I believe I have at least one more world title left in me. How do I know? Because Barry Hearn has told me so. And as I have told you, Barry is always right – even when he is wrong. When we observe that pact to bow out on the same day, it will be one hell of a retirement party.

24

OUTDOORS

May 2014

THE Dubai Duty Free Masters is like a breath of fresh air – because it's the only darts tournament in the world that's played outdoors. And it's still also one of the few titles on the PDC world series roster that I've never won.

Even though there is hardly a whisper of wind on the Arabian peninsula, it's weird playing outdoors. It makes your darts wobble all over the place. Whether it's the humidity or the heavy atmosphere that makes the flight a bit of a lottery at times, I don't know. You don't get draughts blowing across the stage, or sea breezes wafting in off Jumeirah beach – your darts just wobble. But conditions are the same for all the players, so there are no sour grapes from me that I lost 10–5 against Peter Wright in the quarter-finals.

It's also notable as the hottest tournament of the year – even hotter than Blackpool. Don't laugh, if the weather is hot in Blackpool at the end of July, and the Winter Gardens is packed with thirsty punters cooling off with jugs of lager, it can be like a steam bath. But the Dubai Tennis Centre, where they play a Masters event annually, is like playing in a greenhouse.

As well as tennis A-listers, the 5,000-seater Centre Court hosts pop concerts, and I was surprised to discover Chris Eubank even fought there back in 1997, on his comeback from retirement. But first and foremost, I can tell you it's bloody hot on that stage – even at night. By day, the temperature at the end of May nudges 100 degrees in the shade, and even though it slips down into the eighties after nightfall, when you are playing under the stage lights it's like standing in an oven.

Following the disappointment of missing out in the Premier League play-offs, I arrived in the United Arab Emirates after experimenting with a new set of stems. 'The Genius' at Target, and his team of engineers, had again pulled out all the stops for me to make tiny adjustments to the grip and I had been practising for three hours a day with my new weapons. I was excited by an early chance to use them in competition. It's like test-driving a new car – you can't wait to see how it handles, and to hit the open road if you feel like you're made for each other.

With prize money of $250,000, it was well worth the trip for a two-day tournament featuring the world's top six in the Order of Merit – Michael van Gerwen, the defending champion, yours truly, Simon Whitlock, Adrian

Lewis, Dave Chisnall and James Wade – plus two wild cards, Raymond van Barneveld and my quarter-final opponent, Wright. Let me also say a word about the trophy itself: it's a work of art. I don't keep many trophies at home (without bragging, in past years there would not have been much room for anything else in my living room), and sometimes your souvenir from winning a competition is to be presented with a breeze block or a crystal sculpture that looks like it's been made from a damaged car windscreen. But I would put the Dubai Masters trophy on my mantelpiece or sideboard all day long. It's a large silver coffee pot, similar to the one they award the winner of golf's Dubai Desert Classic, a proper collector's item.

Unfortunately, I didn't get anywhere near to taking it home with me. In my best-of-nineteen-legs encounter with Wright, who was proving to be a real thorn in my side in 2014, I started well enough and led 5–4 around the halfway stage. The new stems seemed to be landing largely where I wanted them to go. But, not for the first time in recent months, it all fell apart for me like a cheap suit. Just as I had lost seven legs on the bounce against Van Gerwen in the Premier League and the Players Championship final, this time Wright won six on the trot as my game unravelled. I believe I was averaging 100 at one stage, but when the darts started wobbling in the humidity, I probably started to overcompensate, and my final average of 91.72 was nothing to write home about. Playing outdoors probably favours the players who deliver their darts with a bit of force – I guess tungsten travelling through the air at higher speed is more aerodynamic and less susceptible to deviation. That's no excuse for me losing 10–5 against Wright, but it was no surprise to me that Van Gerwen – whose arrows hit the board with a resounding thud – retained his title and took home that lovely coffee pot.

So Dubai remains a frontier I have yet to conquer among our world series events outside Europe. I will be back next year, trying to tick the box, because I would love to win every competition on stage at least once before I retire. My only consolation was that an early exit from the Dubai Masters – the second year in a row I had fallen at the first hurdle – gave me a bit more time to look round the place and do a bit of duty-free shopping. After all, everyone remembers the famous signal Admiral Horatio Nelson sent out: England expects that every man will do his duty free.

Back home, I had a pressing appointment to keep – a check-up at the opticians. I was disappointed, but not surprised, that my eyesight had deteriorated and, sooner or later, I would have to revisit an experiment I had first tried in 2010: wearing glasses on stage.

My first dabble with the old 'bins' during competition was not a resounding success. I already wore glasses for driving and reading before I played on stage at the 2010 Grand Slam in Wolverhampton in a pair of metal-rimmed specs. Without playing especially well, I made it through to the knockout phase, despite losing to Ted Hankey in the group stage, but no sooner had I disposed of the glasses than I came a cropper against Steve Beaton in the quarter-finals. It's no big deal – some people need false teeth, others need hearing aids and, when you turn fifty, it's a fact of life that many of us who have reached half a century without glasses find themselves squinting at the paper or the football scores on TV.

And it's not easy to be a darts champion, at any level, if the bullseye is a blurred red blotch instead of a crystal-clear dot, or if you are aiming at the wrong side of the wires. As far back as 2008, I did investigate the possibility of having laser surgery to adjust my field of vision, but it wasn't possible to correct my short-range eyesight without leaving the long-range vision blurred. And I don't fancy contact lenses – my eyes have always been sensitive – so if it means finishing my career in glasses, so be it. James Wade, for one, has enjoyed a pretty good career wearing glasses, and you never hear him using them as an excuse for losing.

Although I had no hang-ups about practising in my specs, I do remember being very self-conscious wearing them on stage. From certain angles, it made the board clear again, and at the time I compared it with swimming in a pair of goggles for the first time. In theory, it turns the clock back twenty years and gives you the eyesight of a young man again, but on stage you are throwing with white stripes from the TV lights reflecting off your lenses. It is a bit strange, too disconcerting. Now I've been prescribed a new pair of bifocals with tinted lenses that react to the light. Up until now, I've not worn them in competition, but the time is approaching where I'll need to give them a try. There's no point in worrying about the result because I'll have to get used to them in other aspects of everyday life. You never know, wearing glasses might extend my career.

In 2010, I tried to slow down the tempo of my games, make sure everything was right and maximise my improved long vision. But those white stripes reflecting from the stage lights made me lose confidence. Several darts clipped the wrong side of the wire, but a miss is as good as a mile. I would rather squint at the board and hit 180 than enjoy high-definition clarity and score only 60. I know that next time I wear glasses in a match, there will be a few idiots calling me 'four-eyes' and maybe the odd sarcastic wolf-whistle. Specs may have done nothing for my darts last time, but you never know – next time they may turn me into the ace of shades.

25

ORANGE

June 2014

ENGLAND reached the World Cup final in 2014 before losing 3–0 to Holland. Do not adjust your sets, this is not a misprint.

There may have been a football tournament going on in Brazil to keep us glued to our sofas for five weeks in high summer, but the weekend before a ball was kicked in Rio de Janeiro, Sao Paulo or Belo Horizonte, Adrian Lewis and I flew the flag in Hamburg for the fourth edition of the World Cup of Darts. As holders, England were the No.1 seeds and we did all right – until the final, which was one-way traffic in a tale of oranges and lemons.

I love playing at the World Cup – on the PDC circuit, it's usually every man for himself and the last man standing takes home the loot, but this is a chance to represent your country. A lot of people don't realise how much it means when you stand up there in an England shirt – it brings out the patriot in me, just as it does when Aussie crowds are on my case at the Sydney Masters or on Premier League nights in Glasgow in front of baying Bravehearts. Aidy and I had won the last two World Cup competitions, and we travelled to Germany with high hopes of completing a hat-trick.

Elsewhere in this book, I may have been critical of Aidy when he won his first world title and airbrushed my part in his rise to the top out of his celebrations, but let's put the record straight here and now: I love playing darts with him on my team. He's great fun, and just what the doctor ordered for an old man trying to recapture his past glory. If you are ever down in the dumps, or suffering from depression, don't bother taking a prescription to the chemist – have a night out with Aidy. You won't be feeling sorry for yourself if he's on the cabaret, although he always takes it seriously when it's time to get down to business for Queen and country.

In 2012, we had beaten Australia in a sudden-death leg in the final before retaining the trophy twelve months later against Belgium. Unlike England, whose World Cup pairing came from the same city, the Belgians had gone one better by picking their squad from the same family – Kim and Ronny Huybrechts. This time, our campaign in an expanded 32-nation tournament was starting against Thailand debutants Thanawat Gaweenuntawong and Watanyu Charoonroj in the first round. I felt confident we would progress to the last sixteen, although I feared for the Sky Sports commentators if they had not been practising their pronunciation!

Our best-of-nine legs doubles opener was straightforward enough, a 5–0 whitewash, but the USA's Darin Young and Larry Butler would be dangerous underdogs in the second round. At the same stage of the 2013 World Cup, the Dutch were shocked by Finland, so we could afford to take nothing for granted in the expanded format of two singles matches and, if necessary, a doubles to settle the best-of-three rubber. Sure enough, after I had seen off Butler 4–1, the States took it to a decider when left-hander Young beat Aidy, ranked No.3 in the world, by the same score. I would not say I carried Aidy through the doubles, which we won 4–1, but he was not at his best and I teased him on Twitter: 'What was all that about? You were shite tonight Ade.'

Lewis took it in good heart. Two years earlier, when I was struggling in my singles matches, he had pulled me through. Now it was the other way round, but that's the beauty of teamwork. We were through to a quarter-final against South Africa, which was a good deal closer than the 2–0 scoreline suggests. In my 4–3 win against Devon Petersen, every leg went against the throw, and I was grateful for the 167 checkout which maintained that trend. Aidy's 4–2 win against Graham Filby set up a semi-final date with Australia, a repeat of the 2012 final, and we were up for it. The Aussies hate losing against 'The Poms' at anything, from cricket to sheepdog trials, and it was never going to be anything other than close. Fortunately, after I had beaten Simon Whitlock 4–1 and Aidy had been edged out 4–2 by Paul Nicholson in the singles, England reached the final with a convincing 4–0 win in the doubles decider.

I must admit, I thought we were going to go all the way and win it. In a sweepstake for the football tournament in Brazil, among the ten lads who had contested the Premier League, I had drawn England – which I considered to be a good omen, either for me and Aidy or for Roy Hodgson's team. And, would you believe it? the other country I drew was the Netherlands. Had the sweepstake covered the World Cup of Darts, I would have been laughing all the way to the bank. As it turned out, that privilege belonged to Peter Wright, who drew Germany and Argentina in the football, the jammy bugger.

Between us, I was confident that Aidy and I would have the firepower to beat the Dutch, who had scraped through their semi-final 2–1 against Northern Ireland, needing an incredible 117.88 average – the third highest in televised history – to win the doubles. But Van Gerwen and Raymond van Barneveld's finishing in the final was scintillating, absolutely exceptional. MVG whitewashed me 4–0, with a 103.66 average, even though I did not play badly. Michael took out 129 on the bullseye to win the second leg, and in the next he scored 140, 180 and 149 before nailing double 16 for a brilliant ten-darter. There is no point in beating yourself up when your opponent plays like that.

The only double I missed was for tops, which would have made it 3–1, but otherwise Van Gerwen never gave me a chance. When Barney thrashed Lewis by the same 4–0 score, we needed to win both return singles legs to force a deciding fifth match in the doubles. Van Gerwen, however, was on a roll and he powered past Aidy 4–2 to render the two remaining games obsolete.

It hurt to hear Michael say afterwards that the Dutch had 'walked all over England in the final with some awesome darts' but he was right. We had got to the final, and given ourselves a chance to win our third World Cup in a row, but we were simply outgunned by the better pair. There was no shame in reaching a third consecutive World Cup final, especially as I was still tinkering with my equipment and trying a few different stems. And my two trips to Germany this year had yielded £30,000 in prize money, my first TV title of 2014 and runner-up representing my country in a 32-nation field. But I hope Michael and Barney will forgive me for borrowing one former England manager's line: Do I not like orange.

When we got home, you could tell the football World Cup was just around the corner. Everywhere you looked, the Cross of St George was hanging out of bedroom windows, on flagpoles and in shop windows. I spent a couple of days at Staverton Park, where the PDC's peerless master of ceremonies, John McDonald, had organised a golf day and gala charity dinner for the Afghanistan Trust, a fund for wounded paratroopers who came home from the war with serious, life-threatening injuries. To put us in the mood for the football, two of the special guests were England 1966 World Cup heroes Gordon Banks and George Cohen. Banks – one of the nicest, most self-effacing people you could ever wish to meet – still lives near Stoke. Although it happened forty-four years ago, people still ask him every day about that incredible save he made from Pele's header at the 1970 World Cup in Mexico. All these years later, it remains an incredible feat of agility and I asked Banks if it hurt to land on the hard ground which had made the ball bounce chest-high off the surface. 'Put it this way, it was like lying down in the middle of the road,' he replied.

Remarkably, England were knocked out in Brazil barely a week later. Now Banks and Cohen's feat will be more than a half a century old before England get another chance to emulate the Boys of '66. That's a sad indictment of the country that gave football to the world. But it was a fantastic night to be in the presence of football royalty – and humbling to be in the presence of the brave servicemen and women of our armed forces who put their lives on the line for us. When I saw the incredible fortitude of wounded soldiers supported by the Afghanistan Trust, all my troubles melted away.

26

MUM

I STILL think about my dad every day, even though it's seventeen years since we lost him, but of course the person who has been hardest hit by his absence is my mum, Liz. Although I was born into poverty, and grew up in a household where we had to make do and mend, she has never asked for, nor accepted, a single penny from my earnings. She has always been a rock, in good times and bad, and I have been struggling to find words that are adequate enough to project my admiration and affection for her. Even now, as she battles on against the ravages of rheumatoid arthritis, she won't even let me put the kettle on to make her a cup of tea. Instead of floundering for adequate tributes to her, I have decided to turn over the next few pages to the best mum in the world herself, so she can tell you what it's been like to have a son who plays darts for a living. Over to you, Mother . . . and don't mention the ghost in the wardrobe.

To me, Our Philip is not just the greatest sportsman in Britain. More important – much, much more important than that – he is the best son in the world. Mothers always stick up for their sons, don't they? It's what mums do. But I mean it when I say that I'm very proud of everything Philip has achieved because he has had to work for it.

He wasn't born with a silver spoon in his mouth. We were so poor that we had no electricity in the house and had to wash in the back yard. The only way we could afford to watch TV was by feeding a wire through to a neighbour's house. I used to collect five shillings a week from members of a catalogue club, and the lady who lived next door was one of the customers. In return for letting us hook up our TV to her electricity supply, I let her off her subs for a few weeks. I think we both got a good deal.

Philip always used to play downstairs after his first encounter with a ghost in one of the bedrooms upstairs. He used to pretend he was a pirate, with a tricorn hat made out of the local evening paper, in a wardrobe laid flat on the floor. But one day I was downstairs in the kitchen when he came running in shouting, 'Come quick, there's a ghost upstairs', and that was it. He wouldn't go upstairs after that – we even had to bring his bed down. (Sorry, son, I had to mention the ghost.)

He was always a cheerful boy, even on the four-mile round trip to the shops when I would come home with a bag of coal on his pushchair. Although he was always handy at darts – my husband used to play, and I could find my way round a dartboard as well, so there must have been something in the genes – Philip used to play out in the streets with the other kids in the neighbourhood. Cricket, rounders, football, you name it, they played it. Not many households could afford a car in those days, so it was a lot safer to play in the road than it is now. The kids who had bikes would go for rides along the canal, because it was nice and flat on the towpath, and on hot days in summer he would wear a swimming costume under his clothes and cool off on the way home.

Although he was never any trouble, Philip could be a cheeky beggar. Once I was briefly featured on a TV documentary showing where he lived and he rang me up the next day, putting on a fake Scottish accent, asking if I was interested in doing more TV work. I was intrigued by this offer, so I said yes, I would be interested – until the caller asked me, 'Would you be interested in a bit of porn?' I didn't have time to be outraged, because the voice on the other end of the line broke into hoots of laughter and it was our Philip and his mates, playing one of his little pranks. Another time he rang up and pretended to be a man from the council investigating a complaint about us chucking our rubbish next door, and asking if he could go rummaging through our bins. He could be a proper little rascal.

A few years ago, he told the newspapers that I used to get him out of bed in the morning by throwing buckets of cold water over him. It's true, I did that once. He said,

'Mum, I'm having a day off work today,' and I replied, 'No, you are not' – he got up quick enough when I tipped the pail of water over him, and, funnily enough, the next day he was up bright and early. In fact, I don't remember having any more trouble chasing him out of bed first thing.

I suppose you could call it tough love and, yes, he did have a hard upbringing. He was our only son – I wanted more children, but medically it was too dangerous – and if you have just one child, you don't want him growing up to be soft or a waster. We didn't have much money, and we had to graft for everything we had, but we were determined to bring him up the right way: showing a bit of respect, doing your best, and if that meant I had to be strict with him, so be it. After he won his last World Championship, he told the press that I was harder than Roy Keane, but I wouldn't know about that. Is that the Roy Keane I see on the telly commenting on the football? He always seems like a nice lad to me.

Philip knows I never watch his matches live on the telly these days. It's not because I don't care, or because I don't love him, but I can't stand it when he loses, and it's not much easier when he wins. The tension, and the upset, is too much for me. I went to watch him live once, I think it was at Blackpool, and I spent the whole night hiding my face in my hands. I found it incredibly hard. Now, if I know he is due to be playing and his match is on the box, I wait for him to ring me, or sometimes my niece will phone to say how he got on. Over the years I've had a lot of happy phone calls – more recently, the news has not been so good, but I'm not surprised.

I used to play darts myself and I know one of the hardest things about the game is getting used to a new set of darts. I thought it was a big risk when Philip changed his manufacturer, and I told him, 'Do you think Roger Federer would find it easy to win more tennis matches if he changed his racquet? Do you think Tiger Woods would win more golf tournaments if he changed his clubs?' But it's his decision, and I hope it pays off for him in the long run.

More than anything, I just wish his dad was still alive to see how our son has won sixteen World Championships – not only that, but all the titles he's won at Blackpool, at Wolverhampton, in the Premier League and the Grand Prix. In my opinion, nobody will ever go on to match what Philip has achieved: not in darts, tennis, snooker, golf or any other sport. Even as a boy, he was a really good player, but I hope his dad is looking down on him and feels as proud as I do when he walks on stage and the announcer introduces our Philip as 'the sixteen-times champion of the world'.

One of my proudest moments – which I did watch – was seeing him voted runner-up in Sports Personality of the Year in 2010. I was just thrilled that he had made the top ten, but I didn't think he would finish in the top three. I'm not as mobile as I used to be, but I almost jumped out of my armchair. Almost, but not quite. It was an incredible time for him, and he still talks about it now.

He says that when he walked into the arena, before the programme went on air, there were thousands of people in the audience singing that song that begins 'There's only one Phil Taylor . . .' Other sportsmen came up to him and treated him like royalty. Even David Beckham, the biggest sport superstar of them all, made a point of coming over to say hello, asked how the family was and said some nice things to him. I must admit I did shed a tear that night. Normally I'm pretty good at keeping my emotions in check, but I was one proud mother. Fancy that – a lad from Stoke-on-Trent who plays 95 per cent of his games on Sky Sports coming second in the BBC's biggest sporting vote of the year.

It is not always easy when your son lives his life in the public eye. Philip has never asked to be a celebrity, and it does make me sad when the papers write about his private life as if he were public property. It has been painful for me to watch him going through a divorce. He doesn't like me worrying about it, but I have four grandchildren, and great-grandchildren, who deserve a private life, too.

The other thing that has always upset me, and where the evidence was disputed, was the court case in 2001. He hates talking about it, I never talk to him about it and I hate anyone else talking about it because nobody else knows what really happened. The worst part of it was that Philip had been awarded the MBE for his services to darts six months earlier, but it was withdrawn as a result of the case. That really hurt him – not just because he felt sorry for himself, but because he missed out on the chance to take his old mum for a day out at Buckingham Palace to meet the Queen. (I'm not sure whether you are allowed to turn up for an investiture by driving a mobility scooter through the front gates of the Palace, but that would have been amazing.) I still hope that, one day, he will be recognised for everything he has achieved. Lords, knights and peers who have been sent to prison have kept their titles. One of my dearest wishes is that Philip should be allowed to collect his honour.

Around Tunstall, the area of the Potteries where I live, people stop me in the street and tell me, 'Your son is the greatest darts player who ever lived, he is the greatest living sportsman in England, and yet he never gets any recognition fot it.' Some of these people are from abroad – Koreans, Thai, Japanese – and they will say, 'In our country, Phil Taylor is a god – why don't you treat him like that in England? You should respect him.'

I'm not sure about a god, but he is a good lad – and if he takes me for a big shop at the supermarket, he is always stopped by people asking for his photo or an autograph. Ordinary people do respect him. And Philip tells me it's not like that just in Stoke, he is recognised everywhere he goes. The man in the street knows what he has achieved, but I think the people in authority in this country are slow to recognise greatness. He hasn't been a champion for five minutes, he has been winning trophies for twenty-five years, but it has not changed him. He still comes round to visit his mum, but I don't like him doing things for me. I hate it when he tries to do the washing-up or to make me a cup of tea. I still regard myself as independent, and if independence is one of the last things I've got, I'll try to hang on to it for as long as possible.

Let me tell you what the real Philip Taylor is like. When he's not away, playing in a tournament or an exhibition at one end of the country or another, he offers to take me out somewhere – for a drive, for a cup of tea or to see his Auntie Mary – and when we get back, there will be a new, upgraded model of mobility scooter parked in the living room for me. If I protest, he will tell me it's all taken care of and he won't let me refuse it. He has always been generous, and does a few appearances every year for charity, but that's a side of Philip the public doesn't always see.

So, twenty-five years after he won his first world title, and nearly fifty years since he was first spooked by that ghost in the wardrobe (sorry, son, I mentioned it again), I'm more proud than ever of my boy: not only Britain's greatest sporting champion, but also its most appreciated son.

27

SID

IT meant the world to me that I was the first player to lift the Sid Waddell Trophy, commissioned in the great man's memory for the winner of the PDC World Championship, on New Year's Day in 2013.

With a plinth cast from Eritrean red marble, plus a towering sculpture on top, it weighed half a ton. Apparently, the marble came from the same quarry as Michelangelo's ornate ceiling in the Sistine Chapel. Dear old Sid would have appreciated that because when he was in his pomp as a commentator, his words painted a picture of darts that made professional sportsmen perspiring in polyster sound like Michelangelo was playing Da Vinci in the Circus Tavern.

For a lot of people, darts will never be quite the same without its genial Geordie bard, but as far as I'm concerned his spirit will live on forever. Everyone knows I was probably closer to Sid than most of the players, and he was my collaborator when my autobiography was published in 2004. We shared more laughs, more nights out and more plates of crispy duck in Chinese restaurants than I could ever remember. Because I was so close to him, I think some of the players were jealous. But as far as I can make out, his commentaries were always fair, balanced and in no way did he act as a cheerleader for me when he was on the air.

He used to call himself the 'thief of bad gags', and he wasn't kidding. Sid came up with more great sound bites and memorable one-liners than any commentator who has ever broadcast live sport to the masses. If he had been around in Shakespeare's day, we would not have been quoting *Hamlet* or *Julius Caesar* now. English literature students would be marvelling at the lyricism of a man who could compare three darts landing in the same bed with 'knocking three pickled onions into a thimble'.

I still smile now whenever I hear his name because he was a genius. A crackpot genius, perhaps, but a genius all the same. I used to tell Sid to his face, 'You are nuts,' but he always took it as a compliment, which is exactly how it was intended. He was a one-off, a unique character. No matter how many commentators try to impersonate his style, none will ever come close to matching his cocktail of wisdom and wit. There's only one Sid Waddell, and if you are looking down on us now from the celestial commentary box in the sky, Sid, we all miss you, buddy.

Although his knowledge of darts was encyclopaedic (Eric Bristow used to call him 'The Sponge' because he could absorb so many facts and figures) Sid was the ultimate professional. He didn't just pitch up at the darts, snuggle into a pair of headphones and busk it, he used to carry around a briefcase crammed with folders about each player – reams and reams of notes, statistics, records and anecdotes. It was a real Aladdin's cave of information, a treasure trove of everything he needed to know. There were times, especially while he was researching books, when I thought Sid knew more about me than I knew myself.

He was always very proud that he came from a humble, working-class background, in a Northumberland pit village, to earn a scholarship at Cambridge University, but he never seemed preoccupied with the material things in life. Sid was never happier than when he was having a pint and a game of pool with his son, Daniel, down at their local. I think it's fair to say he was more comfortable using his head than his hands – he was no DIY expert around the house, and on one occasion when I paid him a visit, I ended up fixing a couple of doors for him. They were fairly simple jobs, hinges and that sort of thing, but he was happy to leave me in charge of the screwdriver.

But who needs a tool kit when you are blessed with a vocabulary, and general knowledge, as colourful as Sid's? I never knew, until comparatively late in his life, that he wrote the children's TV serial *Jossy's Giants*; that he used to work as a bus conductor before he went to university; that he once hired a voice coach because he feared he was suffering from irreversible laryngitis; and that he was hired by the BBC as their voice of the National Lottery, only to be fired after one show because he sounded 'too Geordie'.

Too Geordie? What did they expect from a darts commentator born and bred in Ashington – plums in his mouth and 'How now brown cow'?

Sid's greatest gift, of course, was the vivid phrases he would bring to his sport's coverage on TV. A lot of people still say he was the main reason why they started watching darts on the box – and I believe them.

There are so many Sid gags and one-liners that have made me laugh down the years that I can't record them all for posterity here – there are enough to fill an entire book in its own right. But I have selected my own top forty – with a little help from my friends – and I hope you enjoy this assortment as much as viewers enjoyed hearing them first time round.

'It's like giving Dracula the keys to a blood bank.'

'Bristow reasons . . . Bristow quickens . . . aahh, Bristow!'

'This lad has more checkouts than Tesco.'

'As they say down at the DHSS, we're getting the full benefit here.'

'Jocky Wilson – what an athlete!'

'His eyes are bulging like the belly of a hungry chaffinch.'

'Well, as the giraffes say, you don't get no leaves unless you stick your neck out.'

'These players are under so much duress it's like Duressic Park out there.'

'He's been burning the midnight oil at both ends.'

'It's like giving Billy Bunter the keys to the pantry.'

'Over on BBC1, they are showing Shakespeare's *Othello* – but if you want real drama tonight, get yourselves down to Jollies in Stoke-on-Trent.'

'Painter's not bothering with an undercoat tonight – he's gone straight to gloss.'

'He's sweating like a swamp donkey.'

'Eric's chops are covered in lipstick like he's been mugged by an Avon lady.'

'Four legs on the trot! This is Strictly Come Dancing.'

'Denis Ovens has just goosed the cook . . .'

'Bobby George is done up like an electric-purple liquorice allsort.'

'He looks as happy as a penguin in a microwave.'

'Deller's not just the underdog: he's the under-puppy.'

'Keith Deller is like Long John Silver – he's badly in need of another leg.'

'It's like trying to pin down a kangaroo on a trampoline.'

'There's only one word for that: magic darts.'

'I can think of only one word to sum up that performance: world class darts.'

'If you had to throw a knife at your wife on the spinning wheel at the circus, you'd want to throw it like that.'

'Seeds are falling like chaff in a field.'

'The crème de menthe of darts, doing their thing in Blackpool.'

'The atmosphere is so tense, if Elvis walked in with a bag of chips, you could hear the vinegar sizzling.'

'Look at the man go: it's like trying to stop a water buffalo with a peashooter.'

'Big Cliff Lazarenko is so excited he's jumping up and down like a gorilla who wants his banana back.'

'Lazarenko's idea of exercise is sitting in his front room with the windows open while he takes the lid off something cool and fizzy.'

'Cliff Lazarenko's idea of a workout is a firm press on a soda syphon.'

'Big Cliff is off and looking for something golden in a tall glass . . . and I don't mean daffodils.'

'There hasn't been so much excitement since the Romans fed Christians to the lions.'

> 'The Circus Tavern is so packed even a garter snake smothered in vaseline couldn't slide in here.'

Sid was always complimentary about me, and my contribution to the history of darts, so I hope you will forgive me for being a little bit self-indulgent by including half a dozen of his best lines about me:

> 'William Tell could take out an apple perched on your head – Taylor could take out a processed pea.'
>
> 'Taylor is snapping at Gregory's heels like an alligator with toothache.'
>
> 'Taylor is so hot he could hit the bullseye standing on one leg in a hammock.'
>
> 'Meeting Phil Taylor in this mood is like finding an alligator in your lily pond.'
>
> 'If we'd had Phil Taylor at the Battle of Hastings, the Normans would have gone home.'
>
> 'They won't just have to play out of their skins to beat Taylor – they will have to play out of their essence.'

When Sid welcomed actor, comedian, darts fan and all-round good egg Stephen Fry as a guest in the commentary box, and Sky made a programme about it – *A Little Bit Of Fry and Waddell* – he was in his element, reworking the lyrics of Bonnie Tyler's No.1 hit *Total Eclipse of the Heart* to fit a match where I was playing well. 'Once upon a time he was breaking all records but now he's only breaking a heart, there's nothing I can say – it's a total eclipse at the darts.'

There you go, I told you he was a genius. For me, Sid is up there as the defining voice of his sport, along with Richie Benaud (cricket), Peter O'Sullevan (horse racing), Murray Walker (Formula One), Ted Lowe (snooker), Dan Maskell (tennis), Bill McLaren (rugby) and Peter Alliss (golf). All of those names have been feted with the same compliment: they have all been impersonated by more amateur mimics than you could fit into Wembley Stadium. That is probably the true measure of Sid's broad appeal – he used to arrive at the World Championship every year quoting one of his favourite phrases, 'Bring me your huddled masses,' and to the huddled masses he was synonymous with their night out. He was part of the show.

When I am on stage, I normally try not to be distracted by songs in the crowd, but in December 2012, four months after Sid passed away, it brought a lump to my throat when they broke into a chorus of 'Stand up for the Sid Waddell', and 2,500 people inside Alexandra Palace all stood to attention. That's what he meant to them.

Sid was not afraid to poke fun at himself, or to put his money where his mouth was – quite literally, in one instance. Shortly after Rod Harrington's thrilling 18–16 win at the World Matchplay final in 1998, Sid agreed to a William

Tell-style stunt on Channel 4's *Big Breakfast* programme, where Rod had to knock a 20p coin off the great man's tongue with a dart. On the exhibition circuit, it was a regular trick for one pro to knock a cigarette out of another's mouth, but not live on national TV with millions watching. I'm not sure Sid was his usual, cheery self when Rod's first dart flew narrowly over the coin, the second made faint contact – but not enough to make it drop – and the third sent Sid's loose change clattering to the floor, although the barrel took out more flesh than silver and momentarily left the Geordie Lip tongue-tied.

In a more conventional sense, he was prepared to put his money where his mouth was and back his judgement at the bookies occasionally. Four years later, also in Blackpool, I heard on the grapevine that Sid and a few of the Sky Sports production team had laid a tidy wager at odds of 25–1 that I would hit the first nine-darter live on TV. Normally that would have been the kiss of death, because when Sid tipped you to win a tournament or do something special, you would invariably be knocked out in the first couple of rounds. Among some of the lads, he was known as 'the Black Spot' in terms of his tips, because if Sid backed you to win a major tournament, it was as welcome as contracting bubonic plague!

To be fair, Sid was not a bad player himself. I had a good chuckle at an interview in the *Guardian*, back in December 2002, when he recycled a story from his Varsity days about his time as captain of the darts team at St

John's College, Cambridge: 'We got to the final of the inter-collegiate competition, where we were up against Selwyn College, whose team consisted of four trainee priests. We arrived and thought, "Wye aye, they are hopeless, man, they're bloody vicars" and immediately drank four pints of Greene King bitter each. They may have been wearing dog collars, but we were pissed and they hammered us. Golden rule of life – never underestimate your rivals.'

The most amazing thing about Sid was the celebrity he reached from such a humble background. His father, Bob, crawled under the North Sea every day as a coalface drawer, wedged in a claustrophobic tunnel, hoping the roof would not cave in on top of him. I wonder what our friends at Health and Safety would have to say about those working conditions today. Sid used to complain that his old man worked for forty-eight years at the same colliery and, when he retired, they presented him with a commemorative scroll with his surname spelt wrong. I read somewhere that his dad used to stay on guard at night, guarding the prize leeks in his vegetable patch with an unloaded shotgun because he took so much pride in his back garden.

Sid was one of those people who was capable of finding himself in the unlikeliest places and in the unlikeliest of circumstances – just because he was Sid. One story that tickled me, in *North East Life* magazine, pre-dates any involvement with me by about twenty-five years. On his first trip to the BBC, after winning a national competition for writing plays and literature, Sid found himself at

Television Centre when *Top of the Pops* was being recorded. Backstage he stumbled across The Animals chatting up Pan's People, the scantily clad dance troupe, but he managed to make friends with Eric Burdon, the lead singer, and Sid reckoned the band asked him to become their road manager for the night. Several hours later, they ended up in Soho, in one of those bars that Sid used to call 'upholstered sewers', drinking with Burdon and Manfred Mann, who had also been booked to appear on *Top of the Pops*. He didn't just have star quality as a commentator – he had this knack of being drawn to it, although he never got anywhere by driving there himself.

He travelled everywhere in Britain by train, or got his wife, Irene, to ferry him around, because as a younger man he had traumatised a series of instructors and never passed his driving test. The last time he got behind the wheel of a car, he said the instructor went white as a sheet as Sid turned the streets of York into a race track before slamming on the dual-control emergency brakes, throwing him out and barking: 'The only place where you should be let loose is bloody Brands Hatch!'

When Sid announced, in September 2011, that he had been diagnosed with cancer of the bowel, I knew he had been struggling for some time. He had gone on holiday to the United States to celebrate his seventieth birthday and did not feel chipper for most of the trip. Needless to say, he faced up to his illness with great humour, memorably comparing his chemotherapy treatment with spreading weedkiller on your garden: 'It kills the weeds, all reet, but it knocks out your pansies and dahlias too.' It was incredibly sad when I landed in Australia, on an exhibition tour, in August 2012 and found out Sid had passed away during the last weekend of the London Olympics. On a Sky Sports message board, I read one viewer's tribute to the great man that said, 'It feels like the English language has lost a limb.' That neatly sums it up.

For me, Sid was not just a commentator, a friend and a potty Geordie genius. At times he was almost like a brother. When I found myself two sets down against Michael van Gerwen in the 2013 World Championship final, at 2–0 and again at 4–2, I remember thinking, 'Come on, you're doing this for Sid.' It was one of the happiest nights of my life when I lifted the Sid Waddell Trophy, and it will always remain that way.

28

ROBBIE

June 2014

THERE are only a handful of global superstars who could sell out any venue, anywhere in the world, from Las Vegas to London, from New York to New Zealand, from the Ryan Hall Catholic Club in Tunstall to Knebworth Hall. One of them happens to be the son of a close friend I have come to regard as my guru.

Elsewhere in these pages, I discussed my special relationship with Peter Conway (to use his stage name) and how I have come to regard him as a second father with whom I can share any problems, day or night. I call him 'my little Yoda' after the character in the *Star Wars* films, the Jedi grand master who was diminutive in stature but wise beyond compare. Pete's son, Robbie Williams, is a rock and pop phenomenon I am lucky enough to call a friend, and while the rest of the country was gripped by World Cup fever, I nipped over to Belfast to watch the great man in concert.

I felt right at home because the gig was in the Odyssey Arena, where we play in the Premier League every year. It's always one of the noisiest venues for playing darts, so I knew the acoustics would be brilliant for Robbie to belt out his hits. No complaints, either, about the seats he reserved for me and his old man, only a few rows back and just to the side of the stage. Did I sing along with every song? You bet I did – I sang my little heart out. And backstage afterwards, Pete and I chilled out watching England play Italy in their opening World Cup group match in the VIP bar, while Robbie unwound upstairs with his band and security entourage. England played well, I thought we were unlucky to lose 2–1, but I enjoyed watching an artist in his pomp, with the audience like putty in his hand, far more. Robbie didn't fluff his lines once – Wayne Rooney and his chums missed several chances to equalise in the football.

It feels a bit unreal to be part of the backstage crew at a Robbie Williams gig. I don't consider myself famous, or a celebrity in a showbiz sense, but Robbie is the ultimate boy from Burslem made good. Back in 2005, after I had won the Las Vegas Desert Classic, I extended my trip for a few days and stayed at Robbie's place in Los Angeles. It was an unreal experience, driving through Beverly Hills with this megastar, as we passed some palatial properties. 'See that big house behind the wrought iron gates,' he would say. 'Brad Pitt and Angelina Jolie live there.' I strained my neck and peered up the driveway, hoping to catch a glimpse of two Hollywood stars washing the car or mowing the front lawn. No sign of anybody home.

'That big house with the convertible parked outside? Shaquille O'Neal used to own that one,' said Robbie a couple of hundred yards further down the street. 'Here, on the left, is where the Governor of California himself, Arnold Schwarzenegger, hangs out. And down there, Clint Eastwood's mansion.' Eyes left, hoping for a glimpse of a legend. Spaghetti Westerns, *Dirty Harry*, pick your own favourite Clint movie, he's made a few good 'uns. I was so excited to be surrounded by all this stardust. Here I was, being driven along Sunset Boulevard by a chart-topping hit machine, on the lookout for film stars in their natural habitat.

Finally, we pulled in at our destination, and Robbie broke into one of those cheeky grins. 'You know all that stuff about Brad and Angelina's place, and all those Hollywood stars' homes I pointed out? Actually, it was all a load of bollocks – I haven't a f****** clue who lives there!' He dissolved into a giggle, happy that I had fallen for his little party trick – and I couldn't help but share his laughter. Evidently, it was true that a lot of film stars and showbiz sorts lived in Beverly Hills, but millionaires and minted businessmen are two a penny in that postcode. That was typical of Robbie's mischievous humour, though.

It's amazing to spend time in his company and see a genius at work. Every now and then, our conversation would contain a phrase or a sound bite and his eyes would light up because it would make a great lyric or a song title. He's brilliant at what he does – he could be doing something really mundane, an everyday chore, when something clicks in his mind and Bob's your uncle: another title for an album track, or another lyric, is logged. That's a special gift.

He's a great example to all of us, sportsmen included, that you can achieve anything if you follow your dreams. He used to do a blog on his website – all of it in capital letters (probably something to do with him being dyslexic) – and I loved the way he tried to keep it real, as they say in showbiz circles: 'If I had followed the rules and listened to people I wouldn't have got anywhere. I'm from Stoke-on-Trent, I have no qualifications, I didn't come from money, I didn't go to stage school, I didn't have any training to be a singer, I didn't have any special talents, I didn't excel at anything . . . If you're reading this and thinking, "It's only me, I'm not big enough or good enough to achieve", then that's exactly what you'll get. Live in the light or live in the dark – you choose.'

Robbie has been at the top of his profession for about the same length of time as I've been competing at World Championship level. When I moan about the public killing me with kindness, of course it's only a tiny fraction of the non-stop attention and paparazzi-stalking that he has to put up with twenty-four hours a day, 365 days a year. So when he has these brainwaves, these flashes of inspiration, and he jots down a few lines of the next No.1 hit, it's inspiring to be there when it happens. Robbie reckons some of his best numbers have basically taken him only twenty minutes to compose: obviously all the fine detail in the recording studio takes a lot longer, but I'm totally in awe of people who come up with original songs at the drop of a hat. It's the mark of a genius.

As far as I'm concerned, my mate is one of live music's last real icons. He'll belong in the same bracket as Frank Sinatra, Tom Jones, Engelbert Humperdinck, George Michael, Julio Iglesias and Elton John as great entertainers who could fill any arena and have the audience eating out of the palm of their hand.

One of my biggest ambitions, outside darts, is to sing a duet with Robbie – maybe not in front of a live audience, I'm not sure I could handle the stage fright – or to appear among the credits of an album cover for contributing some lyrics to a track. I've sung along with him at home loads of times, especially to 'Starstruck', my favourite song on his 2009 album *Reality Killed The Video Star*, but it takes real bottle to stand in front of 70,000 people and sing your heart out every night on a stadium concert tour. I might leave that to the experts. But as I headed back towards Gibraltar, where there was an unpleasant sting in the tail for me in 2013, one night in Belfast with a VIP view of a superstar at work warmed the cockles of an old crooner's heart. All together now: Babylon back in business, can I get a witness? Every girl, every man, Houston do you hear me? Ground control, can you feel me? Need permission to land – I don't wanna rock, DJ . . .

29

ROCK

June 2014

It's little wonder that Mozart could hold a tune if he was born in Salzburg. Next stop on the PDC European tour was the Austrian Open, and I loved the place. The two-hour journey from Munich airport was like driving through a rack of postcards, the Bavarian Alps rising in the distance, and if Julie Andrews had come skipping over one of the hilltops warbling a few bars from *The Sound Of Music*, I wouldn't have been at all surprised. Salzburg itself, with its imposing castle rising high over the old town, was a setting to inspire any sportsman; a gorgeous place to spend the summer solstice.

By the time I threw my first dart in the tournament, England were already out of the football World Cup after only a week. Thanks for coming, lads – but at least there were no distractions for those of us with an eye on the £20,000 winner's cheque from a long weekend on the border between Germany and Austria. To tell the truth, I did not expect too much of myself from the outset: I was still experimenting with the stems and grips of my darts, getting closer to the optimum combination but not yet 100 per cent convinced by the end product in terms of the numbers they were hitting. One or two people thought my chances of winning it were helped when Michael van Gerwen pulled out on the morning of his second-round tie with Dean Winstanley due to an ankle injury – yes, darts players do sometimes miss tournaments because of fitness issues – but for me, it was never going to be about the quality of the field. It was all about the quality of my darts, and in that regard I had no quibbles with my performances in seeing off qualifier Alex Roy (6–3) and Simon Whitlock (6–2, with a 102.35 average) in my first two games.

But in the quarter-finals, against Jamie Caven – a clever player who is nobody's mug – I was edged out 6–5 and I could have no complaints. When it came to the decider, 'Jabba' produced an eleven-dart leg – absolutely brilliant. He went on to reach the final by seeing off Peter Wright before Vincent van der Voort, a genial chap whose fast delivery and self-effacing character have always made him popular with players and fans on the circuit, produced a fine comeback from 5–2 down to win the title 6–5. I loved it when Vincent adopted KC and the Sunshine Band's big hit 'Give It Up' as his walk-on music, sharing the chorus with a chant Tottenham football supporters used to serenade his fellow Dutchman Rafael van der Vaart. The following year, during the World Championship, Van der Vaart and Van der Voort met at Spurs' training ground, a photo opportunity far too good to turn down.

Without much slack in the events calendar, there was little point in going home after Salzburg for one night and then turning round, heading back to the airport and catching a plane to the Iberian peninsula for the Gibraltar Darts Trophy. We flew straight from Austria to the Rock via Copenhagen, admittedly not the most direct route to get the sun on our backs and catch our breath before the next assignment. Ah, Gibraltar . . . this was where I had encountered some local difficulty with the lighting, double 12 and the firestorm of unpleasant 'cheat' jibes that followed twelve months earlier.

As defending champion, I was determined to make a decent fist of it again, and although I found plenty of time to do some shopping and look around the place before the show started, I was practising for two or three hours daily at a local club. One morning Aidy Lewis and I went up to the summit of the Rock to admire the view, and on the return descent we got lost on the way back to our apartments. It may sound daft that we could lose our way in a tiny colony that's only about two square miles, most of it a giant monolith, but we were looking for a short cut through a narrow back alley, so we stopped a lady walking her dog to ask for directions. We could tell she seemed very pleased to meet us because by the time we got back to our hotel she had tweeted a picture of two strapping

English mountaineers with a caption along the lines of, 'Look who stopped to ask for directions on my walk today.'

Much as I enjoyed the climate and the tourist attractions in Gibraltar, I never lost sight of the fact that I was there on business, but I was also mindful that it would be difficult to retain my title while I was still searching for my best form and tinkering with my darts. I had now reached the stage where I wasn't playing badly, as my close-run encounter with Caven in Salzburg suggested, and, tinkering with equipment aside, now my game was perhaps missing only a small ingredient – luck, killer instinct, confidence or simply taking my chances when they came along.

At the Victoria Stadium, where the stage lighting had been on the gloomy side in 2013, I was glad to see they had found a couple of spare light bulbs this year and there were no issues with visibility. Sadly, however, I wasn't on stage long enough to form any other opinion because my defence of the trophy only lasted about twenty minutes. Joining the 48-man field in the second round, I came unstuck 6–4 against a familiar nemesis . . . Michael Smith. No complaints, he played better than me on the night, and my 93.59 average tells you everything you need to know about my stumbling, fitful performance. And for the long-term health of darts, it cannot be a bad thing when the old guard get their cage rattled by talented youngsters like Smith. When I'm reclining in a rocking chair, enjoying my retirement, I'll be looking to the likes of 'The Bully

Boy' to project their personalities and lead the new generation at the vanguard of our sport.

Of all people, it had, of course, to be Michael who knocked me out in Gibraltar. It gave the doom-mongers and nay-sayers fresh ammunition to declare that I was on the way out. And when the draw was made for the World Matchplay in Blackpool, while we were still out in Gibraltar, it did not go unnoticed among the darts fraternity that my potential second-round opponent at the Winter Gardens would be – you guessed it – Michael Smith.

Sky Sports commentator Wayne Mardle advised people to lump on Smith to knock me out in Blackpool, believing he had become a bogeyman who had learned how to spook me at big tournaments. That's fine, people are entitled to their opinions. But neither Wayne nor Michael himself knew that I was planning another visit to the Target factory on my return home, and that I was convinced I was close to solving the puzzle of how to make the darts land where I wanted. When I heard about the draw, I told my faithful pal Bob Glenn, 'Good – Michael Smith is a proper player, but next time he will be facing the real me.' And I was gratified that Charlie McCann, a tipster with World Matchplay sponsors Bet Victor, said he would stake his last pound on me to win in Blackpool. Thanks, Charlie, you made a doubting champion believe in himself again.

Smith underlined what a good prospect he is by going on to beat Jamie Caven and Adrian Lewis before falling 6–2 in the semi-finals against James Wade, who went on to win the competition – his first tournament victory for three years. I was particularly chuffed for Wade – as outlined earlier, he has had some major health issues and he was left off the Premier League roster in 2014 to help him regain confidence away from the glare of playing on TV every week. We have enjoyed some great battles, and it was Wade who pushed me to twin nine-darters at Wembley in 2010, so it was good to see another member of the old guard back among the silverware. At the time of writing, James is probably the finest player of my era never to win a world title, but the way he played in Gibraltar over that weekend will hopefully give him the confidence to believe he can still make it across that final frontier.

Next stop for me, after my career was caught between a rock and a hard place, was London – for a photoshoot with Argos to help them launch their Christmas catalogue – and then I went to see the engineering wizards at Target for the fine tuning that I believed would make all the difference. After a visit to the sanding stone to adjust the grip, making the friction marginally less abrasive as the dart leaves the hand, and giving the stem a haircut . . . wallop! What a difference. Design and production manager Steve Reed has bust a gut to find the right combination of weight, grip, stem and balance for me, and I'm told his dad had been giving him a bit of playful stick: 'What have you done to Phil? What have you done to the best player in the world?'

Of course, Steve was never the villain of the piece – but

now he was the hero. The arrows he produced for me on this visit were bang on the money. They landed at the perfect angle, I wasn't snatching or trying to fling them, and from the moment I let go of the first batch, I knew they were perfect. I would be heading to Blackpool with renewed confidence in my game, all thanks to a little TLC from Steve's grinding block and lathe. I hadn't lost at the Winter Gardens for six years, and all of a sudden there was the scent of a seventh heaven.

30

QUICKFIRE

IF you don't know me by now . . . that's fine. I hope you have enjoyed a few snapshots of my battle to regain the No.1 spot in the world rankings, and if it hasn't happened by the end of 2014, it's not the end of the story.

Golf legend Tom Watson was nudging sixty when he missed a putt to win the Open championship, which proves it's never too late to be a contender for the biggest prizes in sport. I may have plenty of miles on the clock, and the terrain is not getting any easier, but if I have one more World Championship left in me, all the personal heartache and all the professional anguish I have been through in the twelve months covered by these pages will not have been in vain.

Although it's not the same as flicking through a photograph album, and a single picture often tells more than a thousand words, I thought it might help to join a few dots and help you to build a wider profile of my character by giving a brief insight into some of the jigsaw pieces in my life. As I said in the Foreword, top darts players in the twenty-first century owe much of their earning power and celebrity status to you, the public, who buy the tickets and reward us with gratifying viewing figures on TV. By way of thanks, perhaps it is only fair that I share with you a quickfire assortment of biographical nibbles and titbits about the lifestyle that has given me the motivation to keep fighting for those big prizes.

HOME: A four-bedroom detached house on the outskirts of Stoke-on-Trent. Sadly, it is no longer the marital home, and nor is there sufficient space to show off all of my trophies on the mantelpiece. Gone, too, are some of the more elaborate fixtures and fittings – like the 5-foot statue of Cleopatra that once adorned my living room. It got pulled over by accident with the vacuum cleaner flex and was damaged beyond repair. To be honest, I can't say I was too distressed.

CAR: Currently it's a Mercedes S-Class with a personalised number plate, which purrs along motorways and turns 200 miles of tedium into a swish way to travel. In the past, I've also had two Bentleys, a Jaguar and, back in the day, a Toyota Prius. It wasn't really suitable for long-distance hauls.

MOST PRIZED POSSESSIONS: Easy – the grandchildren. Nice homes, flash cars and material wealth are all well and good, but nothing brings me more pleasure – or wears me out – like a day with Matthew, Nathan, Jack and Lola or taking them to the cinema. They can be a handful, but they are also great fun. Isn't that what grand-kids are for?

HOLIDAY DESTINATION (UK): Blackpool. If it's good enough for Freddie Flintoff, who grew up only 15 miles down the road in Preston, it's good enough for me. My days on the ghost train or the Big One rollercoaster at the Pleasure Beach may be behind me, but I love the Golden Mile and I love playing at the World Matchplay. There's something magical, something very British, about the place. (**Abroad**): It used to be Tenerife, or anywhere with a sunnier climate than the Potteries, but in recent years I've fallen in love with Austria – the scenery and all that Alpine fresh air is only a couple of hours' flight away.

FOOD: Chinese – I love anything with a bit of spice or a bowl of rice, and you can't beat a nice plate of crispy duck, sweet and sour or Chow Mein. And I've always been partial to a bit of rice pudding for dessert.

DRINK: Beer doesn't suit me any more, so I've tended to swap quantity for quality if I'm on a night off or winding down after a tournament. A glass of wine is my tipple these days – more red than white, maybe a nice South African Pinotage.

TV PROGRAMME: You can't beat a good sitcom to lift the spirits – *Mrs Brown's Boys* is a new favourite, but if laughter is the best medicine, I'll volunteer for a taste. Soap operas have always been a guilty pleasure, too, but we travel so much these days that it's easy to lose the thread of a storyline or plot if you miss a week.

MUSIC: Surely you didn't expect me to say anything except Robbie Williams or Take That, did you?

NEWSPAPER: Anything with a crossword, but I don't have as much time to sift through a paper now as I once did. The best darts coverage is usually in the red-top tabloids, and if I've won a tournament or played half-decent, I'll stop at a petrol station and buy a few papers to pore over the back pages. My kids used to keep scrap-books with hundreds of newspaper cuttings and photos of their old man, but I've never looked through them because it's better to keep one eye on the future than to dwell on the past.

FAVOURITE OTHER SPORTSMEN: Too many to mention as a definitive list, but I always loved Daley Thompson. He was a winner, like Roy Keane, Denis Irwin, David Beckham and those great Manchester United sides. Joe Calzaghe, Ricky Hatton, Carl Froch . . . they are not just warriors, they are winners. Ronnie O'Sullivan is a great entertainer. And I discovered a new level of respect for cricketers like Freddie Flintoff after playing in a pro-celebrity game and facing a Zimbabwean fast bowler who was so quick it felt like he was firing bullets. When the wicketkeeper started walking back about 40 yards behind the stumps, I asked where he was going and one of his team-mates replied, knowingly, 'You'll see in a minute.' The first ball nearly took my head off, the second hit my bat (not the other way round) and the third flattened my middle stump. You've never seen anyone so relieved to get a duck.

BEST HABIT: Winning, or winding people up with harmless pranks.

WORST HABIT: Probably being too much of a 'Yes' man. If I'm asked to do somebody a favour, or make a special effort to help publicise a tournament, I wish I was strong enough to say 'No' sometimes.

POLITICS: I come from a working-class background, and I used to be a factory worker, so I've always been a Labour voter. I probably get it from my dad, who was always standing up for the poor. I don't like seeing the rich get richer at the expense of people who are less well-off, it's immoral.

IF I WERE PRIME MINISTER . . . I would look after the National Health Service like beefeaters guard the crown jewels. I know we all like to have a moan about the state of our country, but I'm proud that people who are taken ill in Britain are treated – without fear or favour – on the NHS. In certain other countries I could mention, they won't even send an ambulance before you hand over your credit card.

BEST NIGHT OUT: The older I get, the less glamour I can find in painting the town red. These days, I get the most enjoyment from having the grandkids round for a few hot dogs, a game of cricket in the yard and having a few drinks with the family.

IDEAL FOUR DINNER PARTY GUESTS: Mum, Dad, Barry Hearn and Robbie Williams. At least we would have plenty in common. And it would be a good sing-song.

IDEAL DARTS TEAM: Me, Eric Bristow, John Lowe and Bob Anderson. We might not be invincible, but it would be great fun.

PORT VALE: We played Arsenal in the Cup once, and we ran them bloody close. I think Wayne Corden scored for Vale and Dennis Bergkamp – who had done nothing all game – chipped our keeper in extra time. It went to penalties, and Arsenal missed their first one in the shoot-out, but they had David Seaman in goal and inevitably we fell just short of a big upset. Our manager, John Rudge, had the fire brigade in all week to water the pitch so

Arsenal couldn't move the ball around in their customary style. Then, in 1988, we had better luck against Tottenham, knocking them out 2–1 after Jimmy Greaves had said on ITV's *Saint and Greavsie* show that Spurs' only problem would be finding the ground. Can you imagine the stick he would have copped on social media if he had made such a remark in this day and age?

TEA OR COFFEE? Given the choice, I'm probably more of a coffee man.

***CORONATION STREET* OR *EASTENDERS*?** Easy – Corrie wins every time. *EastEnders* is too depressing. And you wouldn't expect me to say anything else after my walk-on part as Disco Dave when we thrashed the Rovers Return at darts, would you?

ROAST BEEF OR RACK OF LAMB? It's got to be lamb – roast beef doesn't taste so good with mint sauce.

SPICY OR BLAND? Spicy – but I'm not one of those kamikaze diners who always goes for the hottest dish on the menu just for the sake of bravado. If I'm ordering an Indian takeaway, or eating out in a curry house, I'll usually go for the medium-strength dishes, not the nuclear options that make your eyes water.

MY FIRST CURRY: Everyone remembers their first

curry, don't they? Mine was at the Kismet, just down the road from our house, and it's still the best in the area. I remember it only cost £3 for the whole meal – poppadoms, rice, the lot – and although my chicken curry was nothing too ambitious, I could feel the sweat pouring off me. And, yes, I remember shitting through the eye of a needle the next day. It's all part of the learning experience!

ANY CONFESSIONS? Playing tricks on people, juvenile stuff – I've never really grown out of it. If you came to our house and never took a shower under a bucket of water perched on top of the door, you were lucky.

BEST FILM: I must have watched all the *Rocky* films about 100 times each. That scene where he reaches the top of those steps and celebrates like he's on top of the world gets me every time. But my all-time favourite is probably *Zulu*. I must be able to identify with all those people lobbing spears, it must be a darts thing.

BEST STAGE SHOW: I'm not a big theatre-goer, but I went to see *Billy Elliot* in Drury Lane and it was brilliant. The musical score – by Elton John, I think – was spot-on and somehow they even managed to transfer the scenes with riot police and secondary pickets from the big screen to the stage. And the lad who played Billy was a fantastic athlete as well as a handy ballet dancer. He could have won an Olympic gold medal in the high jump.

TOP THREE KARAOKE HITS: Now we're cooking, duck! I've never been able to walk past an open microphone if it's karaoke night, but if I had the chance, I would belt out 'Mack The Knife', 'My Way' and Robbie Williams's 'Rock DJ'. I might need a Zimmer frame afterwards if I tried to swivel my hips like him, though. The best karaoke nights I've had were in a pub next to the old bus station. It's all been knocked down now – I hope that wasn't a comment on my act.

CLOTHES: I live in T-shirts, tracksuit bottoms and Stanley Matthews baggy shorts. I don't need to practise in a tuxedo and bow tie, or ripped jeans and a nightclub shirt, so why be uncomfortable when you don't need to dress up? I'm just as happy in a £2 T-shirt from Sports Direct as a designer label.

SHOES: Off stage, I wear trainers all the time. They are kinder to my feet than winkle-pickers or the stiff leather of a bank manager's brogues. I've always been happy to experiment with shoes – I've even tried wearing a pair of Nike golf shoes recently – because you are not going to throw darts with pinpoint accuracy if you are distracted by footwear that pinches your feet. David Beckham wouldn't have been such a good player if he had to tiptoe around the pitch because his boots were too tight, and the same principle applies on the oche.

ROYALIST OR REPUBLICAN? I would love to meet the Queen, and I am a Royalist, although I don't think the taxpayer should pay for a never-ending extended family of privileged earls, barons and duchesses who have never done a day's work in their lives.

BEST OTHER SPORTING EVENT ATTENDED? One of the best days out I've ever had was at a Wales v England Six Nations rugby international, at the old Wembley Stadium. I think the Welsh played their 'home' games there for a year or two while the Millennium Stadium was being built. I can remember Neil Jenkins's first kick of the match, from the halfway line, and I said to my mate, 'Where's he going to put it?' Back came the response, 'Straight between those posts' – and, blow me down, he made it look like shelling peas. That was the game where Wales snatched it 32–31 right at the death, with a Scott Gibbs try in the corner. In the hotel afterwards, Welsh fans were taking the piss out of me all night, but I didn't mind too much. They kept buying me drinks to anaesthetise the disappointment. Not long after, at an exhibition night with Richie Burnett in Wales, I played in a pro-am charity game, and who should be my first opponent? Neil Jenkins. His place-kicking was more accurate than his darts!

TWITTER OR FACEBOOK? Twitter for me.

PASS DRIVING TEST FIRST TIME? Not only did I pass my test first time, but I did so after only three weeks. I had my first lesson on a Thursday night, my second lesson the following Thursday, and the following week I tore up my L-plates. I'm not sure I would be able to do it so quickly these days – you have to sit an exam and all sorts now, don't you?

STEADY DRIVER OR IMPATIENT? It depends whether I'm trying to get home or make an appointment on time. If it's late at night, and I'm just yearning for a few hours' kip in my own bed, I might put my foot down – but not if I've lost. It's dangerous if you take your frustration on to the road. Recently Bob Glenn, my trusty driver, has taken much of the strain behind the wheel. He's very responsible, and he understands there is no point in having a lovely car to drive if it's going to end up in a ditch.

FAVOURITE MOTORWAY SERVICES? Believe it or not, I'm sad enough to know the distance from almost every motorway service station in the country to my house. In fact, on some major routes I just about know every tree. My favourite pit-stop is northbound at Watford Gap, which is about halfway between London and Stoke. It's like a mini-supermarket there now – if you leave home without any spare clothes, it's no problem. You can virtually buy whole new outfits, from top to toe. Motorway services are not everyone's cup of tea, but I've had twenty-minute power naps in less desirable places.

BEST SUBJECT AT SCHOOL? I left school at fifteen, with few qualifications, so it's fair to say I was never going to be a professor of nuclear physics. But I did take an interest in geography when one of my uncles emigrated to Australia – I was fascinated by all the countries you had to fly over to get there, and how vast the Aussie mainland is. It still makes me shudder to think that it takes four hours to cross Australia by air. It takes less time to fly from London to Moscow.

MAXIM OR PROVERB? We're here for a good time, not for a long time. Or, in a professional environment, winning takes care of everything.

WHAT WILL IT SAY ON MY HEADSTONE? I intend to keep the stone masons hanging on for a few years yet, but the alleged message on Spike Milligan's grave always makes me laugh: 'I told you I was ill.'

IF NOT DARTS, WHAT WORLD TITLE COULD I WIN? Beat the intro. As a former pub landlord with a jukebox knocking out hits all day, pop music – especially from the 70s, 80s and 90s – was the soundtrack to my life. As soon as a familiar song comes on the radio, TV or as background music in a hotel or restaurant, I like to identify it before the DJ can announce what it is. My record is one second, calling the song title after one drum beat. Alternatively, friends tell me I'm a world-class name-dropper. As I was saying to my mate David Beckham the other day, I can't say I've noticed it myself . . .

31

SHRINE

July 2014

As my daughter, Lisa, dropped Target managing director Garry Plummer at his hotel late at night, he ducked his head through the open passenger door. 'Thanks for the lift,' said the man I call The Genius. 'And thank your dad for saving our company.'

Everybody loves a happy ending, even in a 54-year-old grandfather's book about darts, and after an exhilarating week, that was probably the greatest compliment of the lot.

Garry had flown in from a holiday in Dubai, headed straight to Blackpool and managed to catch the last instalment of a tournament which felt like a resurrection or, as the *Daily Mirror* put it, 'more like the rebirth of a champion than an old stager's last stand'. To the end of my days, I will always cherish my fifteenth World Matchplay title, and my seventh in a row, as one of the best weeks of my life. Of course, each world title is special, winning the Premier

League with twin nine-darters in the final was special and runner-up at Sports Personality of the Year was special.

But none of those milestones was achieved against a backdrop of personal heartache off stage and the fight of my life to regain a winning formula with new darts in my hand. And I felt I owed Garry a nice trophy – my first major title since I had changed my dart manufacturer – because it was high time I repaid his sponsorship by landing a big fish. All the time I had been searching for my best form, I was acutely aware that I was being paid to catch great white sharks and, in the first six months of our arrangement, all I had reeled in was a few cod.

Some players don't really understand the principle behind sponsorship. They seem to think they are doing companies a favour by endorsing their products, but I've never really seen it that way. If I go shopping, and the supermarket hands me a bill for £50, I expect to see some shopping in my basket. That's the way commercial deals should work in sport, but there are plenty of people in golf, snooker, football, darts, you name it, who are happy to trouser thousands of pounds by way of sponsorship, yet they have never won a thing. I could not look The Genius in the eye if I kept making a dent in his company's cash flow. As I have explained to some of the younger lads on the circuit, a sponsor might have to shift £1 million worth of gear to pay their star signing £100,000. They need something by way of return. I've never been able to work out the mentality of players who take their thirty pieces of silver, put a patch on their shirt for a year and never even threaten to win a goldfish at the fairground hoopla stall.

After my latest trip to the factory, and the practice sessions that had given me 100 per cent confidence in the updated version of my customised arrows, I headed for Blackpool with a conviction that I was going to win. If an Englishman's home is his castle, then the Winter Gardens is my fortress. I had not been beaten there since 2007, and there is something about the place that brings out the best in me. It is also the hottest venue of any PDC major – and just to add to the electric atmosphere, I arrived at my Ribby Hall hideaway with the Fylde coast lit up by spectacular electrical storms. Either the gods were pleased to see me back in this part of the world or there was trouble in store.

Bob Glenn drove up ahead of me to get the place ready, and I followed with my long-time pal Shaun Rutter (my bosom honcho, as Sid Waddell used to call him) in a separate car, happy to find a cuppa and a sandwich waiting for us on arrival. The first few years I played at the World Matchplay, I used to go up there just hoping I would not come a cropper in the first round; now I was up for the fight, relishing the contest, eager to put these new projectiles to the test. There was never any question of my taking anything for granted in darts, you get bitten on the arse the moment you get ahead of yourself, but immediately I felt settled, in a contented state of mind.

One of the best things about Ribby Hall is that, as a

five-star luxury holiday park and village, everybody is there for the same reason: they want to relax, chill out, and there are no silly herberts making a nuisance of themselves. There is 24-hour security and I know of only one occasion, while I've been there, when a couple of tanked-up idiots started making a racket late at night. They were escorted from the premises without their feet touching the ground. It's not cheap, but for your five stars there are no scallywags or silly beggars spoiling it for everyone else. I've had some nightmare weeks in Blackpool itself when I couldn't get a wink of sleep because of rowdy drunks on all-night benders, fighting in the streets and the sound of smashing glass. At Ribby Hall, you don't get stag parties of twenty-seven lads all piling into one semi-detached house offering bed and breakfast at £10 a head and waking up the whole street. Everyone respects each other's private space, which means nobody bothers me. I can practise, go for a walk or go fishing in the private lake at my own leisure.

Once the electrical storms had shifted north, and taken their spectacular light shows with them, the Fylde coast was consumed by a heatwave. Some like it hot, including me, but that meant the Winter Gardens ballroom would be like an oven – and stamina, especially in the later rounds, was liable to be an issue. From the moment I checked in, I knew that keeping well hydrated would be important. No big nights on the sauce, no necking pints of lager and waking up with a mouth like sandpaper.

My first-round opponent, on Sunday 20 July, was my old practice partner Darren Webster. Known as 'The Demolition Man', he has never quite managed to give the wrecking ball a full swing in major championships, but he is a handy player and a dangerous customer to meet first up in a big knockout competition. Darren will not mind me saying he has never reached his full potential, but when he relaxes and gets into a rhythm, he can be absolutely brilliant. In the first round of the 2014 World Championship, Darren missed six darts to knock out James Wade, which is a fair reflection of his career: good enough to trouble the best players, but never quite cracked it.

For the walk-on, I added a new prop to my 'act' – a white Power baseball cap, which I had signed in advance. I picked out a young fan in the crowd and handed it to him as a souvenir. Fans pay good money to come and watch us play, and although it's only a token gesture, you can't put a price on goodwill. Former England striker Michael Owen joined the fashion critics on social media, tweeting, 'Phil Taylor's cap in the @BetVictor World Matchplay darts, it's an absolute rascal #shocking.' The general reaction was positive – it's not as if I'm going to play on stage wearing a baseball cap – and it's something I'll be doing more often in future.

While other people's attention may have strayed briefly towards my crown topper, for me there was much more serious business on the agenda. This was my first competitive outing with the new darts – the moment of truth. Would they fly as straight and true in matchplay as they did in practice? From the outset there was no apprehension, no hang-ups. They just felt right – and it showed in the way I played. Not only did I beat Darren 10–4, but it was the best I had played all year. My confidence in the new stems and grips was not misplaced.

Now it wasn't a question of whether I was ready for Michael Smith, it was a question of whether he was ready for me. 'It's going to be a cracker,' I said in my post-match interview on Sky Sports. 'I'm going to give Michael a proper game now.' The stats backed up my renewed optimism – against Webster I averaged 101.79, hit five maximum 180s and took 43 per cent of my chances on the doubles. When it was 8–4, I produced a 132 checkout that felt as good as anything I had delivered in 2014: bullseye, bullseye, double 16. If that sounds a bit flash, or smacks of showboating, let me explain why I took that route. If you aim for the bull and hit 25, you can still take out 107 in two darts (treble 19, bullseye). If you hit the bull with your first dart, you still have two ways of taking out 82 with two arrows (bullseye, double 16 or treble 20, double 11). It's just a question of maximising your options.

Full of bravado, I took to my soapbox and said I was so pleased with the way my darts were now coming out of the hand that I fancied my chances of a nine-darter against Smith. The tournament sponsors, Bet Victor, chalked up odds of 18–1 on a perfect leg and I went around telling anyone who would listen that it was worth a tenner, although I was careful not to shout the odds about my chances of beating Michael. There were no thoughts of revenge for what happened at Ally Pally and in Gibraltar, and I was mindful that he had taken care not to rub my nose in it when he had knocked me out of the World Championship. There was no need for any gamesmanship, no need to ramp it up into a grudge match. As far as I was concerned, Michael Smith was a stepping stone on the path towards another World Matchplay title. But above all else, this time he would be meeting the real Phil Taylor, not the exhausted version he had shocked seven months earlier.

'I want to have a scrap with him and I think it will be great,' I said on pdc.tv after the first round. 'The fans will be in for a treat and I think there could be a nine-darter, too.' After hitting the sack early – it can be difficult to sleep at night in hot weather, so I turned in before 10 p.m. – I was up with the larks, and on the practice board, on Wednesday 23 July. From the first darts I let go before breakfast, I knew it was going to be my day, a fine day to hit a nine-darter. I spoke to Eric Bristow, told him the darts were hitting the board a treat and said, 'Just watch – there's a nine-darter on the way tonight.' Eric relayed the tip to all the regulars in his pub, and by the sounds of it, they all lumped on. Backstage at the Winter Gardens, I bumped into Sky pundit Rod Harrington and told him what I thought would happen.

Rod's colleague, Wayne Mardle, did not share my confidence, however, and had been telling punters in his online betting column that Smith would turn me over again. 'I'll be very surprised if he [Taylor] reaches the final,' Mardle told readers of his Betfair blog. 'The draw, on paper, has been kind to the fourteen-time champ, but I think his World Championship conqueror Michael Smith can get the better of him in the second round should their paths meet.' Everyone is entitled to an opinion, and I have no problem with Wayne backing me to lose. I just hope that anyone who took his advice did not stake their mortgage on it!

Walking on, in a red cap this time, which also went to a well-wisher in the crowd I picked out at random, I couldn't wait to get stuck in. Not only did I believe I was going to win, but I had a feeling in my water about producing another nine-darter in the venue where I had hit my first televised perfect leg, against Chris Mason, twelve years earlier. Maybe I was just a little bit over-excited because I shipped the first two legs and, had Michael taken his chances, he might have gone into the first interval 4–1 ahead.

Once I found my range, however, I built up momentum faster than the Big One rollercoaster on the Pleasure Beach funfair. Over the next eight legs, everything clicked into gear with three 126 checkouts before, at 6–2, I slipped into overdrive. The first set, all hitting treble 20, was the perfect swingers' party – three in a bed. It's always nice to hit 180 for openers in any leg because immediately it puts your opponent under pressure. Michael responded with only 60, which gave me a licence to go big again. Treble 20 and another treble 20 landed snugly in the middle of the bed, but there wasn't much room around the outside so I switched 'downstairs' to treble 19, which has been a reliable alternative down the years. Yep, that went in clean as a whistle as well. And with each dart, the noise around the Winter Gardens cranked up from noisy towards an ear-splitting din.

Without wishing to sound conceited, from that moment I knew I was going to complete a nine-darter. There was no scoreboard pressure from Michael, who was way back on 348, when I stepped up to finish the job. I had three darts to clinch the tenth televised nine-darter of my career, and my twentieth in professional matchplay. But, more importantly, I had three darts to let the world know I was back in business, and that The Power was back at full voltage again. The first two hit the treble 20 lipstick as if I was throwing on autopilot. Lovely. Now the target was double 12, another old faithful, around 10 o'clock on the dial. Don't rush, don't snatch at it, don't try and ram it into the board as if you're nailing a picture hook into the living room wall . . .

In she went, like a thirsty builder's pint – without touching the sides. Good old double 12. As the crowd went nuts, I turned to my pals Bob Glenn and Shaun Rutter in the crowd and pointed at them, as if to say 'There you go, what did I tell you?' The night before, I had told them I could feel a nine-darter around the corner. I was pleased that two of my best mates, who have been as loyal to me as a mother hen to her chicks, were there to celebrate the moment. Shaun, who has part of his right ear missing, used to make people squeamish if they asked him how it happened by telling them a crazed girlfriend chewed it off. Whether he has been helping me to knock down walls in houses I've renovated, stumbling into our twin hotel room at 3 a.m. after rising to the challenge of draining pints of Guinness at the World Grand Prix in Dublin, or just been a reliable sidekick in good times and bad, Shaun has been one of my biggest supporters.

I went on to win the game 13–6, clinching the deal with a ten-dart leg, and posting an average of 105.64, with more than half my shots at doubles landing bang on the money. As a present for caller Kirk Bevins, who had never called a nine-dart finish before, I signed the board and presented it to him. In 2009, Bevins was champion on *Countdown*, Channel Four's popular daytime jungle of letters, numbers and anagrams. I hope he enjoyed counting down from 501 to game shot in nine stages as much as I did!

Needless to say, I was pretty euphoric after reaching the quarter-finals in fine style, although I was keen to keep the lid on my celebrations with potentially three hard games to come on consecutive nights at the weekend. But it's not easy to pretend that a thumping win, garnished with a nine-darter, is just another day at the office, and I said:

> It was a phenomenal game, a memorable night for me and everyone who supports me. I'm pleased as punch. The three 126 finishes were the killer and the nine-darter was the icing on the cake. But I think I can improve, especially on my stamina. I did forecast it, by the way. There were a few people in the crowd who had a bet on it – I said before there could be a nine-darter. There's nothing wrong with my form – everyone in the world kept telling me, 'There's something wrong with you'– but it was all about the equipment. We've been experimenting and something just clicked into place tonight.

Coming off stage, one of the first people I saw among the miles of TV cables and production boxes behind the curtains was my old pal Rod Harrington. He knew what was coming next, but he let me say it anyway: 'I told you!' Soon afterwards, I got a text message from Eric Bristow. He was full of it – the regulars in his boozer had all had a nibble at those 18–1 odds, and they were all toasting their extra pocket money. And when Wayne Mardle, who had tipped me to come unstuck against Smith, came backstage, the first thing he wanted was a peek at my new darts. 'What are you throwing there, Phil?' he asked, before examining the workman's tools and pronouncing: 'Oh. My. God. He's back!' I think Wayne was quite impressed.

Next day, after a couple of hours on the practice board, I paid a visit to my old mate Joe Longthorne at his home in Blackpool. When I think of the ups and downs I have had to face in the last twelve months, they are utterly trivial when you compare them with Joe's twenty-year battle with leukaemia, culminating in a life-saving bone marrow operation in 2006, before he was hit by another bolt from the blue eight years later. One of the great entertainers of my lifetime, with a wonderful singing voice, Joe needed more surgery in the summer of 2014 to remove a tumour from his throat, and I know he was terrified he would not be able to sing again. I found him in good heart and, best of all, the latest operation had gone well. I can still remember Joe winning a TV talent competition, *Search for A Star*, back in 1981, and it was uplifting to spend a couple of hours with him in between games at the World Matchplay. I enjoyed the change of pace and, of course, the good company.

Back on the oche, on a steaming hot Friday night in Blackpool, my quarter-final was not as easy as it looked on paper. According to the stats I had read beforehand, my head-to-head record against Wes Newton – a tough cookie and a local hero from just down the road in Fleetwood – in all competitions was twenty-nine wins and two defeats in thirty-one meetings. Thanks for that. No pressure, then. Sure enough, I was soon presented with another test of my born-again confidence, and those remodelled arrows, when 'The Warrior' broke my throw twice early on to lead 4–2, and I settled in for a long night.

What happened next showed how quickly confidence can snowball when you get on a roll. After being on the receiving end of several legs without reply in my darkest hours during the winter, it was nice to be the one dishing out the punishment – although I'm sorry it had to be Wes, a good lad and a fine player in his own right, who happened to be caught in the whirlwind. I won seven legs on the bounce, and it should have been eight: I missed three darts at double tops to make it 9–4. It's never too late to kick yourself for getting too cocky in this game. As we went off at the third break, with me leading 10–5, I was still muttering sweet nothings to myself and slapping my hands angrily because I was annoyed by surrendering the winning streak in such a casual, arrogant fashion.

Yes, I was in a strong position, but there was still work to do. I was six legs away from the winning post, which is a country mile in darts if your opponent gets the bit between his teeth. Newton is a real competitor, and if I needed any reminder of his tenacity, he soon came up with a perfect example. Although I picked up the next two legs to go 12–5 up, Wes picked off a brilliant 149 finish (treble 20, treble 19, double 16). Wow, I thought. This fella isn't going down quietly. I'd better get out of here. I rattled off the next four legs to take the honours 16–6 and line up a semi-final against Gary Anderson.

'Trust me, Wes was in it to win it,' I said on TV afterwards. 'He was 4–2 up, he was giving it large and I was worried. But when he started losing, his head went down. It wasn't a great match in terms of quality, but it was a tough match to win.' For the first time in the tournament, my average dipped below 100 at 99.70, but that may have been due, in part, to the intense heat. The players' room upstairs was like an oven – it was too hot to practise, and the only time I spent in there was to bull up for first throw. Anderson, I noticed, was not impressed by the standard of his 16–8 win against Adrian Lewis in the last eight, which was played on the same night as my game with Newton, and blamed the oppressive heat that had turned the Winter Gardens into a sauna.

I love Gary to bits. He is one of those people who calls a shovel a shovel, and his analysis was brutally honest. 'I thought it was a bad game – Aidy was rubbish and my rubbish was a wee bit better,' he said. 'As soon as we walked in today, the heat up there in the players' room was past the point of a joke. It's terrible in there. I was so uncomfortable coming down the stairs . . . I don't know how hot it is in there, but it's too hot and I think Adrian felt it as well, to be honest.' Gary was a bit harsh on himself, and I found his comments slightly worrying. If he could average 100.63 when he was basically melting, he would take some stopping if the temperature was more to his liking. Twenty-four hours later, we found out just how much it would take to stop him.

On reflection, the ingredients for a classic semi-final were all there. A hot, summer Saturday night in front of a packed, thirsty crowd in a seaside resort, and two players returning to form after a brief tour of the doldrums and deciding it wasn't really their scene. Elsewhere on these pages, I relived the 2013 Grand Slam semi-final against Adrian Lewis as the greatest game of darts I've ever been involved in – and some of the scoring bursts were so ridiculous, it would take something mind-blowing to top it. But as a see-saw contest and gripping drama, this was pure gold. When two players average 105.27 and 105.68 (mine was slightly lower than Gary's), and it takes thirty-two legs to settle a best-of-33 course, you know it's been a real humdinger, and I've had people come up to me and say it was one of their most exciting nights in front of the telly.

When I mentioned stamina after the second-round nine-darter against Michael Smith, this is what I had in mind. Durability in a World Matchplay semi-final is not the same as a long-distance athlete's stamina, which is based on physical endurance, but when you have to squeeze every last drop of nervous tension from your system over two hours, with a heatwave outside and ferocious TV lights indoors, let me tell you it's not for slouches. And I knew Gary would be a monumental test of my revival because his own career had been enjoying improved fortunes after a difficult year struggling with his eyesight. This was the guy who had come within a whisker of knocking Michael van Gerwen out of the World Championship seven months earlier, and who came up just short against MVG in the Premier League play-off semi-finals. On his day, Anderson is probably the heaviest scorer of the lot, knocking out 180s for fun. If he added just a little more consistency on the doubles, he would be unplayable.

Following the same pattern as before – wearing a signed

baseball cap for the walk-on, picking out a friendly face in the crowd and passing it on – I sort of knew what to expect. In the Premier League season, I had lost one game 7–5 against Gary and drew the other 6–6. A major semi-final was bound to be just as tight . . . and I wasn't wrong. It did my confidence no harm to win the opening leg with a 119 checkout on the bullseye, and it went with the throw until the first interval. Immediately after the restart, Gary missed a 36 checkout and I nipped in to claim the first break of throw to open up a 4–2 lead.

Over such a long course, and against a player as gifted as Gary, chinks of light can soon be snuffed out, and before I knew it he had hit an eleven-darter, back-to-back finishes of 108 and 105 and broken my throw again. Suddenly, I had gone from 7–4 up to 8–7 down, and I was right. It was going to be a long night. The standard was relentlessly high, and neither of us was able to shake off his opponent. Fortunately, the third interval gave me a chance to cool off with a glass of water, gather my thoughts again and come out swinging. I broke back, with a clinical finish on double 18, straight away, and the Winter Gardens was a madhouse of excitement as we traded blows before I rustled up a 146 checkout, my highest of the match, to edge two legs ahead again at 12–10.

With the Commonwealth Games in Glasgow underway, there was no shortage of live sport on the box that weekend. But there was no mistaking, from the feverish atmosphere at the World Matchplay, that a perfect storm was brewing.

People have told me that as word got round of a titanic battle, darts 'virgins' – viewers who had never really watched the sport before – were switching on in droves, and they were spellbound by the drama. It was like a good book you can't put down because you feel obliged to turn the page and see what happens next.

Just when I thought I had shaken him off with that 146 finish, Anderson broke straight back. A brilliant eleven-darter. Bedlam. I responded well, breaking his throw again, and when I pulled further ahead at 14–11, it felt like a tipping point, especially when Gary missed a 170 finish by a whisker and I maintained my three-leg cushion to make it 15–12. Nearly there. The next three legs went with the throw, leaving me needing just one leg to reach the final, but there was one last twist, one last outbreak of pandemonium to keep everyone on the edge of their seats. Resolute but weary, I missed four darts for the match on double 18, and when Gary nailed double top to stay alive, the atmosphere was at fever pitch. Fortunately, I had one last chance to prevent it going the full distance – and just when I needed it most, I produced my best leg of the night.

Although nine-darters are the holy grail, what we all strive for is consistency under pressure. That's often what separates champions from contenders in sport, and I had to dredge twenty-five years of experience to find the bottle that hauled me over the line. At 16–15 Gary must have fancied his chances of taking it all the way, but right on cue I managed to hit 140, 140, 140 and take out 81 with two darts (treble

19, double 12). The relief when that winning dart landed was incredible, and the thunderous ovation for both players nearly took the roof off. As I said, the Grand Slam semi with Adrian may be the benchmark for heavy scoring, but for pure drama this one takes some beating.

I was so elated afterwards that I could barely speak. 'Wow – what a player this fella is,' I said, raising his arm like a referee declaring the winner of a boxing match on points. 'That's one of the best games of my life. I don't actually watch games back on DVD, but I'm going to watch that one. Every time you hit him with a right hander and it wasn't good enough, you had to hit him with a left hander as well – and I still couldn't put him away. I hit him with everything I'd got, but I just couldn't get on top of him. He kept putting me under pressure, he wouldn't stop. I haven't got a bad word to say about him.'

Gary was as dignified in defeat as his protégé, Michael Smith, had been humble in victory when he knocked me out at Alexandra Palace. As well as being a formidable opponent, he is a gracious man away from the oche, especially when there's a decent cup of freshly ground coffee brewing. It was the best I had seen him play for four or five years. We certainly brought out the best in each other in Blackpool.

Some people wondered if there would be much left in the tank after my white-knuckle ride as I came back down to earth and turned my attention to the final against Michael van Gerwen, whose semi-final win against Simon Whitlock had also been a hard-fought tussle. But in many ways, I felt it was the best preparation of all. Under gut-wrenching pressure, my form had stood up well and I was in a fantastic frame of mind. The sponsors were delighted because they had got the world's two top-ranked players in their final, and I was delighted because I would get a shot at my seventh World Matchplay title in a row.

At this point, let me say a word or two about Van Gerwen. He is a really nice kid. When darts needs a volunteer as standard-bearer for the younger generation, you won't have to look very far. Michael's fluorescent green shirt stands out like a hitch-hiker's thumb. His ability to compute different combinations for every possible finish, and the pace at which he plays, bring a real buzz to every game. Every match involving MVG is an event. It is like going to watch Ronnie O'Sullivan at the Crucible – as I did in April, at the World Championship final against Mark Selby – big occasions bring out the biggest stars. One or two players had become a bit wary of Michael's habit of fist-pumping and chest-beating when he lands a big shot, but he's not breaking any rules and I like to see players showing a bit of passion, or wearing their heart on their sleeve . . . because it's easier to read their minds!

Less easy to unravel, however, was the head-to-head formbook as I began the walk to my favourite stage, complete with limited-edition baseball cap, on Sunday 27 July 2014, for my golden shot at redemption. Since our meeting in the final at Ally Pally on New Year's Day 2013, when I twice retrieved a two-set deficit to win my sixteenth world title 7–4 with one of my best performances, Michael and I had served up a real mixed bag where neither of us could really claim the upper hand. He had scalped me in two major finals at the Premier League play-offs and the Players Championship, not to mention that horrible 7–0 whitewash in Liverpool I would prefer to forget. But I had enjoyed my moments at the German Masters and the Sydney Masters, and I was keen to find out if he could handle the pressure in an arena I regarded as my domain, my kingdom.

Michael had been the tournament favourite all the way through to the final – until he had to face me. Suddenly, after the thrilling nature of my duel with Gary Anderson, the bookies jumped ship and made me the narrow 4–5 favourite. Good judges, those bookies. I had rested up well after cooking on stage for two hours against Gary, and everything about the night just felt right. From the word go, I was in the mood to let the world know I was back in business. Backstage I had won the bull and wanted to make an early statement by throwing first and putting the reigning world champion under pressure right away. A thirteen-dart leg, starting with 140 and finishing on double 16, was just the job.

I should have broken Michael's throw with a twelve-darter in the next leg, but after answering his 177 with my first 180 of the night, I missed the bull for an 84 finish and MVG picked off 76 to level it up. But remember what

I was saying earlier about consistency? In a major final, that is your magic ingredient – and with my newly crafted arrows flying like a dream, I seized the initiative with three consecutive fourteen-darters, garnished by another pair of 180s, and sealed on double 16, double eight, double eight. I went into the first interval leading 4–1, averaging around 115 and my finishing was deadlier than a German from the penalty spot. I had got Michael just where I wanted him – under pressure. Lovely.

The break did not interrupt my supremacy, nor did it bring MVG much respite. Although Michael hit his first 180 of the match – I was surprised it took him six legs, because he normally drills them into the board from the word go – I took out 78, 74 and 88 to go six legs clear. I looked into his eyes, and all I could see was fear. I wanted to keep him thinking because Michael is such a dangerous player when you let him play on instinct alone. When he has to work out ways of stopping you, when you can get inside his head, you can draw the sting from his game a little bit. Even when he stopped the rot by taking the ninth leg against the throw, much to my annoyance, it was only because I had wired the bullseye on a 161 finish that would have brought the house down. But I paid him back with a nice eleven-darter – 180, 140, 100 and a clinical disposal of 81 in two darts – to reach the second interval leading 8–2. It was just like the good old days: I was confident, ruthless and, best of all, I had a winning mentality again. No panic attacks, no doubts, no hesitation.

I picked up where I had left off at the second interval as another eleven-darter, sealed with a 121 checkout, kept my average above 111, and nobody is going to beat you when you sustain that level of performance. I was always conscious that Michael would throw the kitchen sink at me at some stage, and was capable of stringing a few legs together, and after going 11–2 ahead I let my guard down briefly. When he took out 127 on the bull, I was thinking, 'Ay up, here comes the cavalry.' But after he had clawed back three legs, I stemmed the tide with a nice 124 finish of my own, and by the time the fourth interval came round, I was still well clear at 13–7 with eight 180s and a 177 in the bank.

Michael was now peppering the treble 20 bed, but I knew that holding my throw would be enough to keep him at a safe distance. Even when he landed his ninth 180 and finished 81 for an eleven-darter, the cushion was still six legs. And I killed him off by taking the next three, moving to within one leg of the title by cleaning up 109 on tops, to reach the edge of heaven. I'll never forget the moment of victory. I can still see it now, in glorious 20-20 vision – or double top on the dartboard – and the feeling was just lovely as I clinched an emphatic 18–9 win. To average 107.19 in a major final, with nine 180s and a 55 per cent strike rate on the doubles, is decent by any yardstick. I was so happy that Lisa and her two boys were in the crowd, and I beckoned my grandkids Matthew and Nathan on stage to join me for the presentation ceremony.

I wanted to share the moment with them because grandchildren are the reason I still do this.

Michael was in tears afterwards – he is an emotional kid and, win or lose, he cries a lot backstage in the players' room – but he had an even bigger match the following weekend, when he tied the knot in Holland with his fiancée Daphne. I wish them all the luck in the world, they make a smashing couple. Some players get the hump when they lose and are nice as pie in front of the cameras, but once they get back in the practice area, they can turn nasty and just snipe. Not Michael – he's a genuinely nice fella. You always feel for an opponent who's in tears, but he will be back and we are going to have some rollicking battles against each other. He reached No.1 in the world for a reason – and that reason is he's a bloody good player.

I'm sure he will forgive me for basking in the glory. It felt like a real 'eureka' moment because I've never had to work so hard for a trophy. If Michael had beaten me, I would have been the one in tears. 'I'm going to enjoy every minute of this because the last six or seven months has been the worst time of my career. It's been an absolute nightmare,' I told pdc.tv after cooling off backstage.

> I've been going through a divorce, I've been in court, I've been tinkering with my darts and I've been trying my socks off to get it right. I wasn't close to tears – I was close to cashing that winner's cheque and going down the casino.

> 'It was so embarrassing for me – I was being ridiculed in the street and getting stick like I've never had before, but I'm back with a vengeance now. I've played rubbish this year, but everything has come together and I think I can hit averages better than ever before. The other players know they will have to play well if they want to beat me now. They know I want to win another world title and I want to be No.1 in the rankings again. I don't feel sorry for Michael because he's beaten me a few times this year, but I wanted to prove to myself that I can still do it once more.

How did I celebrate my fifteenth World Matchplay title? The same way I celebrated most of the others – by going for a curry. It's become a bit of a ritual for me in Blackpool: work hard for a week, live like a monk, lift the trophy on a Sunday night, then sit down to a nice plate of tandoori king prawns. I'm too old, by about thirty years, to go nightclubbing. A nice meal, then home to watch a bit of TV and the quiet life, is my idea of a night on the town now. And on the Monday morning? I was back on the practice board, getting ready for the next one. Yes, really. There is no rest for the wicked in this business – because if you put your feet up and take your eye off the board, there is a whole gang of bounty hunters who will take care of the next big cheque for you.

People are seeing a few chinks in Van Gerwen's armour now, but he's going to be around for years to keep us on our toes. Peter Wright, who sent me a nice text message after my win in Blackpool, is a cracking player who does amazing things with darts and even more incredible things with his hair. Adrian Lewis, Gary Anderson, Barney and James Wade are all great lads and great talents. The standard of the top ten is rising all the time. If I want to go out at the top, they will be raising the bar, pushing me all the way.

Once traffic on the M6, which can make a 100-mile journey seem like a lifetime, had finally speeded up to a crawl, and I reached home, sweet home in Stoke-on-Trent, there was one last ritual to observe. For the last seven years, I haven't needed to bring my mum a stick of rock home as a present from Blackpool – because I bring her a trophy instead. I'm delighted to say the World Matchplay pot, which looks like the FA Cup, is back in the spare room she has turned into a little shrine to my career. She knows how much this one meant to me and, of course, I wouldn't have chosen anyone else in the world to look after it for me.

It's the trophy that says I'm back in business. It's the silver lining to a difficult year that says I want to win another World Championship and be No.1 again. And after all the trials and tribulations of 2014, it's the trophy that says The Power has staying power.

MATCH RECORD

BetVictor World Matchplay

July 20-28 2013, Winter Gardens Blackpool

First Round	10-1	v Stuart Kellett
Second Round	14-12	v Terry Jenkins
Quarter-Finals	16-10	v Justin Pipe
Semi-Finals	17-12	v James Wade
Final	18-13	v Adrian Lewis

Sydney Darts Masters

August 29-31 2013, Luna Park, Sydney

First Round	6-1	v Kyle Anderson
Quarter-Finals	8-2	v Paul Nicholson
Semi-Finals	10-6	v Simon Whitlock
Final	10-3	v Michael van Gerwen

Championship League Darts - Group One

September 24 2013, Crondon Park GC

League Game	6-2	v Michael van Gerwen
League Game	6-2	v Wes Newton
League Game	4-6	v Andy Hamilton

League Game	5-6	v Adrian Lewis *Nine-Dart Finish
League Game	6-4	v James Wade
League Game	6-3	v Simon Whitlock
League Game	6-5	v Dave Chisnall
Semi-Finals	6-2	v Wes Newton
Final	6-2	v Adrian Lewis

Players Championship

October 5 2013, Citywest Hotel Dublin

First Round	6-2	v Brian Woods
Second Round	1-6	v Keegan Brown

partypoker.com World Grand Prix

October 7-13 2013, Citywest Hotel, Dublin

First Round	2-1 (Sets)	v Jamie Caven
Second Round	3-1	v Paul Nicholson
Quarter-Finals	3-0	v Gary Anderson
Semi-Finals	5-1	v James Wade
Final	6-0	v Dave Chisnall

Championship League Darts - Winners Group

October 24 2013, Crondon Park GC

League Game	6-5	v Andy Hamilton
League Game	6-5	v Kim Huybrechts
League Game	6-5	v Ian White
League Game	6-4	v Wes Newton
League Game	3-6	v Michael van Gerwen
League Game	6-5	v Terry Jenkins
League Game	6-3	v Richie Burnett
Semi-Finals	6-1	v Wes Newton
Final	6-3	v Michael van Gerwen

The Coral Masters

November 1-3 2013, Royal Highland Centre, Edinburgh

First Round	6-3	v Terry Jenkins
Quarter-Finals	8-2	v Wes Newton
Semi-Finals	10-1	v James Wade
Final	10-1	v Adrian Lewis

William Hill Grand Slam of Darts

November 9-17 2013, Wolverhampton Civic Hall

Group Stage	5-0	v Stuart Kellett
Group Stage	5-1	v Paul Nicholson
Group Stage	5-0	v Kevin Painter
Second Round	10-5	v Gary Anderson
Quarter-Finals	16-12	v James Wade
Semi-Finals	16-9	v Adrian Lewis
Final	16-6	v Robert Thornton

Cash Converters Players Championship Finals

November 29-December 1 2013, Butlins Minehead Resort

First Round	6-2	v Paul Nicholson
Second Round	9-3	v Peter Wright
Quarter-Finals	9-2	v Raymond van Barneveld
Semi-Finals	10-4	v Justin Pipe
Final	7-11	v Michael van Gerwen

Ladbrokes World Darts Championship

December 13 2013-January 1 2014, Alexandra Palace, London

First Round	3-1	v Rob Szabo
Second Round	3-4	v Michael Smith

Betway Premier League Darts

February-May 2014

Week One (Liverpool)	0-7	v Michael van Gerwen
Week Two (Bournemouth)	3-7	v Adrian Lewis
Week Three (Belfast)	4-7	v Peter Wright
Week Four (Glasgow)	7-3	v Simon Whitlock
Week Five (Exeter)	5-7	v Gary Anderson
Week Six (Nottingham)	7-5	v Dave Chisnall
Week Seven (Leeds)	7-1	v Wes Newton
Week Eight (Dublin)	6-6	v Raymond van Barneveld
Week Nine (Cardiff)	7-4	v Robert Thornton
Week Ten (Sheffield)	7-4	v Adrian Lewis
Week 11 (Aberdeen)	7-4	v Michael van Gerwen
Week 12 (Manchester)	6-6	v Gary Anderson
Week 13 (Birmingham)	6-6	v Raymond van Barneveld
Week 13 (Birmingham)	7-2	v Dave Chisnall
Week 14 (Newcastle)	6-6	v Peter Wright
Week 15 (Brighton)	7-5	v Robert Thornton

Play-Offs

Semi-Finals (London)	5-8	v Raymond van Barneveld

Coral UK Open Qualifier One

February 7 2014, Robin Park Tennis Centre, Wigan

Second Round	2-6	v Keegan Brown

Coral UK Open Qualifier Two

February 8 2014, Robin Park Tennis Centre, Wigan

Second Round	6-4	v Joe Cullen
Third Round	6-0	v Darren Johnson
Fourth Round	6-4	v Peter Wright
Fifth Round	6-3	v Mervyn King
Quarter-Finals	6-3	v Justin Pipe
Semi-Finals	4-6	v Andrew Gilding

Coral UK Open Qualifier Three

February 9 2014, Robin Park Tennis Centre, Wigan

Second Round	6-2	v Jack Tweddell
Third Round	6-2	v Michael Mansell
Fourth Round	6-2	v Keegan Brown
Fifth Round	6-1	v Andy Hamilton *Nine-Dart Finish
Quarter-Finals	6-1	v Gary Anderson
Semi-Finals	6-3	v Peter Wright
Final	6-2	v Adrian Lewis *Nine-Dart Finish

Coral UK Open Televised Finals

March 7-9 2014, Butlins Minehead Resort

Third Round	7-9	v Aden Kirk

Players Championship

March 22 2014, K2 Centre, Crawley

First Round	6-4	v Keegan Brown
Second Round	6-2	v Kurt Parry
Third Round	6-2	v Andy Hamilton
Fourth Round	6-5	v Michael van Gerwen
Quarter-Finals	6-4	v Terry Jenkins
Semi-Finals	6-0	v Nigel Heydon
Final	5-6	v Gary Anderson

Players Championship

March 23 2014, K2 Centre, Crawley

First Round	6-0	v Brian Woods
Second Round	6-1	v Mareno Michels
Third Round	6-3	v Paul Nicholson
Fourth Round	6-2	v Vincent van der Voort

Quarter-Finals	6-1	v Michael Smith
Semi-Finals	6-2	v Mervyn King
Final	6-0	v Ian White

Players Championship

April 12 2014, Robin Park Tennis Centre, Wigan

First Round	6-1	v Rowby-John Rodriguez
Second Round	4-6	v Jamie Bain

Players Championship

April 13 2014, Robin Park Tennis Centre, Wigan

First Round	6-0	v Ross Twell
Second Round	6-3	v Ross Smith
Third Round	6-0	v Paul Nicholson
Fourth Round	6-3	v Terry Jenkins
Quarter-Finals	6-4	v Raymond van Barneveld
Semi-Finals	4-6	v Robert Thornton

German Darts Masters

April 19-21, Maritim Hotel, Berlin

Second Round	6-0	v Magnus Caris
Third Round	6-3	v Dave Chisnall
Quarter-Finals	6-0	v Michael Smith
Semi-Finals	6-3	v Stephen Bunting
Final	6-4	v Michael van Gerwen

Dubai Duty Free Darts Masters

May 29-30, Dubai Duty Free Tennis Stadium, Dubai

Quarter-Finals	5-10	v Peter Wright

bwin World Cup of Darts

June 6-8, Sporthalle Hamburg, Germany

* Pairs event, playing with Adrian Lewis

First Round	5-0	v Thailand
Second Round	2-1	v USA
Quarter-Finals	2-0	v South Africa
Semi-Finals	2-1	v Australia
Final	0-3	v Netherlands

Austrian Darts Open

June 20-22, Salzburg Arena, Austria

Second Round	6-3	v Alex Roy
Third Round	6-3	v Simon Whitlock
Quarter-Finals	5-6	v Jamie Caven

Gibraltar Darts Trophy

June 27-29, Victoria Stadium, Gibraltar

Second Round	4-6	v Michael Smith

BetVictor World Matchplay

July 19-27, Winter Gardens, Blackpool

First Round	10-4	v Darren Webster
Second Round	13-6	v Michael Smith *Nine-Dart Finish
Quarter-Finals	16-6	v Wes Newton
Semi-Finals	17-15	v Gary Anderson
Final	18-9	v Michael van Gerwen